Juke box Britain

Manchester University Press

STUDIES IN POPULAR CULTURE

General editor: Professor Jeffrey Richards

Already published

Healthy living in the Alps
The origins of winter tourism in Switzerland, 1860–1914
Susan Barton

Working-class organisations and popular tourism, 1840–1970
Susan Barton

Leisure, citizenship and working-class men in Britain, 1850–1945
Brad Beaven

The British Consumer Co-operative Movement and film, 1890s–1960s
Alan George Burton

British railway enthusiasm
Ian Carter

Railways and culture in Britain
Ian Carter

Relocating Britishness
Stephen Caunce, Ewa Mazierska, Susan Sydney-Smith and John Walton (eds)

From silent screen to multi-screen:
a history of cinema exhibition in Britain since 1896
Stuart Hanson

Smoking in British popular culture, 1800–2000
Matthew Hilton

Popular culture in London, c. 1890–1918:
The transformation of entertainment
Andrew Horrall

Horseracing and the British, 1919–39
Mike Huggins

Amateur operatics: a social and cultural history
John Lowerson

Scotland and the music hall, 1850–1914
Paul Maloney

Films and British national identity: from Dickens to Dad's Army
Jeffrey Richards

Looking North: Northern England and the national imagination
Dave Russell

The British seaside holiday: holidays and resorts
in the twentieth century
John K. Walton

Juke box Britain

Americanisation and youth culture, 1945–60

ADRIAN HORN

Manchester University Press

Manchester and New York

distributed exclusively in the USA by Palgrave Macmillan

Published by Manchester University Press
Oxford Road, Manchester M13 9NR, UK
and Room 400, 175 Fifth Avenue, New York, NY 10010, USA
www.manchesteruniversitypress.co.uk

Distributed exclusively in the USA by
Palgrave Macmillan, 175 Fifth Avenue, New York,
NY 10010, USA

Distributed exclusively in Canada by
UBC Press, University of British Columbia, 2029 West Mall,
Vancouver, BC, Canada V6T 1Z2

British Library Cataloguing-in-Publication Data
A catalogue record for this book is available from the British Library

Library of Congress Cataloging-in-Publication Data applied for

ISBN   978 0 7190 7907 8 hardback

First published 2009

18 17 16 15 14 13 12 11 10 09   10 9 8 7 6 5 4 3 2 1

Typeset in Adobe Garamond with Gill Sans display by
Koinonia, Manchester

Printed in Great Britain
by Bell & Bain Ltd, Glasgow

STUDIES IN POPULAR CULTURE

There has in recent years been an explosion of interest in culture and cultural studies. The impetus has come from two directions and out of two different traditions. On the one hand, cultural history has grown out of social history to become a distinct and identifiable school of historical investigation. On the other hand, cultural studies has grown out of English literature and has concerned itself to a large extent with contemporary issues. Nevertheless, there is a shared project, its aim, to elucidate the meanings and values implicit and explicit in the art, literature, learning, institutions and everyday behaviour within a given society. Both the cultural historian and the cultural studies scholar seek to explore the ways in which a culture is imagined, represented and received, how it interacts with social processes, how it contributes to individual and collective identities and world views, to stability and change, to social, political and economic activities and programmes. This series aims to provide an arena for the cross-fertilisation of the discipline, so that the work of the cultural historian can take advantage of the most useful and illuminating of the theoretical developments and the cultural studies scholars can extend the purely historical underpinnings of their investigations. The ultimate objective of the series is to provide a range of books which will explain in a readable and accessible way where we are now socially and culturally and how we got to where we are. This should enable people to be better informed, promote an interdisciplinary approach to cultural issues and encourage deeper thought about the issues, attitudes and institutions of popular culture.

Jeffrey Richards

For Jeanne and Harold

Contents

List of plates   *page* ix

List of figures   x

General editor's foreword   xiii

Acknowledgements   xv

Introduction   1

1 Context: British acceptance and resistance to American popular
culture before 1945   14
   I: music and dance   14
   II: Americanisation and World War II   20
   III: pre-war juke boxes   24

2 Americanisation and the post-war juke box   34
   I: 1945–54   34
   II: 1954–60   49

3 American music, juke boxes and cultural resistance   66

4 British teenagers   90

5 Spivs and Teds: changing meanings of 'rebellious' male dress
styles   115

6 Cutting your coat according to your cloth: dress styles for
young women after World War II   142

7 Venues: from arcade to high street   161
   I: Legal implications   162
   II: Venues and style   169
   III: Social uses   176

Conclusion   186

Bibliography   196

Index   212

List of plates

Colour plates appear between pages 114 and 115

1   Wurlitzer 24 of 1938, courtesy Rich Leatham – Always Jukin'
2   The Music Maker Mark II of 1946, courtesy of Music Hire
    Group, Leeds
3   The Filben Maestro of 1946, courtesy Rich Leatham – Always Jukin'
4   The Wurlitzer 1015 of 1946, courtesy Rich Leatham – Always Jukin'
5   AMI's colourful juke box selection in Chris Pearce, *Jukebox Art*, p. 94
6   The 40-selection BAL-AMI Junior from 1956 manufactured by
    Balfour Engineering Co., Ilford, Essex, UK, courtesy Terry Lovell, The
    Jukebox Co.
7   The BAL-AMI G80 from 1954 manufactured by Balfour Engineering
    Co., Ilford, Essex, UK, courtesy Terry Lovell, The Jukebox Co.

List of figures

1.1 Hawtin's Bunny Shooter, Hawtins Trade Catalogue,
circa 1945   *page* 26

2.1 Hawtin's advertisement in *World's Fair*, 23 December 1944,
p. 24   35

2.2 Wurlitzer Victory, contemporary advert in Chris Pearce,
Jukebox Art, p. 46   36

2.3 Artist's impression of the Jack Hylton Music Maker, Hawtins
Trade Catalogue, circa 1945   37

2.4 Juke box assembly at Hawtin's factory, Hawtins Trade
Catalogue, circa 1945   38

2.5 The 'Tank', Hawtins Trade Catalogue, circa 1945   39

2.6 1954 Cadillac series 6, courtesy Dan Vaughn, http://concept-
carz.com   41

2.7 The Ditchburn Hideaway of 1955, from contemporary
advertisement, courtesy John Crompton   46

2.8 The Minstrel, courtesy Music Hire, Leeds   48

2.9 'Culture Shock', AMI Super Forty in contemporary
advertising   51

2.10 Advertisement for Seeburg Selectomatic 100JL in *World's Fair*,
25 May 1957   54

2.11 Advertisement for Fanfare 60A, Seeburg 100EL and Wurlitzer
1900 in *World's Fair*, 19 April 1958   55

2.12 Advertisement for the Belgian Renotte in *World's Fair*, 24
March 1956, p. 32   56

2.13 Advertisement for reconditioned Wurlitzer 1015s from
Singapore in *World's Fair*, 24 March 1956, p. 32   57

2.14 The Ditchburn Music Maker 100 made in West Germany by
     Tonomat – Contemporary Ditchburn advertising, courtesy
     John Crompton   59
2.15 The Ditchburn Music Maker 200 made in West Germany by
     Tonomat – Contemporary Ditchburn advertising, courtesy
     John Crompton   59
2.16 The Ditchburn Music Maker 30 – Contemporary Ditchburn
     advertising, courtesy John Crompton   60
 4.1 Cost of living 1920 to 1940   97
 4.2 Cost of living 1940 to 1960   97
 5.1 Zoot suits, 22 June 1948. Three Jamaican immigrants (left to
     right): John Hazel, a 21-year-old boxer, Harold Wilmot, 32,
     and John Roberts, a 22-year-old carpenter, arriving at Tilbury
     onboard the ex-troopship *Empire Windrush*, smartly dressed in
     zoot suits and trilby hats. Getty Images   117
 5.2 Artist's impression of Cecil Gee's American Look   118
 5.3 Spivs loitering in London's Notting Hill area, *Picture Post*,
     1954. Getty Images   120
 5.4 London Spivs, *Picture Post*, January 1954. Getty Images   121
 5.5 A Teddy Boy in a London Street, *Picture Post*, 1954. Getty
     Images   128
 5.6 Cool Ted – A Teddy Boy gets admiring glances from his
     friends. Getty Images   129
 6.1 Fans wait for Bill Haley at London Airport, 1957 © TopFoto   147
 6.2 Elsie Henden, aged 16, Jean Rayner, 14, Rose Henden, 16 and
     Mary Toothy, January 1955, from the exhibition 'Bombsite
     Boudiccas' © Topfoto/Ken Russell   150
 6.3 Pat Wiles and Iris Thornton, both aged 17, from Plaistow,
     January 1955, from the exhibition 'Bombsite Boudiccas' ©
     Topfoto/Ken Russell   151
 6.4 Jean Rayner, aged 14, January 1955, from the exhibition
     'Bombsite Boudiccas' © Topfoto/Ken Russell   152
 6.5 Eileen, aged 16, January 1955, from the exhibition 'Bombsite
     Boudiccas' © Topfoto/Ken Russell   153
 6.6 On the first London to Aldermaston march of Easter 1958,
     CND supporters wore duffle coats and donkey jackets which
     became symbols of nonconformity and protest © TopFoto   154

6.7 June 1956: Juliette Gréco, French actress and singer at the
Festival of Dijon © TopFoto   155

6.8 October 1953: Belgian-born actor Audrey Hepburn (1929–93)
with American actor William Holden on the set of director
Billy Wilder's film *Sabrina*. Hepburn wears a black sweater,
black Capri pants, hoop earrings, and flats. Getty Images   156

6.9 1955: French-born actress Leslie Caron in Jean Renoir's *Orvet*,
Theatre of the Renaissance, Paris © TopFoto   157

7.1 Herbalist and Surgical Stores, 1960. Upper Moss Lane,
Hulme, Manchester © Manchester Central Library   172

7.2 Regent Snack Bar, 1958. Collyhurst Road, Collyhurst,
Manchester © Manchester Central Library   173

7.3 Snack Bar, 1958. Ardwick, Junction of Hyde Road and
Marshland Road, Manchester © Manchester Central Library   174

7.4 A. Chiappe, Italian Café, 1958. Stockport Road, Ardwick,
Manchester © Manchester Central Library   175

General editor's foreword

The phenomenon of Americanisation has long been recognised as a key character-istic of British youth culture in the period 1945–1960. In his thoroughly researched and eminently readable book Adrian Horn advances a revisionist interpretation which questions the notion of wholesale Americanisation and argues instead for a fusion of American and British influences creating a cultural hybrid which was new and distinctive. He examines in turn the juke box, popular music, youth venues and youth fashion. His work on the history, function and design of the juke box in Britain is particularly innovative and revealing. He demonstrates convincingly that between 1945 and 1955 juke boxes in Britain had a specifically British form and only after 1955 did a modified American style appear. He also argues persuasively for the role of the juke box as a disseminator of raw and undiluted American music in a business otherwise limited by the Musicians' Union, copyright restrictions, industry practices and the generalised disapproval of American rock 'n' roll by the BBC. His ethnography of youth venues, milk bars, coffee bars, amusement arcades and youth cafés is thorough and well documented. He thoughtfully deconstructs teenage fashions, male and female, identifying their various British and American elements. The book makes excellent use of hitherto neglected primary printed sources and a good range of oral interviews. Not only is this a significant work of scholarship, it is also a nostalgic evocation of a now lost and vanished era.

Jeffrey Richards

Made by Me

Manchester University Press operates a training and development scheme called Made by Me, in which one member of staff follows the progress of a particular book through all of the publishing processes. As the book passes from department to department they are shown exactly what is involved at each stage, and wherever possible they do the work themselves. At the end of the process the book will have had special care and attention given to it, and the staff member will have a full understanding of the life of a book.

This book has been made by Laure Pernette, who works as a publicity executive, and has special responsibility for our history and media lists.

Acknowledgements

I would like to thank Annette Kuhn, without whom this book might never have been written. I would also like to express special thanks to Michael Seymour and many other scholars have also shared their knowledge and time with me. These include Jeffrey Richards, John K. Walton, Moira Peelo, Jackie Stacey, Kevin Hetherington, Phil Mitchell, Suman Ghosh, Ian Lewis, David Fowler, Bill Osgerby and Rod Ireland. The order is not significant and I apologise for inevitable omissions.

I am most grateful to all of my interviewees, who happily and freely gave their time, particularly Barry Stott, Harry Isaacs, Dave Fagan, John Farmery, Jim Cheetham, Terry Mitchell and Laura Dowding.

I would especially like to thank the juke box experts Tony Holmes, John Crompton, George Whittaker, John Johnson and all the staff at H and D Leisure in Crosby. Dan Vaughn, Rich Leatham, Ron Murdoch and Terry Lovell have provided me with photographs and Brian Downey with artistic impressions.

The following organisations are just a few of those that have been extremely helpful: *World's Fair* in Oldham, National Fairground Archive at Sheffield University, Jack Hylton Archive at Lancaster University, Manchester Central Library, Music Hire Group, Leeds and TopFoto.

I owe a great deal to my kind and long-suffering friends, who have indulged my ideas, hopes and grumbles for long periods. These include Colin Pritchard, Dave and Carole Smith, Steve Garnett, Shannon Lowe and Jo Stanley.

Most of all I would like to thank my partner, Christine Downey.

Introduction

Juke box Britain was born out of a desire to understand the impact on young people of American popular culture and design in the first fifteen years following World War II. It presents a revisionist history of youth culture and provides a case study in cultural and design mediation with reference to American influences. Too many studies of post-war youth have been concerned with accounts of England's southeast, particularly London, and this regional bias has led to a general impression of glamour, Americanisation and increasing modernity for young people across the country. *Juke box Britain*, however, unearths a more mundane reality and shows that with the exception of American rock 'n' roll music young people were not overly influenced by American popular culture.

Juke box Britain offers contributions to Cultural and Design History as well as Cultural Studies.[1] The research is anchored in two separate ways: firstly, through an examination of juke boxes, their changing styles, technical development, expansion and distribution; and secondly, through a broad, and often localised, investigation of British youth between the end of World War II and 1960. By balancing a regional investigation with an exploration of wider and various national trends within, for example, broadcasting, small catering establishments like café and snack bars, and young people's dress styles, it makes an original contribution to our understanding of youth culture in the period.

I make a distinction between mass culture and popular culture, taking popular culture to refer to a wide range of popular tastes and customs; for example, after World War II rambling and cycling were popular pastimes for young people, as were eating fish and chips and attending sporting events – these were popular-cultural activities. Mass culture, however, refers to manufactured and mass-produced cultural commodities like gramophone records, Hollywood films and cheap make-up. For cultural commentators of the period mass culture was synonymous with America and perceived American values. Popular culture may include mass culture but mass culture specifically refers to manufactured cultural products.

As I was growing up in the Greater London suburb of Harrow in the late 1950s and 1960s images of rock 'n' roll were very fresh. Young men in Teddy Boy clothes, for instance, were still visible, and the 'super groups' of the day, particularly the Beatles and the Rolling Stones, paid regular homage to their rock 'n' roll roots. John Lennon said that 'before Elvis there was nothing'[2] and Keith Richard's guitar style paid tribute to its enormous debt to Chuck Berry and his driving guitar riffs.

When I was 18 we moved to the town of Ilkley in Yorkshire's West Riding (now West Yorkshire) and I was immediately struck by the difference in youth cultures between Ilkley and Harrow. The northern and less-urban influences on youth had apparently been very different from mine, and it appeared to me that the local teenagers were culturally isolated. In Harrow the musical styles that my friends and I had listened to were predominantly American, or British versions of American styles like blues, r & b, soul and Tamla Motown. All of these were musical genres that had not apparently reached the consciousness of the young people that I met in Ilkley,[3] who, despite Jimi Hendrix's attempt to play a gig there in 1967, preferred a diet of either progressive rock or pop music.[4] Moreover, Ilkley's youth were divided socially along the musical lines of British rock and commercial pop.

I wondered, and still do, that if youth culture was so different in these two different parts of the country then why was it so regularly written about as a unified whole? The idea was fixed in my mind, even at this early age, that there were probably whole areas of youth history that were regional and unexplored. It was glaringly obvious that there was in Britain at least a north/south divide and an urban/rural split and probably many variations on these. It took me twenty-five years to decide, albeit in a very narrow area, to look into youth experience, and *Juke box Britain* is the result of my investigations.

I initially set out to test the extent of several seemingly widely unchallenged assumptions about youth culture and its relationship with American popular cultural influences: namely, that British youth were strongly influenced by America and that their adoption of American cultural symbols was seen as part of a cultural dilution or 'levelling down' process that was robustly criticised by the older generation and state apparatuses.

There was certainly a tradition of British prudity in the twentieth century that saw mass culture as a threat to artistic values and originality. The arguments were generally anti-American, and the word America became a metaphor for mass culture; as a consequence the prudity was directed at American products. In the 1950s 'the debate about mass-culture became an explicit debate about American culture'.[5] My assumptions on the extent of American influences were based upon the many retrospective accounts that catalogue a pronounced hostility to what was known as 'Americanisation' – accounts that are expertly summed up in Dick Hebdige's influential essay 'Towards a Cartography of Taste, 1935–1962'.[6] One of my intentions was to examine further this apparently general anti-Americanism using, as a case study, juke boxes in Britain and the music they played in the period 1945 to 1960. Juke boxes provided a particularly appropriate mass-cultural icon. Juke boxes in Britain are, to all intents and purposes, a post-war phenomenon and contain multitudes of American and mass-cultural associations and signifiers. In this respect they were a paradigm of American popular culture. Moreover, they have been predominantly linked with youth and youth culture both aurally and visually.

The well-documented anti-American feeling had apparently been part of an historical tradition dating from at least the mid-nineteenth century with the writings of Matthew Arnold and through the first half of the twentieth century with intellectual commentators on all sides of the political spectrum such as F.R. Leavis, Bertrand Russell, Richard Hoggart and the Communist Party of Great Britain.[7] My research, however, suggested that these critics were a vociferous minority that overshadowed a massive popular acceptance. Moreover, it became apparent that this was not a simple intellectual/popular split, as scientists, intellectuals and well-known figures are reported to have praised American cultural influences over the same period. Undoubtedly many pro-American examples would be found if I had the time and inclination to direct my research in that area.[8] So when American cultural influences entered Britain they did so in an atmosphere that was just as likely to embrace as to resist them.

'Americanisation' has been a dominant subject in Cultural Studies and it is my contention that the recorded extent and effect of American influences in popular culture have been overemphasised through a selective bias within the discipline. This has been the case particularly when reactions to perceived Americanisation by influential figures and 'Establishment' bodies like the BBC have been recorded. My point is not that these views were insignificant, simply that they have been overemphasised. American cultural influences certainly had been significant in the period 1945 to 1960 and this was the case in the realm of youth styles and musical tastes, but not exclusively so.

When I started this project my intention was to explore the reasons why young people in post-war Britain had apparently so enthusiastically adopted American influences because, in common with other post-war analysts and theorists, I had accepted that 'Americanisation' was an overwhelming cultural feature of the period. I found, however, through closer examination of specific phenomena in primary-source material, that American cultural influences, in the area of style and design, had been less influential than previously suggested. Moreover, I noticed that the influences that *were* imported had been mediated through British social, economic and cultural conditions to create style fusions that were distinctive and particular to Britain at that time. The questions that these mediations raise for this book are concerned with exploring the extent of the American influence.

Another of the initial intentions of my research had been to examine some of the cultural issues that Americanisation raises for young people and to test some of the assumptions of extensive American influence through a detailed examination of juke box reception by young people. What has evolved, though, has been a wider remit that explores the distinctiveness and regionality of British design and youth culture in the post-war period and the reasons for this distinctiveness. This localised approach suggests that strong regional variations existed and that youth culture was neither a monolithic nor an integrated whole.

My research is informed by reference to a diverse range of primary historical sources that are at the core of most historical writing. These include material drawn from trade papers, local and national newspapers, magazines and periodicals, contemporary advertisements, local directories, Mass-Observation reports, archives, survey data, oral testimony, memoirs and fiction. Prominent among these sources is the trade paper *World's Fair*. Moreover, much of my argument is explored through visual sources.

World's Fair was first published in 1904 and is an important primary source for researchers into the fairground and amusement arcade industries.[9] It has played a central role in my research because it records the development of Britain's juke box business through trade advertisements, editorial commentary, gossip and comment columns that closely followed the industry. There are three major areas of academic value in using *World's*

Fair: firstly, it records the commercial, political and social attitudes that concerned the amusement machine business at the time; secondly, as long as any editorial bias is taken into account (and the bias itself is of historical significance), it allows a view from the standpoint of the trade in the post-war period; and thirdly, *World's Fair* provides a day-to-day chronology of events that lends an historical structure.

Many of the attitudes that the *World's Fair* illustrates so graphically were incidental at the time of writing and were part and parcel of the 'common sense' thinking of the era. This was a 'common sense' that frequently ran counter to 'Establishment' orthodoxy. These unconsciously provided attitudes and assumptions are significant to this enquiry because they are the views of an 'oppositional' force to the 'dominant' cultural hegemony. Discourse that is particular to the period is illuminating and unquestioned attitudes towards delinquency, for example, are apparent in *World's Fair* reports and are significant as examples of the moral climate. Indeed, the reports of music licence litigations allow us a singular insight into some attitudes of the time, exposing a widespread belief in a link between amusement machines and delinquency.

Secondary sources include literature from cultural commentators and investigations into British youth culture: for example, work by the Centre for Contemporary Cultural Studies (CCCS), T.R. Fyvel, Peter Laurie, George Melly, Stan Cohen and Dick Hebdige. Literature on juke box design and history comes primarily from writers with a specialist interest like Frank Adams, Chris Pearce, John Krivine and Ian Brown. Non-written primary sources include oral testimony, films, TV and radio programmes, and recorded music.

Three important books on youth culture were published in the 1980s and 1990s, namely John Springhall's *Coming of Age: Adolescence in Britain 1860–1960*, David Fowler's *The First Teenagers: The Lifestyle of Young Wage-earners in Interwar Britain* and Bill Osgerby's *Youth in Britain Since 1945*, and I have drawn heavily on all of these.[10] Both Osgerby and Springhall examine the relationship between youth and popular music, and teenage dress codes are a consistent theme with all of the authors. None, however, addresses the subject of design fusions in a regional context outside of the area of youth fashions.

In the 1990s and the first few years of the twenty-first century British youth culture in the immediate post-war period has been a neglected area of study within Cultural Studies, and I can only suggest some possible reasons for this. The influence of structuralist approaches, which so informed the vast body of literature from the CCCS, had waned within the discipline whilst ethnographic and empirical research took a back seat along with historical perspectives. This led to a shift of methodological emphasis that has generally favoured theoretical perspectives and research in more contemporary areas.

Juke box Britain does not aspire primarily to take forward theoretical debates on culture; nevertheless, theoretical lines have been influential and, although this is not the place to list them all, several prominent cultural commentators, historians and social scientists do deserve mention. Those that have informed my approach are not necessarily referenced directly within the text so I would like to credit their influence here.

A theoretical framework informs my research methods which broadly follows Raymond Williams' definition of 'social' culture as a 'way of life'. The three main ingredients for his 'analysis of culture' are outlined in *The Long Revolution* (namely 'documentary', the 'selective tradition' and the 'lived experience'), all of which have their own particular view or angle.[11] My research is based on a triangulation of these three areas. For Williams the 'significance of documentary culture is that, more clearly than anything else, it expresses that life to us in direct terms, when the living witnesses are themselves silent'.[12]

I have used a wide range of documentary evidence in this project that has been chosen from a variety of archival sources that include: contemporary national, regional and specialist newspapers and periodicals; archives, record offices and reference libraries; Mass-Observation reports; and illustrations from a variety of sources like advertising, the *Picture Post*, and 1950s photographs of Manchester streets (housed in the Manchester City Library).

For the 'selective tradition' I have looked at how a 'structure of feeling' of the period has been extracted and perhaps partly constructed by cultural commentators and researchers.[13] For Williams these can never be objective because the sources of the selective tradition are governed by a variety of special interests that reflect particular attitudes of the period in which they were written:

> Just as the actual social situation will largely govern contemporary selection, so the development of the society, the process of historical change, will largely determine the selective tradition. The traditional culture of a society will always tend to correspond to its 'contemporary' system of interests and values, for it is not an absolute body of work but a continual selection and interaction.[14]

In order to gain a view of the 'lived experience' and to analyse what Williams writes of as the 'most difficult thing to get hold of, in studying any past period, [the] sense of the quality of life at a particular place and time: a sense of the ways in which the particular activities combined into a way of thinking and living,'[15] I have conducted ethnographic research that focuses around taped interviews with people who were a part of that 'lived experience'. Williams describes this as the 'lived culture of a particular time and place, only fully accessible to those living in that time and place'.[16] These people enjoyed their teenage years within my period of study and have volunteered retrospective information about their personal reception of juke boxes and youth culture in England's northwest between 1945 and 1960. Around fifty years have elapsed since the interviewees were teenagers and therefore their memories cannot be taken as a definitive record; they are nevertheless central to my ethnographic perspective.

I observed, when reading through returned questionnaires and in my interviews, that the respondents remembered their teenage years as being the most exciting of their lives. I suspect that this would have been the same for any generation and in this respect all memories of youth have a particular perspective or bias. To attempt to recapture the cultural history of a generation of young people is a difficult task, particularly in a period of great economic and social changes. Although Williams does not discuss youth culture in his works I believe that, bearing in mind that no cultural reconstruction can be truly objective, his analytical methods of triangulation are appropriate for studies of youth culture.

Antonio Gramsci's ideas on cultural hegemony have been highly influential in my understanding of cultural conflicts within the post-war period because he rejects a strictly Marxist base and superstructure model of society as being too restrictive.[17] For Gramsci the situation is more complex and culture is an area where dominant and subordinate ideological values interweave in numerous permutations where each cultural force fights for supremacy and influence. Youth culture, using Gramsci's model, may be seen as struggling for 'cultural space' in symbolic and artistic challenges to the dominant culture. Williams recognises that there are very complex systems of permutations at work and he discusses ideas of 'dominant', 'residual' and 'emergent' cultures that co-exist at any given point, and I use these terms throughout the book.

Gramsci's writings have been central to Cultural Studies since the 1960s and his work still attracts significant attention within the discipline. There are, for example, several Internet sites dedicated to his concept of cultural hegemony and theoretical approaches. *The International Gramsci Society* website, which provides links to other Gramsci-related sites, is probably the best starting point to track current debates.[18]

Informed by Gramscian theory, Raymond Williams' essay 'Base and Superstructure' revisits the subject of the 'selective tradition' central to his 'analysis of culture'.[19] Here he explains that the 'selective tradition' is

> that which, within the terms of an effective dominant culture, is always passed off as 'the tradition', *the* 'significant past'. But always the selectivity is the point, the way in which from a whole possible area of past and present, certain meanings and practices are chosen for emphasis, certain other meanings and practices are neglected and excluded. Even more crucially, some of these meanings and practices are reinterpreted, diluted, or put into forms which support or at least do not contradict other elements within the effective dominant culture.[20]

Williams' analysis of the 'selective tradition' has heightened my awareness that my research and methods are selective and that an authorial bias is inevitable in mine as in any 'analysis of culture'.

Stan Cohen's seminal work into the media's relationship with youth culture has an important role. In *Folk Devils and Moral Panics* Cohen associates post-war 'moral panics' with emergent youth cultures that adopt delinquent behaviour.[21] He argues that there is a process whereby the mass media[22] initiate a circular and amplifying model of deviance through which they create folk devils:

Original act
of deviance by   >   media   >   more acts   >   more reaction=moral panic
'folk devil'   reaction   of deviance

In this period of study Spivs and Teddy Boys were standard media folk devils (see chapter 5). For Cohen a moral panic occurs when the initial impact of youthful deviance

> is followed by a reaction which has the effect of increasing the subsequent warning and impact, setting up a feedback system.
> … each event can be seen as creating the potential for a reaction which, among other possible consequences, might cause further acts of deviance.[23]

My research finds that the moral panic arising from the Teddy Boy phenomenon of the mid-1950s was an exaggeration of the reality, and young people's experience was inevitably more humdrum than had been portrayed by the media. Cohen has also been useful in my understanding of the spread of youth styles because, by adapting his media-amplification model and substituting 'style' for 'deviance', I argue that the media played a key role in disseminating fashions.

Pierre Bourdieu's conclusions on public taste, based on empirical research in France, have provided *Juke box Britain* with an insight into possible relationships between musical tastes and social class in post-war Britain.[24] His model connects with British debates that surrounded Americanisation and mass culture among intellectuals and, for example, the BBC. Following Bourdieu, 'cultural capital' is to be found in a rejection of mass tastes in music like the emergent rock 'n' roll of the mid-1950s.

The following chapters broadly centre on the theme of juke box reception by young people in Britain between 1945 and 1960. Chapter 1 places British receptions of Americana in an historical context and argues that there had been a tradition in the first half of the twentieth century of social adoption of American popular cultural imports demonstrated in mass enthusiasm for American cinema, music and dance: for example, 15 per cent of films exhibited in Britain were of American origin in 1910; this rose to 60 per cent during World War I; and, by 1926, 95 per cent of films on British screens were Hollywood productions.[25] However, style influences that were a result of these cultural imports were subject to an inevitable mediation process. A process, for example, that was manifested in the way American popular culture was re-formed through British interpretations and receptions. I explore this cultural arbitration through the specific example of the take-up by amusement arcade and fairground operators of imported American juke boxes.

Chapter 2 charts the progression of the British juke box industry and demonstrates, through a detailed case study of a British juke boxes between 1945 and 1960, that the American styles of industrial Art Deco and Streamlining hardly affected British juke box design. It notes, however, that this situation changed in the mid-1950s when American styles *did* begin to influence the rapidly expanding industry, and for this reason the chapter is in two sections. The second section argues that post-war conditions particular to Britain meant that these influences, though increasing, never dominated the 'look' of the machines.

Chapter 3 looks at a more orchestrated mediation process that culturally 'filtered' American popular music. BBC radio was broadly resistant to musical forms that did not conform to its founding ideals of public education. Within the BBC particular fears were raised concerning the effect of mass-cultural broadcasting on Britain's youth. To simplify the argument 'standardised' or 'formula' music (in other words, music produced for a mass market) was regarded as bad, whilst 'original' or 'autonomous' music was good.[26] General 'Establishment' concerns over perceived subversive ideological affects in American sound imports were evident but these were not as pronounced as some contemporary media sources and retrospective accounts might lead us to believe. Mediation in Britain, however, was not an all-pervading process and juke boxes were an important exception because they aided the dissemination of American music by bypassing the BBC's near monopoly broadcasting position. Juke boxes in this instance played a remarkably similar role to those in pre-war America where they circumvented restrictions imposed by commercial radio stations.

Chapter 4 provides a profile of post-war teenagers and finds regional differences in youth occupations and culture. It determines that young people's post-war socialisation was influenced by several key factors like educational opportunity, class structure and an increase in disposable income. The social, economic and cultural conditions surrounding British youth before 1960 are important because they influenced teenage receptions of popular cultural forms and were necessarily part of the mediation process.

Chapter 5 observes the way male youth styles spread over the post-war period and finds that the Teddy Boy styles of the mid-1950s were not 'original' expressions of youth culture. Although highly influenced by America and an upper-class London fashion of the early 1950s Teddy Boys were part of a continuum of male display whose dress styles descended from, among others, the London Spiv. Teddy Boy styles and attitudes, moreover, were adapted locally and fused into regional variations that took on the main Teddy Boy signifiers like Tony Curtis haircuts, sideburns, drape jackets or drainpipe trousers, but not the full regalia. The originally highly distinctive expression of London male youth culture was transformed and diffused into a more mainstream youth fashion that lost many of its criminal connotations, except for certain sections of the press.

Chapter 6 looks at style mediations among young women's fashions and argues that they were modified through the widespread use of home dressmaking, and that fashion influences came from sources including magazines and the cinema. It finds there is no substantial evidence to suggest that teenage girls' dress styles were perceived by the public or media as confrontational. 'Oppositional' styles did, however, enter at the end of the decade and took on Continental influences as depicted by Hollywood.

Chapter 7 concerns 'unorganised' youth venues and specifically *not* adult-organised youth venues like youth clubs and church organisations. It shows how casual youth meeting places went through a period of change and crossed over, in parallel with juke boxes, from amusement arcades into small-scale catering establishments that were rapidly expanding in Britain both spatially and in actual numbers. The chapter is in three sections: the first section assesses the legal implications of relaying recorded music to the public. Here it uncovers an intriguing and complex situation regarding juke box licensing and copyright law. This has provided the opportunity to examine some of the legal material and bring to light attitudes toward youth's preferred music and connections that society made between youth, popular music and 'undesirable elements'. The second section looks at the style and type of youth venue, notes regional differences and assesses the extent of imported design influences. The style and type of new youth venues in the post-war era further highlights Britain's cultural regionality. The third section examines the social uses of youth venues and the contemporary discussions that surrounded them.

Juke box Britain maintains that imported cultural forms, particularly those from America, were *influences* on British youth and not part of a domination of popular culture. The fusions that these influences made with existing cultural norms became part of the fabric of the period but not to the extent that previously been argued within cultural studies scholarship.

Notes

1 Throughout this work I use the word 'America' to mean the United States of America; the word 'Americanisation' to mean American cultural influences of on Britain; and 'Americana' to mean American or American-style mass-cultural products. In post-war Britain there were certainly imported cultural and design influences other than the American (from Scandinavia and Italy, for example), but, though the same tendencies to design and cultural fusions still apply, they are not the main subjects of this discussion.

2 Widely quoted: see, for example, Patrick Higgins, *Before Elvis There Was Nothing* (New York, Carroll & Graff, 1994), p. 12.

3 With a few notable exceptions.

4 The Jimi Hendrix Experience were booked to play at the Troutbeck Hotel on 12 March 1967. Two numbers into the set the police stopped the concert, due

to the capacity of the venue being exceeded – and it never resumed. The *Ilkley Gazette* ran an article the following week (Friday 17 March 1967), p. 7.

5 Simon Frith, *Sound Effects: Youth, Leisure, and the Politics of Rock* (London: Constable & Co., 1983), p. 46.

6 Dick Hebdige, 'Towards a Cartography of Taste, 1935–1962'in *Hiding The Light* (London: Routledge, 1988), pp. 45–77. See also John Storey, *Cultural Theory and Popular Culture* (London: Harvest Wheatsheaf, 1993); Dominic Strinati, 'The Taste of America: Americanization and Popular Culture in Britain' in *Come on Down? Popular Media and Culture in Post-War Britain* ed. by Dominic Strinati and Stephen Wagg (London: Routledge, 1992), pp. 46–81.

7 Matthew Arnold, *Culture and Anarchy* (London: Cambridge University Press, 1960); F.R. Leavis, 'Mass Civilisation and Minority Culture' in *For Continuity* (Cambridge: Minority Press, 1933); Bertrand Russell et al., *The Impact of America on European Culture* (Boston: Beacon Press, 1951) – contributions by Bertrand Russell, John Lehman, Sean O'Faolain, J.E. Morpurgo, Martin Cooper and Perry Miller; Richard Hoggart, *The Uses of Literacy* (Harmondsworth: Penguin, 1960); Communist Party of Great Britain. National Cultural Committee Conference 1951, *The American Threat to British Culture* (London: Arena, 1952). See also John Stuart Mill, 'Essays on Politics and Society'(first published in 1836), in *Collected Works* , V, xviii (University of Toronto, 1977); De Tocqueville in Lesley Johnson, *The Cultural Critics: From Matthew Arnold to Raymond Williams* (London: Routledge and Kegan Paul, 1979), p. 150.

8 For example, T.H. Huxley, W.T. Stead, W.E. Curtis, Lord Rosebury, Lord Derby and Cecil Rhodes. See Cyril Bibby, *Scientist Extraordinary – T.H. Huxley* (Oxford: Pergamon, 1972), p. 90; W.T. Stead, *The Americanisation of the World or The Trend of the Twentieth Century* (London: The 'Review of Reviews' Office, 1902) chapters ii and iii part IV, pp. 150–63.

9 Copies dating from 1904 are housed in the National Fairground Archive at Sheffield University and copies on microfiche may be viewed by prior arrangement with World's Fair Ltd., 2 Daltry Street, Oldham OL1 4BB.

10 John Springhall, *Coming of Age: Adolescence in Britain 1860–1960* (Dublin: Gill & Macmillan, 1986); David Fowler, *The First Teenagers: The Lifestyle of Young Wage-earners in Interwar Britain* (London: Woburn Press, 1995); Bill Osgerby, *Youth in Britain Since 1945* (Oxford: Blackwell, 1998).

11 Raymond Williams, *The Long Revolution* (London: Chatto & Windus, 1961), pp. 45–53.

12 Williams, *Long Revolution*, p. 49.

13 For example, the work of the Centre for Contemporary Cultural Studies; Peter Laurie, *The Teenage Revolution* (London: Anthony Blond, 1965); T.R. Fyvel, *The Insecure Offenders: Rebellious Youth in the Welfare State* (Harmondsworth: Penguin, 1963) and many more secondary sources.

14 Williams, *Long Revolution*, p. 52.

15 Williams, *Long Revolution*, p. 47.

16 Williams, *Long Revolution*, p. 49.
17 Antonio Gramsci, *Selections from the Prison Notebooks*, translated and edited by Quintin Hoare and Geoffrey Nowell-Smith (London: Lawrence & Wishart, 1971).
18 www.italnet.nd.edu/gramsci.
19 Raymond Williams, 'Base and Superstructure in Marxist Cultural Theory', *New Left Review*, 5/82 (1973), pp. 1–16.
20 Williams, 'Base and Superstructure', p. 9. Original emphasis.
21 Stanley Cohen, *Folk Devils and Moral Panics: The Creation of the Mods and Rockers* (New York: St Martins Press, 1980).
22 In the 1945 to 1960 period this is typically the press.
23 Cohen, *Folk Devils*, p. 24.
24 Pierre Bourdieu, *Distinction: A Social Critique of the Judgement of Taste*, translated by Richard Nice (London: Routledge & Kegan Paul, 1984).
25 Rachael Low and Roger Manvell, *British Film 1906–1914* (London: Allen & Unwin, 1948), p. 134; C.J. North, 'Our Foreign Trade in Motion Pictures', *Annals of the American Academy of Political and Social Science*, 128 (1926), p. 102.
26 See Simon Frith, *Performing Rites* (Oxford: Oxford University Press, 1998), p. 69.

Context: British acceptance and resistance to American popular culture before 1945

I: music and dance

Youth culture and juke box reception between the years 1945 and 1960 are the main concerns of this book. This occurred within a historical context of mass enthusiasm for, and acceptance of, American cultural products like popular music, cinema and dance that had been apparent throughout the first half of the twentieth century. The eagerness for American cultural commodities, though, was set against a background of intellectual hostility toward the feared effects of American cultural intrusions. Social perceptions of American cultural influences, however, have been more positive than the impressions given by earlier cultural critics like Matthew Arnold and F.R. Leavis.[1] If the negative 'intellectual' impressions of American cultural influence are contrasted with a view of a 'grass roots' reception of American popular culture over the same period, a clearer picture emerges of an overwhelmingly positive public response.

In the early twentieth century the American musical styles of ragtime and jazz, which were originally popularised through sheet music and later by gramophones, became a focus for rebellion against Victorian moral values and perceptions of 'respectability'. The vitality and syncopated rhythms of the American music were in direct opposition to the values of restraint and self-control inherent in the culturally dominant ideals of middle-class gentility. Dances like the Charleston and Blackbottom enhanced the body's versatility, and young men and women could dance closely and suggestively in a more sensuous routine than had been previously feasible, with the possible exception of the waltz.[2] American popular music's appeal was no doubt boosted, especially for the young of all classes, precisely because moralists throughout the early twentieth century deemed it to be unrespectable. Cultural historian D.L. LeMahieu explains that the names and steps of the dances which emerged during the ragtime era reflected this preoccupation with one's fundamental animal nature. The Turkey Trot, Grizzly Bear, Monkey Glide, Bunny Hug, and other whimsically named dance routines allowed the respectable classes to liberate themselves temporarily from the demanding conventions of social propriety. Freer, more spontaneous body movements replaced the precisely ordered, carefully prescribed steps of earlier ballroom dancing. Bodies swayed to the rhythm naturally and unselfconsciously.[3]

African-American influences in American popular music at this time were perceived as suggestive of sensuality and 'savagery' in direct opposition to Arnoldian notions of 'civilisation', and were seen by parts of the 'Establishment' as a retrogressive evolutionary step for society. What British people heard and danced to was admittedly a new sound but one that had been mediated through British social conditions.

The first jazz records were issued by HMV (His Master's Voice) in 1919 with their recordings of the Original Dixieland Jazz Band; the first ragtime records were issued by Columbia in 1921 and both of these supported a national dance craze.[4] This example of Americanisation and music and dance inevitably attracted a widespread British interpretation. James J. Nott notes that

> Older musical forms did persist and although popular music became increasingly Americanized, a separate British interpretation evolved. The British dance bands appropriated the American idiom and adapted it to the relatively conservative tastes of the British public. ... In the decade after the First World War the gramophone was one of the most important elements in the transformation of British popular music from its Edwardian and Victorian roots to a more American style.[5]

On a regional level Robert Roberts' detailed observations of Salford life in the early twentieth century identified aspects of 'Americanisation'. This was in the industrial working-class community of his upbringing, where he recorded how American-style music in the shape of ragtime songs 'flooded' into dance halls, ousting the 'traditional', and widely perceived as inferior, product of the music hall and public house, 'the bulk of which were of a wretched quality, with airs painfully banal and lyrics of an inanity that even the sub-literate rejected'.[6] A major reason for the popularity of the American ragtime tunes was that they were seen as so much better than what went before and consequently improved popular music's entertainment value.

Ragtime was originally a parody of European high cultural music: American musicians and their imitators were 'ragging' the melodies of social elites, and this was a process that was seen as impertinent toward the upper classes.[7] Record companies thought the 'real thing' to be too anarchic for the British consumer, and because of this a sanitised jazz developed for the home and white American market. Black American music had been Anglicised and the resulting musical form bore only a dim resemblance to the original product. A minority following for 'authentic' jazz did exist in Britain, though, and the *Melody Maker*, founded in 1926, supported the 'authentic' in opposition to the sanitised versions.[8] These American imports of 'authentic' jazz were for a predominantly middle-class niche market whose musical demands were 'inelastic'.[9]

It is certainly probable that Americanised popular music had a homogenising effect on British society – perhaps eroding class, regional and gender constraints – and that this was aided through the widespread use of gramophones and gramophone records. Prices of both the machines and the records fell in the inter-war period and they became a significant element in both working- and middle-class culture.[10] LeMahieu explains:

> As an instrument of Americanization, the gramophone helped buttress apparently opposing trends. … The men and women who enjoyed 'Hitchy Koo' and the Charleston came from Bradford and Oxford, from Hampstead and Battersea. Ragtime and jazz drew its public from all classes and regions. Moreover, they were styles particularly suited to youth.[11]

Although American popular music was not socially exclusive, as anyone could listen to it on a gramophone, public performances in many parts of Britain were attended almost exclusively by the 'lower orders' of society.[12] Popular reception of the new dances was strong in England's northwest, where 'the enormous rooms of the dance palaces of Lancashire and the popular seaside resorts' catered for thousands.[13] There was a massive popular welcome for American music and dance, albeit predominantly in its mediated Anglicised form. Ragtime and jazz were a revolt against the musical traditions of an older generation in much the same way that rock 'n' roll would be in the mid- to late 1950s.[14] Between 1913 and 1938, whilst the cost of living was falling, income for those in work nearly trebled and this made gramophone records affordable for many of the working class.[15] By 1914 gramophones were a status symbol that had 'penetrated deep into top working-class homes' where the bourgeoisie looked down upon gramophones and pianos for their 'mass-cultural' connotations.[16] By the start of the World War I the people of Salford were already enthusiastic consumers of American popular music and were familiar with gramophones and records; and by the 1920s, boosted by a developing 'hire purchase' system, gramophones had become commonplace.[17]

The development of recorded sound began in 1877 with Thomas Edison's wax cylinder phonograph, which was superseded in the 1890s by Emile Berliner's gramophone, which played ten-inch discs.[18] The British population ignored arguments raised against the sound of early gramophones that suggested they were simply a novelty with short playing time and poor sound quality and, after a slow start, the industry boomed in the 1920s.[19] Economies gained through mass production allowed the companies of Columbia and Decca to put a gramophone player on sale for around £4 or a fiftieth of the annual income of a railway clerk.[20] This was certainly influenced by the revolutionary effect of portable gramophones that came onto the market in 1914 with prices ranging from £3 to £9.[21]

Gramophones allowed American popular music to be widely disseminated in Britain, thereby accelerating American cultural influences. For the period 1919 to 1939, out of a total of 141 'Most Popular Songs' 132 originated in the US, 47 in the UK and 2 from elsewhere.[22] American music, however, was mediated by British social contexts and this was not 'a straightforward process of cultural displacement or substitution. [Because] [t]radition complicated the pattern of assimilation [and] Americanization became something recognisably British'.[23] Gramophone use affected leisure patterns and was linked to an inter-war craze for dancing: 'In palais-de-danse, church and mission halls, club rooms, municipal halls, swimming baths, hotels, restaurants, and even cinemas, large numbers participated regularly in dancing.'[24] The indications are that this mediation process, through British cultural conditions, was undoubtedly linked to venue.

Due to mechanical limitations gramophones set listening time at around three minutes. In this respect they were technologically deterministic and changed the nature and composition of popular music irrespective of nationality. These transformations occurred on both sides of the Atlantic so that in both Tin Pan Alley and Charing Cross Road songwriters wrote material specifically designed for the ten-inch disc. American jazz had to adapt its style as there was no longer any room for lengthy improvisations on a three- to four-minute recording.

Although in the first half of the twentieth century American popular music came to dominate the British record market,[25] the gramophone was only one part of a tradition of cultural fusion in music. Musical forms from Europe and the Americas had been at large and widely available for fifty years before the gramophone boom of the 1920s and had been vigor-ously promoted with the mass marketing of sheet music.[26] This meant that audiences were not necessarily unsophisticated or uninformed about musical styles in the early years of the gramophone. The importance of sheet music in the 'Americanisation' process should not be overlooked. Ragtime, for example, was music designed for the piano and though there are no accurate sales figures it is widely assumed that Scott Joplin tunes were consequently widely popular.[27]

Initially, however, the record industry pandered to the middle classes, where it saw the industry's future, and subsidised the production of their classical lists:

> Although sales of classical music were generally poor and loss making, such music was central to the industry's long-term strategy of winning over the middle classes. In such a climate popular music was seen as a 'necessary evil'. 'Necessary' because it sold well, 'evil' because of its associations with 'low' culture and 'vulgarity'.[28]

Though F.R. Leavis did not specifically criticise the gramophone in his 'Mass Civilisation' essay, Leavisite intellectuals perceived gramophones as a part of an overwhelming Americanisation of British culture because they were a mass-produced, mechanical commodity.[29] It was certainly the case that the rapid increase in gramophone ownership in the inter-war period meant an Americanisation and commercialism of the content, style and nature of popular music.[30] The gramophone's popularity contributed to a renaissance of live performances, and British musical interpretations neces-sarily rejuvenated and negotiated both ragtime and jazz.[31] The 'mechaniza-tion of music by the gramophone and other new technologies reconfigured rather than displaced the diversity of British musical culture'.[32]

American films dominated the cinema at the same time as American popular music came to dominate the British market in gramophone records: the *Daily Mail* reported in 1926 that 'the cinema today is almost wholly an appendage of the United States. ... The whole world is surfeited with an exclusive diet of American pictures'.[33] The massive cultural effect of the predominantly American cinema was noticed by Roberts and the 'upright' citizens of Salford, who were quick to find fault:

> Cinema in the early years of the century burst like a vision into the under-man's existence and, rapidly displacing both concert and theatre, became both his chief source of enjoyment and one of the greatest factors in his cultural development. ... Moralists were not long in condemning cinema as the tap-root of every kind of delinquency.[34]

Silent films did not necessarily show their place of origin and because of this much of their influence probably went unnoticed by the cinema-going public. Cinema and music in the inter-war period had a 'symbiotic relationship' because in the 1920s, for example, 75 to 80 per cent of British musicians were employed in cinema orchestras playing film scores.[35]

At the beginning of the twentieth century, the leisure industry was characterised by non-commercial or small entrepreneurial providers and this situation changed during the years leading up to World War II through a penetration of the leisure market by large-scale capitalist enterprises. In Rochdale, for instance, 'this transition occurs in the form of the decline of the pub, the music hall and the chapel relative to the rise of the dance hall and the cinema'.[36]

By the late 1930s popular entertainments centring on the pub, the recreational functions of churches and chapels, and music halls had dwindled. These were replaced, in the main, by the cinema and dance halls. In the early stages of this process it was not a simple displacement, as other entertainment premises remained open despite opposition. By 1913 in Salford the 'borough still retained its four theatres, but already thirteen premises had been licensed under the Cinematographic Act'.[37] Between the wars a few major companies took control of the film industry from filming to screening and the same process occurred with the dance halls, where the Mecca group became dominant, so that by 1939 a handful of oligopolies ran the main part of the newly emerged, capital-intensive, British leisure industry. The cinema was undoubtedly the most popular form of entertainment in the 1930s, and the main audience were working-class and predominantly young people.[38]

Mass entertainments have always been frowned upon by sections of the 'respectable' classes – frowned upon but not necessarily actively resisted, and there is an apparent consensus that traditional forms of entertainment in Britain were being discarded in favour of American ones. The novelist and playwright J.B. Priestley toured England in the 1930s and commented on what he saw as an erosion of 'authentic' entertainments by American and mass-cultural influences. In the seaside town of Blackpool he noted that it

> lacks something of its old genuine gaiety, its amusements are becoming too mechanised and Americanised. Talkies have replaced the old roaring variety turns. Gangs of carefully drilled young men and women (with nasal accents), employed by the music publishers to plug their 'hot Broadway hits', have largely replaced the Pierrots and Nigger [sic] minstrels. The entertainments

are more calculating, their shows more standardised, and the audiences more passive. It has developed a pitiful sophistication – machine made and not really English – that is worse than the old hearty vulgarity.[39]

John K. Walton, commenting on the Blackpool entertainment industry before World War II, agues that a mass-cultural, more American style of entertainment had emerged: 'the entertainment industry more generally was changing in step: more mechanisation, more national and international (or at least American) influences, less local idiosyncrasy and regional distinctiveness.'[40] Cinemas in the inter-war years played to capacity audiences in Rochdale where dance halls and skating rinks were also flourishing. From the 1920s dance schools were teaching 'the Charleston, Black-bottom, fox-trot, tango and Waltz to the youth of Rochdale'.[41]

The spread of American popular culture was aided through church halls and municipal buildings that were regularly hired out for dances and film screenings. The haphazard, local and small-scale nature of these venues of cultural diffusion, however, were in themselves part of a mediation process that necessarily led to a particularly regional audience reception. In Rochdale, for example, until the 1930s films screened in church halls were 'preceded with a prayer and a song',[42] and, more generally, cinema names throughout the UK like the Empire, Regal, Pavilion and Palace expressed a particularly British imperial hegemony.

II: Americanisation and World War II

There was a pronounced American military presence in Britain that began in 1942 and continued into the early years of the 1950s, and the military personnel, both enlisted and civilian, were direct agents of Americanisation. During the years 1942 to 1945 three million American servicemen and-women passed through Britain and this was the first contact that most people would have had with Americans in person.[43] The GIs had a difficult time adapting to what the British media had to offer, as David Reynolds notes: 'The lack of radios, phonographs [gramophones] magazines … was a constant complaint of the 8th Air Force in 1942. The BBC's dominance of the airwaves and the difficulty of importing American papers, magazines and movies also meant that many GIs found little to their taste from the media.'[44]

They were stationed, on the whole, in large out-of-town bases: for instance, at Greenham Common in Berkshire, Burtonwood near Warrington, and Wharton near Lytham on the Fylde coast. A slow uptake of British domestic hospitality was apparent, as noted by, for example, the provost marshal of the 8th Air Force in 1943: 'The British home, the one instrument through which a stronger bond between British and Americans could be forged, is not being entered as much as would be desired. Only two per cent of American troops are accepting existing hospitality.'[45]

However, where they were billeted amongst the indigenous community in houses and farms, positive attitudes toward the GIs were observed, not least because they boosted the local economy.

The GIs had mixed views on British hospitality, and cultural frictions were recorded. Reynolds, for example, notes the American sociologist Margaret Mead's observations that 'home hospitality – centrepiece of official efforts to welcome the GI – was anathema to many American soldiers. Off duty for a precious few hours, they had little desire to put on their manners and venture into the social minefield of an English teatime.'[46] However, even though 'a significant number of GIs never befriended English people and never entered their homes, there are a wealth of stories to show how mutual homesickness made many GIs into adopted family members.'[47] Both oral testimony and written memoirs suggest that the Americans were often liked and welcomed by people of all ages. Interviewee Jim Cheetham's family was among them. Jim's family owned an amusement park in Cheshire and he remembers that his 'father used to like them' and that his 'father and mother got on very well with them'.[48] GIs also helped out at harvest time when so many of the local labour force were away on military service:

> American soldiers [were] on leave from a nearby camp. All worked with enthusiasm and provided a social atmosphere which lightened the isolation which resulted from constant work and difficulties of transport. We housed them either in the farmhouse or in tents about the farmland and fed them either in the kitchen or, if the weather was fine, at a table on the flag terrace at the kitchen door.[49]

The American presence was not confined to enlisted men because there were also support personnel and, again, the impression they made on the local population was often positive. Jim Cheetham explains how these workers boosted both local morale and the local economy:

> Once the Americans came over to Burtonwood, they'd got loads of money and they could buy a bicycle and come out there. It was ten miles/nine miles. They'd got plenty of money and things picked up, and of course where you got the Americans you got plenty of girls, and so business was good, business was very good.

First of all we started off with a lot of Americans staying with us. ... You see they got all these American aeroplanes, the English, and nobody to service them, so they brought dozens of technicians over from – they were civilians – from San Antonio, Texas most of them came from. We used to put them up because we had a large house – about eight bedrooms – and we used to put up so many of them for the weekend, and then they'd spend the night in the club. So it was sort of leased land. They were happy to get into a private house which also had a club attached to it. So it worked both ways and comparatively speaking they were very well paid. They were certainly a lot better paid than the American army because they were being paid at civilian rates and then so much for coming overseas.[50]

An image of 'women and drink' that had built up around the GIs was often dissipated where billeting did occur, and in these cases there were reports of Americans integrating into the community. In January 1943, for example, a regional commissioner talked of the Bury (Lancashire) experience where 'several young officers who are attending a technical course are living in billets. They seem to be finding their way to local churches and forming large circles of English friends.'[51]

The Americans who came to Britain during the war inevitably engaged in mutual cultural exchange, learning and choosing to observe each other's 'ways of life'. A clear change of opinions toward America over the wartime period can be observed from the increase in favourable attitudes indicated by surveys conducted in these years. The words of Sir Godfrey Haggard, Head of American Forces Liaison in the British Ministry of Information in September 1945, for instance, note that a 'noticeably more intelligent and less critical attitude towards the Americans exists among the people of this country than when they arrived. [And that among the young] an unmistakable interest in America has been aroused.'[52]

Areas where the population was frequently in contact with Americans were left with impressions of American abundance. The Cheethams, for example, were shocked by the waste of seemingly exotic food they saw when providing entertainment for Americans from the surrounding area: 'But the food they wasted. We weren't starving but we weren't far off we were permanently hungry. And the food they used to waste it was terrible, just thrown away, potato salad and all sorts of cooked meats, things you'd never seen, just trodden in on the floor.'[53] The difference in diet between Americans and British civilians was so pronounced that it was a matter for cabinet concern where in 1944 questions were raised about the 'excessive' US rations. It was calculated that 'GIs were receiving ... three times the

British civilian rations.'[54] It is unsurprising, then, that for many British people America signified abundance.

Teenage girls, when coming into contact with the GIs, could be smitten by them. Officially these girls were perceived as victims of wartime disruption and many were evacuees who were placed in foster homes and 'forced into a premature and precocious adulthood'.[55] Although the GIs typically made liaisons with young working women in their late teens and early twenties the authorities were concerned about the mid-teenage promiscuity that could come about through the allure of American culture and apparent prosperity. A Home Office report from 1945 voiced these concerns:

> To girls brought up on the cinema, who copied the dress, hairstyles and manners of Hollywood stars, the sudden influx of Americans, speaking like the films, who actually lived in the magic country, and who had plenty of money, at once went to the girls' heads. The American attitude to women, their proneness to spoil a girl, to build up, exaggerate, talk big, and to act with generosity and flamboyance, helped to make them most attractive boyfriends.[56]

American popular culture's dissemination throughout Europe and the Far East characterised the wartime and post-war period and was aided by the juke boxes that followed American forces wherever they went. As 'instruments of subliminal propaganda they were as effective as any amount of political indoctrination'.[57] And the American juke box trade were aware of their cultural influence overseas. A chauvinistic article from the US in 1942 runs:

> We of the coin machine industry have maintained that nothing is more purely American than these machines. They were born and raised in this country. Until we made them no other part of the world had even thought of them. They were invented, built, sold and zoomed into popularity by the Americans.[58]

Juke boxes, however, were seen primarily as morale boosters by the US military command. American military bases in the UK contained juke boxes and, at their dances and social events, a number of invited Britons would have had a chance to see and hear them. More importantly, though, for the future expansion of the industry into new markets, the operators realised that they had a larger potential market outside the traditional British fairground and amusement arcade, and operators 'brought juke boxes out of the fairgrounds and off piers and relocated them in the clubs and public houses that the Yanks patronised. There were several Wurlitzer juke boxes in the Rainbow room in Leicester Square, and it was a learning exercise for the English coin business.'[59]

Indeed, due to the influx of American clientele, dance halls flourished. Among the most famous of these were London's Hammersmith Palais and Lyceum, but the dances were common all over the country. They were sited 'in church halls, town halls, even marquees – to phonograph records if there was no band … most villages had one a week.'[60] The 'Yanks' brought with them the new dance style of jitterbug or jiving that was based on the rather acrobatic African American dance routine of lindy hop.[61] This was an exciting dance where the girl could be spun around with her skirts flying, and the ability to jive added to the attraction of the GIs for young British women. The music that epitomised the period was the Big Band Sound associated with Glenn Miller, Tommy Dorsey and Artie Shaw.

Throughout the early twentieth century, in the areas of music, dance and the cinema, American influences had been overwhelmingly welcomed and absorbed into the fabric of Britain's popular culture. Moreover, the nature of British regional interpretations of American cultural imports had mediated their reception, resulting in a cultural fusion that became the dominant popular culture. The rest of the discussion is set in the context of established and active cultural interactions between Britain and the US.

III: Pre-war juke boxes

The story of juke box reception started within the context of cheap working-class entertainments in amusement arcades, seaside towns and fairgrounds. Before 1938 the juke box business in the UK was insignificant. There were probably fewer than a hundred machines before this date and most of these were second-hand.[62] The juke box companies of Wurlitzer and Seeburg had set up agencies in England in the mid-1930s when a limited amount of advertising for juke boxes in *World's Fair* began.[63] A 1938 advertisement referring to the annual Amusement Devices and Trades Exhibition held at the Royal Horticultural Hall ran

The Wurlitzer Simplex Automatic Gramophones
The world's finest automatic machines made by the makers of the world's finest musical instruments
See Them on Stand No. E6

M.J.Gubay   London Representative:
12 Victoria Avenue   British American Novelty Co. Ltd.
Rhyl   49, Fetter Lane, London E.C.4
Sole British Agent[64]

As the advertisement makes clear, Mr M.J. Gubay of Rhyl had been appointed the sole British agent for Wurlitzer Automatic Gramophones.[65] At this time the Wurlitzer 'automatic phonograph' business was a large industrial concern in America with large markets.[66] It is significant that the hugely successful company in the US chose an agent from the small Welsh coastal town of Rhyl because it reinforces the importance of a seaside connection to the UK's amusement industry. It is also significant that Mr Gubay and the London representatives, The British American Novelty Co. Ltd., launched the automatic gramophone as a fairground/amusement-arcade novelty attraction, because these were not the venues that generally attracted juke boxes in America.

A trade advertisement from 1938 promoted the 'Wurlitzer Gramophone' as an amusement machine along with other fairground novelties such as 'Clown', 'Pussy' and 'Bunny Shooters' and 'Fun Wall Machines' (Figure 1.1).[67] These fairgrounds were distinctly British venues for juke boxes and were quite different from their American counterparts. Juke boxes fitted well into the British fairground atmosphere not only because they were a mechanical novelty but also because, like many mechanical amusements of the time, they had a visible mechanism that offered the appeal of delivering something to see as well as something to hear.[68] Advertisements in the trade press stated that 'every arcade would have the Wurlitzer Gramophone' and that it was 'an arcade necessity',[69] and this is close to the truth because, in due course, most arcades would have a juke box.

The outstanding success of juke boxes in the States did not go unnoticed by the trade in Britain. Throughout the 1930s a regular column appeared in *World's Fair* titled 'U.S. Automatic News', which closely followed developments in the juke box business. British amusement machine manufacturers and operators could have been in no doubt of the potential that a juke box industry in the UK would have in catering establishments when hostilities ceased. Information on the success of the US business in the US was already filtering through before America entered the war in December 1941. A report from 1940, for example, stated that juke boxes in America directly supported 'at least 20,000 families, with at least 400,000 owners of restaurants, taverns and soda fountains sharing in its dividends' and that the industry employed at least 4,500 people in manufacturing new machines, accessories and records, while 146 established distributors employed an average of 1,168 workers. The same report claimed that the average operator owned 70 machines and 8,000 men were required to service them.[70]

Hawtin's Bunny Shooter, Hawtins Trade Catalogue, circa 1945

'Automatic Gramophones' were formally launched to the British trade
at the Royal Horticultural Hall, London in February 1938.[71] The advertising material and trade reports from this date suggest that these early

juke boxes could have been any of several pre-1938 models, which played sixteen selections of 78-rpm shellac discs, 'A' side only.[72] They contained Art Deco features and their visual impact was impressive. From the design of the few machines that were imported into Britain, however, it is evident that they were not stylistically radical as similar designs were already seen in early radio cabinets.[73]

Sales of Wurlitzers by the two British outlets were presumably successful, since in May 1938 Mr Gubay and the British American Novelty Co. Ltd. imported the very latest Wurlitzer model '24'. The model '24' (Plate 1) was an example of flamboyant American, mass-produced, Art Deco ostentation and *was* visually radical because it was the first 'light-up' juke box cabinet that featured illuminated plastics. As its name suggests it offered twenty-four selections of 78-rpm discs. The new arrival was reported in the *World's Fair*:

> New Wurlitzer Model:
> British American Novelty Co. Ltd., have now on show at 49, Fetter Lane the very latest '24' Model Wurlitzer coin-operated gramaphone which they are handling in conjunction with M. J. Gubay of Rhyl. The model is known as '24' for the simple reason that the machine gives clients the selection of 24 records, such selection being made by button stops on a dial indicator. The two front corners of the cabinet are of illuminated glass and inside at the back is an illuminated sunray. Green tube lighting enhances the appearance of the lower front of the cabinet.[74]

A spate of imports occurred in the next two years, indicating that there was a market for the music machines. The main American manufacturers consequently appointed agents in the UK. Mr Gubay opened premises in Leicester Square and Llandudno and started to sell American Rockola juke boxes as well as the up-to-date model '24' Wurlitzers.[75] By the outbreak of war in September 1939 the four major American juke box companies[76] were represented in Britain, though the handful of dealerships were mainly in the London area.[77] At this stage Wurlitzer clearly dominated the market in Britain as well as in America.[78]

Import restrictions imposed as a consequence of the war meant that few new juke boxes entered the country during World War II. In these years, however, some were available for sale, usually second-hand and often reconditioned by specialist companies. Trade press advertisements which regularly appeared in 1940 show that on the whole there was a balance between advertisements for juke boxes *wanted* and those for *sale*:

Wanted on Rent or Shares
One Waltonian / One Wurlitzer
For Arcade in Good Position in New Brighton

Buy Now / Brand New / Rockola / Phonos
In Stock, Write:- Gubay, Llandudno / or phone 6609

Chicago Automatic Machine Supply
Wurlitzers in Stock, Seen on the Premises
24, 16 and 12 record – Buy Now While Stocks Last[79]

Advertisements from 1944 show a continuing trade in juke boxes and also indicate a wide distribution across the British Isles. The following advertisements, for example, are for juke boxes in London, Belfast and Blackpool:

Chicago Automatic Machine Supply
13, St. George's Road, London, S.E.1.
For Sale   One only
Rockola   Almost new condition.   Last one made.
All Lit Up.   Finest Phonograph on the Market
Subject to being unsold. Gilt Edge Security.   Also an Investment
No Reasonable Offer Refused.

For Sale -One Only- 12-Way Wurlitzer   Guaranteed Perfect Condition
£375
Carriage and Insurance Paid in UK
Apply: Manager, Bellevue Amusement Park, Belfast

Two Model 500 Wurlitzers
Press Button Type, With 24 Records: Also
1 Large Keyboard Model
The Above are in Perfect Condition with Quantity of New Valves and
     Needles.
Offers Over £1,500 – Cox, 79, The Promenade Blackpool.[80]

Initial signs that juke boxes could be treated as a business separate from amusement machines are evident from an apparent agreement in the trade that reconditioning and overhauling juke boxes was an expert business:

Phonograph Overhauls:
The work of overhauling coin-operated phonographs is a fairly lengthy job; that is in comparison with similar jobs on bumper games and the like. It is not everywhere that this work can be placed, so operators of musical machines will be interested to hear … that the Scott Supply Company can, at the moment, undertake a limited number of orders for such overhaul and renovation …[81]

The juke box business was late to start in Britain and was minute compared to the established US industry. In the late 1930s and early 1940s all the machines in Britain were imports. Juke boxes were seen as fairground/ amusement arcade novelties and, since they had had no significant cultural impact, the emerging industry received scant attention.

In these venues a long association existed between Britain's youth and mechanical amusements, and connections were made between male youths, amusement arcades and delinquency. Violent male youth 'gangs' have been recorded as present throughout modern British history[82] and it is the 'delinquent' aspect of male youth behaviour that has received a disproportionate amount of press coverage, perhaps influencing the process.[83] There was a public impression that male youths and amusement arcades were a lethal combination. 'Pin tables', for example, were a fad that had raised public concerns in the years before the war. In February 1936, for instance, *World's Fair* printed a lurid account of violent youths armed with razor blades entering 'pin table saloons' intent on violent attack; in 1938 it reported a 'Pin-Table Menace'; in April of that year a review appeared on arcades and 'undesirable' elements and further comment was reported under the headline 'Alleged Stabbing Affray at West End Fun Fair'.[84]

Popular music was a part of the fairground/seaside resort tradition in the first half of the twentieth century and oral testimony suggests that many people's first recognition of pop music was accompanying mechanical rides.[85] Early sightings of juke boxes in Britain were typically at fairgrounds where American machines were positioned prominently. The visible mechanism was part of the experience and integral to the amusement machine tradition.[86] At the same time fairgrounds and arcades were regarded as magnets for deviant male youths, and this perception was confirmed in reported references to deviancy.

Juke boxes in Britain, both before and during World War II, were accepted within the established industry of mechanical amusements. The juke boxes at this time were originally imported and were seen as novelties, and little effort was made to introduce them to more 'respectable' locations. Arcade, fairground and seaside economies were based on low-cost rides and amusement machines. Juke boxes fitted into this tradition because their profitability depended upon minimal financial outlay (2d per record) and high turnover.

In the years leading up to the World War II the juke box industry was poised for 'take off'. The next chapter looks at the position following the war, when Britain started to manufacture and design its own machines, and how this mediated their style, size and capacity. This tailoring of juke boxes to suit British conditions allowed the machines to cross over from their arcade and fairground locations to small catering establishments on the high street.

Notes

1 Matthew Arnold, *Culture and Anarchy* (Cambridge: Cambridge University Press, 1960) first published 1868; F.R. Leavis, 'Mass Civilisation and Minority Culture' in *For Continuity* (Cambridge: Minority Press, 1933).
2 D.L. LeMahieu, *A Culture for Democracy: Mass Communication and the Cultivated Mind in Britain Between the Wars* (Oxford: Clarendon, 1988), p. 93. For a full discussion of African-American dance in America see Katrina Hazzard-Gordon, *Jookin: The Rise of Social Dance Formations in African-American Culture* (Philadelphia: Temple University Press, 1990).
3 LeMahieu, *A Culture*, p. 93.
4 James J. Nott, *Music for the People: Popular Music and Dance in Interwar Britain* (Oxford: Oxford University Press, 2002), p. 49.
5 Nott, *Music*, p. 55.
6 Robert Roberts, *The Classic Slum: Salford Life in the First Quarter of the Century* (Manchester: University of Manchester Press, 1971), p. 119.
7 See for example Edward A. Berlin, *Ragtime: A Musical and Cultural History* (London: University of California Press, 1980), pp. 66–71; Terry Waldo, *This is Ragtime* (New York: Da Capo, 1991), p. 4.
8 LeMahieu, *A Culture*, p. 95.
9 Nott, *Music*, p. 18.
10 Nott, *Music*, p. 36.
11 LeMahieu, *A Culture*, p. 96.
12 See Paul Wild, 'Recreation in Rochdale, 1900–40' in *Working Class Culture*, ed. by J. Clarke, C. Critcher and R. Johnson (London: Hutchinson, 1979), pp. 140–60; Roberts, *Classic Slum*.
13 LeMahieu, *A Culture*, p. 97.
14 See chapter 3.
15 Nott, *Music*, p. 36.
16 Roberts, *Classic Slum*, p. 121.
17 Roberts, *Classic Slum*, p. 185.
18 Gelatt, *The Fabulous Phonograph*, chapter 4.
19 LeMahieu, *A Culture*, chapter 2 'Technology and Tradition'; see also Gelatt, *The Fabulous Phonograph*.
20 Gelatt, *The Fabulous Phonograph*, p. 101; LeMahieu, *A Culture*, pp. 82–3.
21 Nott, *Music*, p. 41.
22 Nott, *Music*, 'Appendix', pp. 237–44.

23 LeMahieu, *A Culture*, p. 82.

24 Nott, *Music*, p. 40.

25 Ironically, however, it probably boosted the dissemination of classical and minority tastes as large revenues created through sales of popular music freed up funds to record and distribute less popular musical forms. In LeMahieu's words 'BiederBieck did not exclude Bach'. LeMahieu, *A Culture*, p. 87.

26 See, for example, Derek Scott, *The Singing Bourgeois: Songs of the Victorian Drawing Room and Parlour* (Milton Keynes: Open University Press, 1989), chapters 2, 'The Growth of the Market for Domestic Music' and 4 'Cultural Assimilation'.

27 LeMahieu, *A Culture*, pp. 91–2.

28 Nott, *Music*, p. 48.

29 F.R. Leavis, 'Mass Civilisation' in *For Continuity*, pp. 16–17.

30 Nott, *Music*, p. 51.

31 Nott, however, maintains that this meant less live music.

32 LeMahieu, *A Culture*, p. 98.

33 The *Daily Mail*, 1926, quoted in William Marston Seebury, *The Public and the Motion Picture Industry* (New York: Macmillan, 1926), p. 201.

34 Roberts, *Classic Slum*, p. 140.

35 LeMahieu, *A Culture*, p. 90.

36 Wild, 'Recreation', p. 140.

37 Roberts, *Classic Slum*, p. 141.

38 Jeffrey Richards, *The Age of the Dream Palace: Cinema and Society in Britain 1930–1939* (London: Routledge & Kegan Paul, 1984), pp. 11–13.

39 J.B. Priestley, *English Journey* (London, 1934), p. 267.

40 John K. Walton, 'Afterword: Mass-Observations, Blackpool and some alternatives' in *Worktowners at Blackpool: Mass-observation and Popular Leisure in the 1930s,* ed. by Gary Cross (London: Routledge, 1990), p. 233.

41 Wild, 'Recreation', p. 148.

42 Wild, 'Recreation', p. 141.

43 David Reynolds, *Rich Relations: The American Occupation of Britain, 1942–1945* (London: Harpers Collins, 1995), p. 24. In October 1944 from a total UK presence of 630,561, Lancashire received 40,480 rising to 45,028 by January 1945. Statistics from Reynolds, *Rich Relations*, pp. 395, 6. It should be noted, though, that there were few GIs in Scotland or Wales and that in Northern Ireland there were a 'distinct set of reactions', Reynolds, *Rich Relations*, p. 257. Much has been written about the cultural interaction between American military personnel and their hosts in these years and I would direct the interested reader in the first instance, to Reynolds' detailed monograph, *Rich Relations*, particularly section IV, 'Real Life'.

44 Reynolds, *Rich Relations*, p. 247.

45 Reynolds, *Rich Relations*, p. 249.

46 Reynolds, *Rich Relations*, p. 254.

47 Reynolds, *Rich Relations*, p. 281.

48 Jim Cheetham, b. 1929 interviewed at Hale, Cheshire, 2 November 2001. Tape ref: T.05.

49 Stella C. Davies, *North Country Bred* (London: Routledge, 1963), p. 239.

50 Cheetham Tape ref: T.05.

51 Quoted in Reynolds, *Rich Relations*, p. 150.

52 BBC Listener Research Report 'America', 17 February 1944, in Reynolds, *Rich Relations*, p. 435.

53 Jim Cheetham Tape ref: T.05.

54 Reynolds, *Rich Relations*, p. 149.

55 Reynolds, *Rich Relations*, p. 267.

56 Richard M. Titmuss, *Problems of Social Policy* (London, 1950), p. 562, quoted in Reynolds, *Rich Relations*, p. 267.

57 John Krivine, *Juke Box Saturday Night* (London: Bucklebury, 1988),, p. 129.

58 Trade article quoted in Pearce, *Jukebox Art*, pp. 44–5.

59 Krivine, *Juke Box Saturday*, p. 129.

60 Reynolds, Rich Relations, pp. 263–4.

61 See Hazzard-Gordon, Katrina, *Jookin: The Rise of Social Dance Formations in African-American Culture* (Philadelphia: Temple University Press, 1990), p. 133.

62 Krivine, *Juke Box Saturday*, p. 128.

63 Krivine, *Juke Box Saturday*, p. 128.

64 *World's Fair* (WF), 5 February 1938, p. 34.

65 Referred to by the Wurlitzer Company in the US as 'Automatic Phonographs' – never juke boxes – and in Britain, initially, as 'Automatic Gramophones'. Wurlitzer always referred to their juke boxes as 'automatic phonographs' in an attempt to avoid the black and sexual connotations of the word 'juke' – in Britain the name held no such associations.

66 In 1936 Wurlitzer sold 44,397 machines – Ian Brown, Nigel Hutchins, Gerry Mizera, *The Ultimate Jukebox Guide 1927–1974* (Brighton: Pla-mor, 1994), p. 115.

67 WF, 5 March 1938, p. 41.

68 Krivine, *Juke Box Saturday*, p. 128. See also Chris Pearce, *Jukebox Art* (London: Blossom, 1991), p. 94.

69 WF, 12 March 1938, p. 41; 19 March 1938, p. 41.

70 WF, 2 November 1940, p. 14.

71 WF, 19 February 1938, p. 40.

72 They used a 'Simplex' mechanism that was superseded in the autumn of 1937 with the 'Model 24' and '24A', which were also Wurlitzer's first models with 'Light-Up' cabinets. See Frank Adams, *Wurlitzer Jukeboxes 1934–1974* (Seattle: AMR Publishing, 1983); Vincent Lynch, *American Jukebox: The Classic Years* (San Francisco: Chronicle Books, 1990), p. 100.

73 See Adrian Forty, 'Wireless Style, Symbolic Design and The English Radio Cabinet 1928–33', *Architectural Association Quarterly*, 4/2 (spring 1972), pp. 23–31.

74 WF, 7 May 1938, p. 41.
75 WF, 28 January 1939, p. 40; 25 March 1939.
76 Wurlitzer, Mills, Seeburg and Rockola.
77 The agents were as follows; Wurlitzer: Mr Gubay, Rhyll, British American Novelty Co. Ltd., London, Gerrard Novelty Co. Ltd., London; Rockola – Mr Gubay, Llandudno; Mills Phonographs: Coin Amusement Supply Ltd., London; Seeburg: Gerrard Novelty Co. Ltd., London.
78 See Krivine, *Juke Box Saturday*, p. 42.
79 WF, 30 March 1940; 11 May 1940 p. 20; 15 June 1940, p. 18.
80 WF, 1 July 1944, p. 14; 2 September 1944, p. 14; 16 September 1944, p. 14.
81 WF, 9 December 1944, 'Automatic Gossip by Sevarg', p. 14.
82 See for example John Springhall, *Coming of Age: Adolescence in Britain 1860–1960* (Dublin: Gill & Macmillan, 1986); David Fowler, *The First Teenagers: The Lifestyle of Young Wage-earners in Interwar Britain* (London: Woburn Press, 1995); Geoffrey Pearson, *Hooligan: A History of Respectable Fears* (London: Macmillan, 1983); Roberts, *Classic Slum*.
83 See chapter 5, and for a full discussion of this phenomenon see Stanley Cohen, *Folk Devils and Moral Panics: The Creation of the Mods and Rockers* (New York: St Martins Press, 1980).
84 *World's Fair*, 1 February 1936, p. 17; 26 March 1938, p. 41; 16 April 1938, p. 33.
85 Conversation with Tony Holmes 11 January 1999; Krivine, *Juke Box Saturday*, p. 128; Adrian M. Horn, *Americanisation and Youth Culture: Juke boxes and cultural fusions, with special reference to Northwest England 1945–1960*, PhD, Lancaster, 2004.
86 Krivine, *Juke Box Saturday*, p. 128; Pearce, *Jukebox Art*, p. 94.

2

Americanisation and the post-war juke box

This chapter continues with the theme of a developing British juke box industry. In part I (1945–54), through predominantly visual comparisons of juke boxes of the period from both sides of the Atlantic, it illustrates how the American styles of industrial Art Deco and Streamlining scarcely affected British juke box design. This situation changed in the mid-1950s, when American styles *did* begin to influence the rapidly expanding industry. Part II (1954–60) shows how post-war conditions peculiar to Britain meant that these American influences, though increasing, never dominated the look of the machines.

I: 1945–54

American visual design was, to all intents and purposes, excluded from the British amusement machine market from 1945 to 1954. During this period American influences on juke boxes, machines that may be seen as archetypal symbols of American popular culture, were minimal, and when they did affect British design, style fusions were created that were identifiably British and of the period. There are several reasons for this state of affairs, ranging from restricted supplies of raw materials and sterling inconvertibility, to ingrained hostility towards American visual aesthetics and style influences. In the decade after the end of World War II juke boxes were manufactured to British specifications to cater for perceived British tastes and pockets.

This section traces the development of a stylistically distinctive British juke box industry from its beginnings in Blackpool in 1945 to the first imported American style influences in British-made juke boxes in 1954. It continues by exploring the reasons behind resistances to American designs, which meant that even with juke boxes British manufacturers did not imitate the distinctive flamboyance of the American product. Indeed, in the post-war climate the idea of 'Britishness' was seen as an important selling point in itself, and a war theme is central to the first production models. A reluctance to adopt American styling was combined with a particular set of economic conditions that made the physical importation of American juke boxes impossible.

The first sign of a British-made juke box appeared in December 1944 in an advertisement for the Hawtins Company of Blackpool. Hawtins were specialist manufacturers of fairground equipment and amusement arcade devices, and during the war their production changed to the manufacture of military aircraft components. By the end of 1944, however, they were preparing to revert to peacetime manufactures.

2.2   Wurlitzer Victory, contemporary advert

The advertisement (Figure 2.1) displayed Hawtin's prototype juke box as part of 'Tomorrow's' production and it stood next to a streamlined locomotive, inserted to signify modernity. The picture includes, along with military aircraft, fairground rides and amusement machines, an artist's impression of the intended post-war juke box. This was probably based on the American Wurlitzer 'Victory' cabinet of 1942 (Figure 2.2) which, though sporting brightly coloured and decorated translucent panels, was, due to wartime restrictions on materials, one of the more staid and unimaginative designs in the Wurlitzer range. In the Hawtins production models the design was then toned down so that these illuminated panels were undecorated, consisting of plain opaque glass.[1]

The first British juke box, the Jack Hylton Music Maker Mark I, was in production by the winter of 1945 (Figure 2.3).[2] It is not certain how many of these Jack Hylton Music Makers were manufactured but the factory

Artist's impression of the Jack Hylton Music Maker, Hawtins Trade Catalogue,   **2.3**
circa 1945

brochure suggests that the number would have been substantial; 2,000 is a reasonable guess. Figure 2.4 shows the factory in full production.

In their advertising the Hawtins Company stressed and made capital from the Music Maker's 'Britishness'. The 1944 advertisement (Figure 2.1) featured military aircraft, and this drew attention to the company's wartime role as an aircraft component manufacturer and suggested that buying from them was a patriotic act. The war theme was understandably fixed in the public imagination of the period and the Hawtins catalogue provided several examples of this along with the requisite patriotic overtones. The large toy 'Tank', for instance (Figure 2.5) 'is decorated in camouflage [and] gaily coloured in red, white and blue'.[3] This military fixation reflected how the British saw themselves as having won the war, and these military images mirrored a feeling of patriotic pride and Britishness. British-made juke boxes throughout the late 1940s and 1950s often stressed their British origin and that they were not overly influenced by American design.

Hawtins' second production model juke box was launched to the trade at the Amusement Devices and Trades Exhibition in London in February 1946. The machine was called the 'Jack Hylton Music Maker Mark II' and the appearance of the cabinet differed dramatically from the 1945 model (Plate 2). The new, imaginative design of the Mark II was born out of necessity as well as a desire for a modern appearance: wood for the cabinets was in short supply but aluminium was relatively plentiful as wartime material was melted down for peacetime purposes.

Jack Hylton's endorsement of both models adds another element to the discussion and is significant because his music was acceptable to the

2.4   Juke box assembly at Hawtin's factory, Hawtins Trade Catalogue, circa 1945

The 'Tank', Hawtins Trade Catalogue, circa 1945   **2.5**

mainstream: it was a form of 'sanitised' American Swing characterised in retrospect as 'sedate and generally bland'.[4] Hylton's endorsement combined with the 'old fashioned' furniture look of the Mark I cabinet and the modernist appearance of the Mark II went against any notion that it might be subversive or rebellious through association or style.

The Mark II was a brave step into a unique British strain of modernist design and as far as its appearance went, artistically, technically and in its dimensions, it bore no resemblance to its American counterparts. It was American only through its associations. It is, however, an archetypal example of the 'Anglicisation' of an American mass-produced commodity, and this point is best illustrated by comparing it with two popular American juke boxes of the period. The American-made Filben Maestro (Plate 3) was a wonderful specimen of 'shocking' flamboyance from the American 1940s that featured a profusion of highly polished chromium plate, subsequently described as 'the marriage between power and beauty'.[5] Taking its artistic influences from pre-war streamlining it also boasted a 'wraparound' windscreen straight from the aircraft industry (a feature that would be

repeated in the Cadillacs of the mid-1950s) as well as a central Aztec Art
Deco gleaming metal cobrahead. It played 30 x 78-rpm records and stood
nearly five feet high and three feet wide.

Arguably the most famous Wurlitzer juke box of all time is the model
'1015' (Plate 4), which has become an icon of 1950s American youth culture.
It was ostentatiously bright and glitzy, featuring multi-coloured bubble
tubes and an ornate front grille. Like the Maestro it was comparatively
large, standing five feet high and three feet wide.[6] Here the differences in
design and technology between the American and the British products can
be seen as striking and pronounced.

Unique pre-war economic influences led to flamboyance becoming a
mainstream factor in American industrial design, and these were not replicated in Britain. These specific market conditions were situated in 1920s
and 1930s America and, in the case of the juke box business, ostentatious
visual design had peaked before the war in the late 1930s, an era that is
known as the 'golden age' of juke boxes. In respect of style and design
the American juke box industry borrowed ideas from earlier American
manufacturers that, in the late 1920s, began to realise the benefits in sales
that could be obtained by employing industrial designers. These professionals were put to use redesigning the outward appearance of all manner
of industrial goods, from locomotives and cars to telephones and cameras.
Penny Sparke explains the conditions that led to the rise of the industrial designer in the 1920s: 'Fierce competition meant that the functional
efficiency of the new goods and … advertising could no longer act as the
only selling tools and inevitably the choice between a number of similar
articles began to be determined by appearance. – A factor that had hitherto
been given only minimal attention.'[7]

This specifically American trend occurred because by the mid-1920s the
market for manufactured goods was 'glutted' at a time when recession was
looming. Industrial design, from this point, was to take a leading role in
presenting industrially produced commodities. 'By giving objects visual
sales appeal' manufacturers could gain a commercial edge.[8]

Design in the American juke box industry became increasingly important by the late 1930s and the trade thought that because a juke box was a
medium of entertainment it needed to *look* entertaining. An industry greedy
for annually increasing sales made certain that juke boxes would stand out
from their positions to be the centre of attention and, like arcade and
fairground machines, almost demand to be fed with money. Obsolescence

came quickly to American juke boxes whose designs were soon upstaged by a stream of new models presented to the market. The 'eye appeal' of juke boxes was as important to the industry as their 'ear appeal'.

Part of the resistance of the British design establishment to 1940s American design was that the styles of Streamline, Art Deco and Baroque were seen as unrestrained. They were perceived as gaudy and in bad taste by such bodies as the Council of Industrial Design (COID), whose orthodoxy was a style of modernism that was often linked to a sense of 'Britishness'. 'In the immediate post-war period the protagonists of 'good design', based on modernist sensibilities, aligned it with the ethos of the war years and a sense of national pride.'[9]

1954 Cadillac series 6   **2.6**

The 'Music Maker Mark II' (Plate 2) is a particularly intriguing example of the restrained, industrial British modernism of the period that was influenced by wartime utility. It was aesthetically simple with clean lines and its form followed its function. It was remarkably subdued for a juke box and with cream-coloured, easily cleaned surfaces it looks rather like a fridge from the same period.

A clear parallel can be made between the American car industry, where re-packaging and re-styling had become commonplace by the late 1930s, and the juke box business, with both industries displaying a commitment to visual obsolescence by regularly producing new models. In terms of style American cars were the antithesis of what was perceived as tasteful in British design. Chrome was a new experience for most Britons, and cars like the 1954 Cadillac included many examples of unfamiliar and aggressive symbols of speed like chromium 'rockets' on the bumper (Figure 2.6).[10] Reyner Banham explains that they 'were like space ships, or visitors from another planet or something',[11] and the COID used phrases like 'does not even look like a motor car'.[12] The British public, however, except around London, would be unlikely to have seen American cars with their own eyes but only in magazines and Hollywood films.[13] American design had little to do with British car design, though minor features were borrowed and toned down.

Stylistic influences, as with the Filben Maestro juke box (Plate 3), came from the jet aircraft industry. Some 1950s Cadillacs, for example, featured simulated air-intakes along their sides that were symbols of performance that did not actually need to work in reality because it was enough for them to *signify* jet performance. Tail fins started to appear in the late 1940s and early 1950s and these spurred the disfavour of an influential British design hierarchy. The *Architectural Review* maintained a consistent anti-American stance. For the British design establishment, dominated by the ideals of modernism and 'form following function', stylised was bad and functional was good, and there was no middle ground. Contemporary hostility within the British design intelligentsia on the part of Edgar Kauffman and other prominent figures is hard to comprehend when looked at outside of the wider mass-cultural debate the background of which has been discussed in the introduction.

There are also some very practical reasons why American-designed cars would never be accepted in Britain at this time, and these were the crux of the style-mediation process. Average Britons were not wealthy when compared to average Americans and this difference was particularly acute in the first decade after the war when widespread rationing was in place. Although there were signs that consumer purchases were increasing, most of the British public were unlikely to be able to afford to buy a car on which unnecessary styling was perceived to have added to the cost. American manufacturers in Britain were aware of this and adapted their styles to suit the presiding cautious tastes. Ford, for example, who had been producing cars in Britain since 1911, designed the 'Popular' and 'Prefect' to reflect British tastes and to sell within the prevailing trading conditions. In the case of juke boxes American influences on British industrial design, and *vice versa*, were extremely limited.

British design in the post-war period is distinctive and symbolic of the particular time and place. The Morris Minor of 1948, for example, was a functional 'people's car', and advertising material from the time stressed its economical use of petrol. It remained in production until 1971 and, although it contained examples of streamlining on the bonnet, these were minimal and had fused with its functional shape to produce a car that is a fitting example of a popular British style from the age. It sold over a million models.

After the war, Britain was unable to import American manufactured goods and this physically stopped, or at least severely inhibited, a dissemination of American styling and design. Britain had accumulated vast debts to pay for its war effort and a re-financing package, subsidised predominantly by America, meant that Britain would be committed to debilitating repayments of $140m per annum for the rest of the twentieth century. The US government insisted that these repayments were made in currency that was convertible into dollars and, because the post-war Labour Government could not meet the demand for dollars, they made the pound 'unconvertible'.[14] To put it more simply, the Bank of England would not exchange a pound sterling for its equivalent value in dollars.

At the beginning of the war the Board of Trade introduced a licensing system that restricted 'luxury' imports. For the juke box industry this meant that throughout the war years juke boxes became available only as second-hand and/or reconditioned and, because of a catalogue of new restrictions and extensive government control, new machines were not imported into the country. In 1946 only one-third of all imports were in private hands; that is to say, outside of the state sector. Of this third, nine-tenths were restricted by import controls – all imported manufactured goods were subject to a government licence, and further restrictions imposed in the summer and autumn of 1947 were specifically intended to move imports away from dollar sources.[15] Moreover, a series of economic crises in the 1950s led to further restraints.[16] After the war there were two main problems for Britain's economy. Firstly, Britain had been living beyond her means and, secondly, Britain's productive capacity had been disrupted through the war effort and it would clearly take several years for its production to return to a peacetime footing.[17]

Press reports from the period claim that the War Office encouraged the Music Maker consortium to manufacture juke boxes. Britain was trying hard to return to stable peacetime production and the government was keen to attract foreign currency, especially dollars, through exports. The *Nottingham Journal* reported that

> **Every Little Helps**
> One of the new British industries to spring into activity under a Labour Government is the manufacture of juke boxes or, to give them their sedate British name, 'Music Makers'.
> A firm whose pre-war business was fun fair accessories and who turned over to aircraft production was asked early this year to make juke boxes by the War Office. It is turning out about 25 a week, mostly for B.A.O.R.[18]

The American connection was evidently a strong one. Wartime influences of American popular culture on Britain and Europe are hard to quantify but a demand certainly existed for juke boxes and the music they played. The manufacturing capacity of much of mainland Europe had been devastated, whilst in Blackpool Hawtins were geared up for full production (the above report suggests an initial capacity of twenty-five or thirty machines per week). The potential market at home and abroad must have seemed huge to the Music Maker consortium.

Jack Hylton introduced some distinctly British 'show biz' glamour to promote the machines. An item in *The Performer* shows Hylton's use of his entertainment contacts for promotion and indicates a desire for mainstream acceptance. The Music Makers were a British product endorsed by British celebrities:

> Almost all the stars of the various Hylton shows were on view and had their photographs taken by zealous press men – usually in clusters around the instrument [Music Maker], looking at it, pointing at it, caressing it. Among those who enlivened the proceedings were Will Hay, Jimmy Nervo and Teddy Knox, Billy Caryll and Hilda Mundy, Peggy Rawlins, Jean Adrienne, Bebe de Roland, Louis Green, Evelyn Dall, Arthur Askey, Erin de Selfa.[19]

Technical differences between American and British juke boxes were considerable, however, and comparisons highlight the lack of sophistication in the home-produced product. Though modern for Britain, Music Makers were technically old-fashioned by American standards. They used a pre-war mechanism and it is unlikely that the British machine would have been technically superior in any area, though Hylton publicity office's hyped claims of technical superiority were all good commercial exposure.[20]

Initially the Music Makers were sold to the trade mainly through agents. Arcadia Automatic Instruments Ltd. of Manchester were prominent among them and started advertising the 'Hawtin Juke Boxes' from September 1946. These regular Arcadia advertisements focused on the main qualities of the Music Makers. They stressed the design –'Introducing The Mark II – Super Modernistic in Operation and Appearance'; and claimed, 'It's the New Music Maker – It's the Best Money Taker'; and invited inspection whilst offering hire purchase agreements.[21]

Though figures are not available it appears that both Music Maker models were popular machines, not least because there was nothing else new on the market. How many of the estimated twenty-five to thirty machines per week (or 1,500 per annum) went to export and how many to the home market, we can only guess. Despite trade for the Mark II being clearly buoyant the Music Maker business was sold in September 1947 to a Mr Norman Ditchburn, from Blackpool. This sale was barely twenty months after the Mark II was launched and this was, perhaps, because the government contracts had 'dried up'. Writing in 1958, Bingo Beaufort noted Mr Ditchburn's commercial foresight in buying the business and predicted that consumer trends in Britain would follow similar lines to those in America:

> After thorough investigation he [Ditchburn] concluded that just as Britain was slowly but surely following America in things like domestic refrigeration so the British public would in time follow the American habit of music while you eat – or drink – and in the Music Maker he saw the opportunity to develop this wonderful market in Britain.[22]

Ditchburn made the decision not to sell the Music Maker juke boxes on the home market but to site them instead, sharing the takings with the site owner: Ditchburn claimed to have 500 on site by 1949.[23] There were still privately owned machines in circulation, however, and Music Makers were available through a buoyant second-hand market: 'Though the Ditchburn policy was not to sell there were still plenty of Music Makers about and

THE *HIDEAWAY* MODEL
WITH MULTIPLE WALL BOX SELECTION

Occupying only about 20in. x 12in. of a wall, the Hideaway is ideal where floor space is limited, or where selector points are required in more than one room, or where more than one point in a room is desirable.

The mechanism of a Music Maker is hidden away in any upper, basement or back room and is wired to the Hideaway. The coins are inserted in the Hideaway and the loud speakers are independently controlled by the site owner.

The Hideaway is attractively finished in gold and chrome.

2.7   The Ditchburn Hideaway of 1955

these were regularly traded both second-hand and reconditioned, privately and through dealers.'[24] An advert from 1953 ran: 'Music Makers Reconditioned, Guaranteed, Delivered and Installed £350 each, Music Hire Service, Burton Road, West Didsbury.[25]

Ditchburn dominated the market and because of a lack of competition there was little commercial incentive to force stylistic and technical improvements and to introduce new models. Indeed, Ditchburn did not introduce a new model until 1954 with their 'Hideaway' wall box which, although new for Britain, still offered only sixteen selections and was unassuming in appearance (Figure 2.7). This machine did, however, suit sedate venues because the idea was to 'hideaway' the workings and not to celebrate them in flamboyance. It was an indication that juke boxes were 'crossing over' into more mainstream locations from the amusement arcades and seaside/fairground venues. *World's Fair* reported from the

British Industries Fair (geared for British exporters) in May 1955, drawing attention to its functionality and stylistic restraint:

> Ditchburn showed and demonstrated, with good trade results, their 'Hide Away' installation for locations where the presence of a juke-box as such is, for one reason or another, not required. In some place away from the music to be sold, the usual mechanism is sited without, naturally, the standard dressy cabinet.[26]

The Ditchburn 'Hideaway' was comparatively dated for 1954: Automatic Musical Instruments (AMI) introduced the twenty-selection 'Mighty Midget' to the American market in 1938 and since then wall boxes had been an established part of the American juke box business. Indeed, by 1955, just one year after Ditchburn's wall box, Wurlitzer were producing 104-selection wall boxes (model 5207) in bright chrome finishes.[27] Ditchburn juke boxes were technically unsophisticated and distinctly British in appearance, and were lagging behind the American product by at least ten years. Ditchburn offered sixteen selections, one side only, from 78-rpm shellac discs. In the US 100-selection machines had been available since 1948 using 45-rpm 7-inch vinyl discs, and 200-play machines were available from 1955.[28] Imported technology would be needed to 'up-date' British juke boxes.

In November 1953 Arcadia Automatics of Cheetham Hill Road, Manchester launched the Minstrel and it went into full production the following year. It is perhaps one of the most peculiar looking juke boxes ever built, and like the Music Maker Mark II it appeared to stand on sledge runners. A caption across the top of the machine reads 'He Who Pays the Minstrel Calls the Tune' (Figure 2.8), and it sold for £395 including purchase tax. Considering that the Minstrel was such an odd-looking machine with a limited play selection it received a very favourable press. Edward Graves called it 'exciting' and 'beautiful' and made reference to modernist tendencies:

> 'The Minstrel', a creation of Arcadia Automatic Acoustics Ltd., which is the most exciting thing in juke-boxes yet to come my way. Following the modern trend, it provides a striking example of what can be done by plastic craftsmen in turning out an eye arresting job made all the more beautiful by cutting out the once-favoured ostentatious ornamentation. Anything other than clean lighting would not suit this type of design and in that respect Arcadia have made no mistakes. The front is boldly curved, the line being continued through the entirely translucent top.[29]

Graves made a telling point when he claimed that it is 'made all the more beautiful by cutting out the once-favoured ostentatious ornamentation'. His comments mimicked the views of the orthodox design establishment, though what the COID may have made of the Minstrel's styling is not recorded. Other *World's Fair* reports impressed its Britishness and modern design, which had been consistent selling points since the end of World War II. Advertising captions read, 'The new all-British juke-box', and this indicated patriotic support for home-built products in an austere age.[30]

Although the *Manchester Evening News* stated that the Minstrel cabinet was made of 'streamlined wood and plastic'[31] it was clearly without American visual design influences. It played sixteen 10-inch 78-rpm discs on both sides,[32] and although thirty-two plays was still not a grand selection for 1954 Arcadia promoted this as an advantage optimistically maintaining that '[m]any years of operating by people all around the world has shown the smaller selective choice to be far more advantageous than the larger totals'.[33] And this is a fair point because individual juke box operators may well have struggled to finance a wider selection of discs; it also illustrates how economic conditions in Britain led to relatively small selections in juke boxes.

2.8   The Minstrel

Arcadia was one of only three major juke box manufacturers in the UK in 1954 (BAL-AMI (see Part II) and Ditchburn were the others)[34] and the Minstrel was unique because it was a British-designed juke box that could be bought new. It was made by an established, reputable company and consequently received preferential publicity in *World's Fair*.[35] Its main selling points were that it was British, comparatively inexpensive to buy and stock, and that it played 78-rpm records. In advertisements it referred to these '78s' as 'normal', highlighting the importance of the 78/45-rpm issue among juke box owners and operators of the day.

World's Fair reported on Arcadia's success with the Minstrel just one year after its initial launch when the owners were extending their premises and production line to meet high demand for the machines. Arcadia were reported as aspiring to a production target of 100 per week:

> **One Year Old:**
> One year ago on bonfire night [5 November] of 1953, the Minstrel juke box was first seen and heard by the public, and what gladdened me (as a profound believer in British possibilities) was the information given (and proved) by the brothers R. and S. M. Morris that the volume of trade goes on, with orders (among them plenty of repeats) exceeding production. Their aim in this latter connection is one hundred a week and towards that they have planned a considerable extension to the factory in Cheetham Hill Road …[36]

In 1954 there was an infrastructure of juke boxes in place across Britain, with predominantly British design features, particularly in seaside towns, fairgrounds and amusement arcades, through which rock 'n' roll could and would be disseminated (see chapter 3). The year 1954, then, provides a suitable 'cut-off' point for this section. Part II examines the period 1954–60, which featured a massive increase in the number of juke boxes sold and distributed in Britain. From 1954 the entry of American style influences became more apparent in British settings.

II: 1954–60

As we have seen, from the beginning of World War II to 1954, the British market for amusement machines was, to all intents and purposes, closed to American design influences in the form of directly imported goods. In the juke box business the full production of anglicised versions of American juke boxes started with the BAL-AMI Company in Essex in 1954. Here it manufactured a selection of models in a variety of colours and cabinet finishes which was a foretaste in Britain of the kind of consumer choice normal in America. The BAL-AMI factory, though, never made a machine with more than an 80-disc selections even though, by 1954, 120 selections were standard in America, which reflected the differing scale of the markets.

The period 1954–59 was one of massive expansion for the British juke box industry. In 1955 the *London Evening Standard* estimated that there were 3,000 machines in the country;[37] in 1957 the Ditchburn Corporation estimated a total of 5,000, increasing at 200 per month;[38] and in 1958 *World's Fair* put the total at 10,000 to 13,000, increasing at 400 per month.[39] Several factors contributed to the demand. Not least among these was the desire of the nation's youth to enjoy their own social space in the form of cafés, and snack and milk bars, where they could play modern popular records, many of them American or American-influenced. The first imported sounds of rock 'n' roll into Britain were immediately popular with many of those young people who had been able to hear it and, as it was largely ignored by BBC radio, juke boxes were one of the first places where rock 'n' roll could be heard (for a full discussion see chapter 3).

BAL-AMI started to manufacture juke boxes in the UK in 1954 and from then to the end of the decade they came to dominate the market usurping Ditchburn's near-monopoly position. BAL-AMI's entrance is important because it denotes the time when American stylistic influences in juke boxes first started to appear after the war, albeit in a minor way.

The US company Automatic Musical Instruments (AMI) saw the potential market for juke boxes in post-war Europe and, as most countries had imposed protective import restrictions, AMI had the commercial intelligence to arrive at a solution – manufacturing in Europe under agreed licences. They initiated production through manufacturing agencies: BAL-AMI in England, IMA-AMI in Denmark and EDEN-AMI in France.[40] The British AMI juke boxes were made by the Balfour Engineering Company of Ilford, Essex and were marketed under the name BAL-AMI. The agreement reached in the UK was that the finished juke boxes would need to contain at least 53 per cent of British-made components.[41]

The situation in Britain by 1954, then, with regard to home-produced juke boxes, was that there were three manufacturers, Ditchburn, BAL-AMI and Arcadia. Ditchburn was the established producer of the Music Makers whilst BAL-AMI and Arcadia Automatics (Minstrel) were new entrants to the market. Having both begun production, to all intents and purposes, at the beginning of 1954 they were poised for expansion in the second and more prosperous half of the decade. The Music Maker Mark II and the Minstrel were clear examples of how an American idea had metamorphosed its appearance when made by British manufacturers operating in different economic conditions. As we have seen, the differences in design and technology between the American and the British product were striking and pronounced and British juke boxes could not have been described as American from their looks or technology. This was because the pre-war economic influences that led to flamboyance becoming a mainstream factor in American industrial design were unique to America and were not replicated in Britain. The technical advances in the American post-war juke box were beyond Britain's capabilities. Indeed, in 1954 when rock 'n' roll came to Britain in the shape of Bill Haley's *Rock Around the Clock* and *Shake Rattle and Roll* American design influences in the British juke box market were negligible.[42]

Advertisements for the AMI model 'E 40' (Figure 2.9) appeared from September 1953 and the following report goes some way to explain its impact on the trade:

'Culture Shock', AMI Super Forty from contemporary advertising   **2.9**

Being Made Here:
When I first read the Samson advertisement heralding the AMI E-40 my reaction was to assume that [they] had got hold of one or two, and that when these had gone that would be the end of them, the ban on imports not having been lifted. But … I was to learn something very different. E-40 is an American juke-box but prototypes [are] being sent over, it will now be made in England under licence.[43]

In line with established trends of mass consumerism in the United States, but new for Britain, the E 40 offered a choice of twelve colours and finishes (see Plate 5), and the first models were constructed using limed oak.[44] This was strong competition for Ditchburn, who had not changed the Music Maker's appearance since 1946. Conforming to American juke box convention the changer mechanism in the E 40, F 40, G 80 and Junior (see Plates 6 and 7) was a visible, dominant feature. A chrome frame held three 'perspex' windows, one across the front with the other two as side panels, and above these were the record title strips. Below the front window, plastic louvre doors refracted coloured light from rotating tubes. This was the first real sign of American flamboyance entering the British juke box market after the war and 'through the back door' as it were. It was in the vanguard of a new strand of British design that was increasingly indulgent toward American influences. The BAL-AMI manufacturing agreement was a compromise and was important in the design mediation process because the machines, although available in the US, were designed to fit in with European functionality and perceived tastes. Although BAL-AMI reproduced many of the smaller models for the American parent company's range, they also created small models specifically suited to Britain's relatively compact venues. The mechanisms were scaled down to take twenty 45-rpm discs, playing both sides. The Junior 40 (1956) (Plate 6), Super 40 (1957) and Super 40 Deluxe (1959) were all popular and BAL-AMI's best-selling model was the G80 from 1955 (Plate 7).[45]

Like the Music Makers, the BAL-AMI models were ideally suited to tight British locations like the snack and milk bars or corner cafés of the period. Only months after the E 40 AMI introduced the E 80: looking much the same as the E 40 it offered eighty selections from forty discs. The E 40 sold for £545 (of which 33⅓ per cent would be purchase tax) and this would have been a vast sum for a small café owner to find, if you add to it the cost of 40 records at approximately 5s. each and two sets of licence fees (see chapter 7); buyers would need to be certain of a good return on their capital. George Whittaker, who sold juke boxes through the mid- and late

1950s, points out that 'often the machine was more valuable than the rest of the contents of the café';[46] and, because of this, a large proportion of juke boxes were sold to specialist operators.[47] The BAL-AMIs were incredibly popular: in the first two years of operation Balfour had sold 'as many juke boxes as had been manufactured and imported in the UK since 1935'.[48]

A major commercial drawback to the AMI machines in the mid-1950s was that they could only be loaded with the new speed 45-rpm records. The changeover from 78-rpm discs had only really just started and the selection of music available on 45-rpm was limited. The British public did not see a switch from 45- to 78-rpm as a foregone conclusion because there were plenty of 78s in the shops and people were generally happy with them. For the domestic consumer a gramophone was a luxury item and the public were not yet ready to write off their investment. The argument for a new size and speed of disc would not be won for several years yet.[49] Britain's reluctance to adopt the 45-rpm single, combined with the high price and cost of loading the American style BAL-AMI machines, meant that there was still room in the market for smaller, cheaper machines offering fewer selections, and this place was filled by Ditchburn's Music Makers and Arcadia's Minstrel.

There is evidence of some 'unofficial' juke box entries into the country through smuggling operations and a small number of more legitimate imports by way of machines, confiscated by Customs and Excise, being sold on. An advertisement in *World's Fair* from 1953 suggested that an illicit trade, however small, did exist for American juke boxes:

> **H.M. Customs and Excise**
> Offers For Sale / Fifty American Juke Boxes / For further Information Apply to:- The Officer / Customs and Excise, / Queen's Warehouse, / 298, Clyde Street, Glasgow, C.1.[50]

A limited number of American-designed machines, however, entered Britain through European countries with which the UK had formed bilateral trade agreements. Initial indications of a relaxation in import controls with the continent were described in *World's Fair* in July 1954. Mr Amory, speaking for the Board of Trade, was reported as saying that a £10,000 bilateral trading quota had been established with West Germany that included 'automatic coin-operated amusement machines including gramophones and phonographs'.[51] Part of a commentary from the same source is worth quoting at length because it was the first step in relaxing import controls since the late 1930s and was significant for the amusement trade and as a record of American style dissemination:

Maybe you don't think that the news is particularly exciting, and we will agree that the concession is not over generous – at present day prices £10,000 doesn't go very far, and in any case there are perhaps few types of German machines that are really suitable for operation over here. But what makes this event of such great significance is that it is a first step.

Since the early days of the last war – for nearly fifteen years, in other words – we have suffered an almost complete embargo on the import of amusement equipment from abroad. Now, for the very first time, we have been able to gain some relaxation, and although it is not a fraction of what the trade wants it is, at least, a first step on the road back to freedom.[52]

This legislation set the scene for American and continental styles to enter Britain through West Germany. A report in March 1955 provided news that the American Seeburg Company were manufacturing in West Germany and that Mr G.A. Whittaker of Blackpool would be their UK distributor.[53] The research needed to establish the exact origin of these European imports is beyond the scope of this book; however, the machines were American-styled and were undoubtedly the first regular post-war import of American juke boxes to the UK apart from those installed on American military bases.

By the mid-1950s juke box design in America had lost its blatant Art Deco flamboyance. Although still mostly featuring visible changer mechanisms, cabinet styling had become relatively subdued, without the promi-

WHITTAKER --- SEEBURG --- WHITTAKER --- SEEBURG --- WHITTAKER

WE ARE PROUD TO ANNOUNCE OUR APPOINTMENT AS EXCLUSIVE DISTRIBUTORS IN THE BRITISH ISLES FOR

- SEEBURG -

IMMEDIATE DELIVERY £875

HIRE PURCHASE ARRANGED—50% Deposit   Trade-ins Welcomed

★ **ONLY SEEBURG HAS THE SELECTOMATIC MECHANISM** ★

G. A. WHITTAKER Ltd., Blackpool
4, LEICESTER ROAD Tel.: 28255

SEEBURG 100JL
100 SELECTIONS

Applications Invited from Reliable Firms with Experience and Capital for the Sole Selling Rights in Scotland, Northern Ireland and Southern England

62% OF ALL NEW JUKE BOXES SOLD IN AMERICA ARE SEEBURG

2.10   Advertisement for Seeburg Selectomatic 100JL in *World's Fair*, 25 May 1957

nence given to flashing lights and bubble tubes epitomised in the Wurlitzer 1015 (Plate 4). The styles of Seeburg and Wurlitzer machines that entered Britain through West Germany and Belgium from 1956 like the Seeburg Selectomatic 100 (Figure 2.10) and the Wurlitzer 1900 were no longer in opposition to British tastes. In the juke box market the visual aesthetics of American, European and British cabinet styling had converged. A Whittaker advert from 1958 (Figure 2.11), for example, showed the American Seeburg and Wurlitzer machines as having no significant or distinctive stylistic differences to the German-made 'Fanfare'.

The mid-1950s, then, was a key moment in the assimilation of styles from America and the Continent. Following on from BAL-AMI's inclusion in their range of 'light-up' cabinets in an array of finishes from 1954, advertisements for other juke box imports started to increase from 1955: some were European-styled machines and some American-styled. Often, new machines penetrated the British market from Belgium where, for example, the Belgian-made 'Ambassador' was advertised for £425[54] in November 1955 and the 'Rennotte', in March 1956 (Figure 2.12). In January 1956 Whittaker offered, along with the Seeburg 100 selection, a 'Rock ola 50' selection, another new American entrant to the market, for £395.[55] One unusual source for American machines was Singapore, where the 'British

Advertisement for Fanfare 60A, Seeburg 100EL and Wurlitzer 1900 in *World's Fair*, 19 April 1958   **2.11**

The Manufacturers of the "RENNOTTE" Juke-boxes wish to thank all their visitors at the A.T.E. for the interesting information they gave in designing a British operator's cabinet. The new Juke-boxes are now almost ready and will be available at an early date on the British market.

2.12   Advertisement for the Belgian Renotte in *World's Fair*, 24 March 1956

Asiatic Equipment Co.' showed ingenuity in circumnavigating British import restrictions direct from America. The company offered reconditioned Wurlitzer 1015s for the relatively small sum of £185 and supplied with them a 'Guaranteed British Empire "Certificate of Origin"' (Figure 2.13).[56] These machines, though, were by this time technically outdated, only playing 78-rpm discs and offering only twenty-four selections whilst Whittaker, by 1956, was offering the Seeburg 100-selection 'JL' and by 1957 was selling the Wurlitzer '2104', 104-selection model.[57]

The Ditchburn organisation was slow to modernise and introduce updated models. They claimed to resist actively what they saw as blatant American influences, and this was a policy founded on their own 'research' into British tastes. When interviewed in 1958, Norman Ditchburn claimed an insight into the British character that lent him an advantage over his rivals. He understood very well that juke boxes needed a certain amount of mediation to be acceptable to British tastes, though with the Music Makers he may have been over-cautious:

> After thorough investigation he concluded that just as Britain was slowly but surely following America in things like domestic refrigeration so the British

Advertisement for reconditioned Wurlitzer 1015s from Singapore in *World's Fair*, 24 March 1956

2.13

public would in time follow the American habit of music while you eat – or drink – and in the Music Maker he saw the opportunity to develop this wonderful market in Britain.

But research soon showed that the British response would be slow. In Britain people did not like noise, preferred quiet in their cafes, didn't like the idea of putting money into a machine and criticised 'popular music'. The very words juke box smacked of American speakeasies and gangster films.

Realising that there was a social problem here and that if the many hindrances were to be overcome public opinion must be won over, Mr. Ditchburn decided in the early stages at any rate the strictest control was necessary.[58]

Ditchburn's views, however, were convenient for a company in a near monopoly position because it meant that they would not need to update their equipment when American technical advancements became available. Economic restraints were understandable factors in this process. A highly competitive market drove the variety of design choice in America whereas the British market, although becoming more spirited in the late 1950s, would never reach the same competitive intensity. Indeed, it was only the home competition, most particularly from BAL-AMI, that forced Ditchburn to introduce machines that were visually eye-catching and technically superior with an increased number of selections. In a brief history of the company from their employees' handbook it recognised this threat from BAL-AMI, explaining that 'A good thing is usually copied sooner or later and eventually competition arrived in the form of the Bal-Ami machine which played 40 records – severe competition to the Music Maker, still offering only 16 plays'. The handbook clarified that 'it was unable, at short notice, to produce a machine with many more selections'.[59] As we have seen, the BAL-AMI machines had a selection of styles and their machines could offer 40 or 80 selections whilst the 16-play Music Makers and the 'Hideaway' model of 1954 were visually dated.

In order to ward off competition, most notably from the BAL AMI 40- and 80-play machines, Ditchburn made the decision not to increase their manufacturing capacity but instead to import superior technology and styling. They made contact with the West German manufacturer Tonomat Automaton, who subsequently supplied them with a 100-selection machine from the May of 1956. These machines were called the Music Maker 100 (Figure 2.14) and were followed up in 1957 by a 200-selection model – the Music Maker 200 (Figure 2.15). These two Tonomat machines were a technical leap for the British market. Their styling had been influenced by market conditions in Germany where youth venues, like those in the rest of Western Europe, were typically small cafés, which were by now becoming more common in Britain. Contemporary advertising material from Ditchburn stressed the lack of ostentation and talked of the 'dignity of the cabinet' in the Music Maker 100-selection, and with the Music Maker 200-selection machine advertisements drew attention to the visible mechanism and observed that '[it] is a handsome piece of furniture, modern in design, beautifully made of first-class materials and its changing coloured lights are entrancing'.[60]

The Tonomat machines have been described as 'eccentric but stylish' and compared favourably with Ditchburn's 'dowdy' Music Maker 30 upgrades from 1958 (Figure 2.16).[61] These Music Maker 30s were created as the

This machine has been a success from the moment we introduced it. It is exceptionally attractive in appearance, a high-class production in every way. Its illuminated fluted glass front with coloured lighting enhances the dignity of its cabinet. As with all our Music Maker models the musical reproduction is of the highest standard. For many premises this is the ideal machine and such installations are making valuable extra profits for snack bars, cafes, etc.

The Ditchburn Music Maker 100 made in West Germany by Tonomat   **2.14**

result of a conversion of the Mark IIs that had been on sites around the UK and particularly in England's northwest for over a decade.[62] Ditchburn offered their Mark II clients a conversion to a 30-play with 45-rpm discs if desired. The tops of the original cabinets were sawn off and substituted with a fibreglass hood, whilst chrome stars replaced the distinctive Mark II flash and the cabinets were repainted.[63] There was a lack of money to buy

The Ditchburn Music Maker 200 made in West Germany by Tonomat   **2.15**

new machines and they were adapted to keep the price down: a further example of British economic conditions affecting the appearance of juke box cabinet styling.

The most important point for the amusement machine business since the end of World War II was the week ending 6 June 1959, because it was the point at which the British market was opened up to direct imports from America. The late 1940s and 1950s were years when Britain had, through direct government control, been protected from the impact of American-style imports in the juke box business and moving into the 1960s American style influences would be felt more strongly. *World's Fair* called 6 June 'little short of epoch making' because restrictions against imports from the dollar area were lifted. In anticipation, *World's Fair* listed some of the concessions:

> All our predictions of recent weeks have come true to the letter. These are the things that have happened. (1) Dollar imports of juke boxes, juke – box accessories, and allied equipment, free of all licence restrictions, are permitted from next Monday, June 8. So, too, is the import of vending machines and

The Ditchburn Music Maker 30

spares. They can be brought in freely from virtually any part of the world whatever their origin. This is a staggeringly quick development, and one which has taken many people by surprise. (2) Dollar (and also Continental) imports of amusement machines – which come into a category of their own and are frowned on by the Board of Trade – still cannot be allowed. They constitute one of the few remaining restricted categories, and are likely to remain so for some considerable time – which leads to point (3), about which we dropped glowing hints last week.

(3) It is this, A.M.I. (G.B.) Ltd., the enterprising Ilford firm that has done infinitely more than any other to put juke boxes respectfully on the map in Britain, has moved into amusement machines in a big way.[64]

The news of British markets opening up to American imports created a flurry of commercial activity and 'a number of top juke-box executives flew into Britain from America and Europe'. Paul Hunger of AMI, for example, reached agreement with BAL-AMI, Britain's largest juke box network, securing the firm as sole distributors of AMI products in Britain, Eire and the Commonwealth. Wurlitzer had anticipated the move to convertibility and its company president flew to London to discuss arrangements with distributors to start shipping Wurlitzer machines into Britain.[65]

Relaxation of trade restrictions was not a completely 'across the board' measure though, because only a small number of countries would be able to export to the UK and, although this point of dollar convertibility had been tipped by *World's Fair* for at least a year, many British companies were said to be unprepared at the prospect of direct American imports. *World's Fair*, however, reported on the excitement of now seeing 'some of the goods that have never been seen in this country'. There was also much discussion of a trade in American second-hand machines:

> It should be simple. The Americans have the goods, new and second-hand, at competitive prices. Some of the goods have never been seen in this country. There is still a hunger for them. They are willing and eager to sell, and are here as proof of it. We are free to buy at long last, but some have no programme that makes sense …[66]

Before 1954 new juke boxes in Britain were limited to the eccentric looking and technically outdated Mark II Music Makers from the Ditchburn factory in Lytham St Annes, which were joined late in 1953 by the more peculiar-looking Minstrel from Arcadia Automatics in Manchester – both machines played a limited number of 78-rpm discs. BAL-AMI's entrance into the market in 1954 produced both 40- and 80-record selections and used new 45-rpm, 7-inch vinyl discs. A variety of cabinet finishes coupled with increased record selections led them to dominate the market, leading the Ditchburn Company to import machines directly from Germany, as and when trade agreements were initiated. Over the same period a spate of other juke boxes were imported into Britain from the Continent and from American manufacturing bases in Europe – some of these perhaps circumventing official import agreements. The American-styled machines, however, by the late 1950s had lost the ostentatious flamboyance that contributed to their popularity as amusement machines and were epitomised by the Wurlitzer designs of Paul Fuller from the late 1930 and 1940s.[67]

By June 1959, when American juke boxes had their first relatively unhindered access to British markets since the beginning of World War II, there were in the region of 15,000 juke boxes on site in Britain and the design influences on these were a mixture of British, West European and American. The music that these machines played, its reception and audiences are the subject of the next chapter.

Notes

1 Ian Brown, Nigel Hutchins, Gerry Mizera, *The Ultimate Jukebox Guide 1927–1974* (Brighton: Pla-mor, 1994), p. 59.
2 Jack Hylton 1892–1965 was a Lancastrian who led the most popular dance band of the 1930s. I know of only one of the Jack Hylton Music Makers still in existence. The cabinets were broken up and updated with the arrival of the Mark II.
3 *Hawtins Trade Catalogue*, circa 1945, reproduced by Gary Goulding (Blackpool: 2001).
4 P. Hardy and D. Laing, *The Faber Companion to Twentieth Century Popular Music* (London: Faber & Faber, 1992), p. 377.
5 Brown et al., *Ultimate Juke Box*, p. 80.
6 56,000 were built. See Frank Adams, *Wurlitzer Jukeboxes 1934–1974* (Seattle: AMR Publishing, 1983).
7 Penny Sparke, 'From Lipstick to a Steamship: the growth of the American design profession' in *Design Council: Fad or Function?*, ed. by Terry Bishop (London: Design Council, 1978), pp. 10–16, p. 10.
8 Sparke, 'Lipstick', p. 10.
9 Michelle Jones, Television and the British Broadcasting Corporation's Promotion of 'Good Design', *Journal of Design History*, 16/4 (2003), p. 308.
10 Reyner Banham, 'Detroit Tin Revisited' in *Design 1900–1960: Studies in Design and Popular Culture of the 20th Century* ed. by T. Faulkner (Newcastle Upon Tyne Polytechnic, 1976), p. 122.

11 Banham, 'Detroit Tin', p. 128.

12 Banham, 'Detroit Tin', p. 124.

13 Dealers in American cars did exist outside London but were rare. George Whittaker remembers that there were two American Car showrooms in Blackpool in the 1950s. Phone conversation 8 April 2002.

14 Convertibility was re-introduced after the war in July 1947, which led to a run on Britain's dollar pool as countries with sterling reserves rushed to change them into dollars. The drain on reserves was so severe that convertibility was abandoned after only a month. See Sidney Pollard, *The Development of the British Economy 1914–1967* (London: Edward Arnold, 1973, 2nd edition), p. 360.

15 J.C.R. Dow, *The Management of the British Economy 1945–60* (Cambridge: Cambridge University Press, 1965), pp. 155–6. See also A.M. Leysham, 'Import Restrictions in Post War Britain' *Scottish Journal of Political Economy* 4 (1957), pp. 177–93.

16 Peter Oppenheimer, 'Muddling Through: The Economy, 1951–1964' in *The Age of Affluence 1951–64* ed. by V. Bogdanor and R. Skidelsky (London: Macmillan, 1970), p. 126.

17 Pollard, *Development of the British Economy*, p. 356. See also Peter Howlett, 'The War Economy' in *Twentieth Century Britain: Economic, Social and Cultural Change*, ed. by Paul Johnson (London: Longman, 1994), pp. 283–99 and Catherine R. Schenk, 'Austerity and Boom' in *Twentieth Century Britain: Economic, Social and Cultural Change*, ed. by Paul Johnson (London: Longman, 1994), pp. 300–19.

18 *Nottingham Journal*, 6 February 1946. B.A.O.R. = British Army on the Rhine.

19 *The Performer*, 14 February 1946.

20 The Simplex Mechanism was developed by a Mr Erikson in the early 1930s and was updated in America by Wurlitzer by 1938 – Krivine, *Juke Box Saturday*, p. 36; Adams, *Wurlitzer*, no page numbers.

21 WF, 21 September 1946, p. 16; 7 December 1946; 14 December 1946; 11 January 1947, p. 18.

22 Bingo Beaufort, 'Juke Box Firm's New Policy is "Sell' Now"', WF, 25 January 1958, p. 33.

23 Ditchburn *Employees Handbook* (early 1970s). Courtesy of Tony Holmes.

24 WF, 25 January 1958, p. 33.

25 WF, 31 January 1953, p. 23.

26 WF, 14 May 1955, p. 29 'Juke Jingles by Coingram'.

27 Frank Adams, *Rowe – AMI Jukeboxes 1927–1988* (Seattle: AMR Publishing, 1988); Adams, *Wurlitzer*, no page numbers.

28 The Seeburg 'Model 100 A' and Seeburg 'V.200'.

29 WF, 23 January 1954, p. 22, 'Automatic Gossip by Edward Graves'; WF, 6 February 1954, p. 52.

30 WF, 6 February 1954, p. 27.

31 *Manchester Evening News*, 26 August 1954, 'My Line in Pictures'.

32 Reported in WF, 23 January 1954, p. 22 – the 16-play 'simplex' mechanism being updated through a claimed Arcadia patented modification which allowed both sides to be played without the record being turned over.

33 WF, 23 January 1954, p. 22, 'Automatic Gossip by Edward Graves'.

34 Other juke boxes were made in Britain, like the Hit Parade of 1954, but they had minimal impact.

35 There is some anecdotal evidence from Tony Holmes (conversation 11 January 2000) that operators found it to be unreliable. Hire purchase conditions were offered.

36 WF, 6 November 1954, p. 18, 'Automatic Gossip by Edward Graves'.

37 *London Evening Standard*, 2 May 1955, 'The juke-box invaders say … It isn't all just hotcha'.

38 WF, 27 April 1957, p. 29, 'Juke Jingles by Coingram'.

39 WF, 16 December 1958, p. 36.

40 Brown et al., *Ultimate Juke Box*, p. 64.

41 Krivine, *Juke Box Saturday*, p. 131.

42 Bill Haley (*We're Gonna) Rock Around The Clock* (Brunswick, 1954); *Shake Rattle and Roll* (Brunswick, 1954).

43 WF, 3 October 1953, p. 22, 'Automatic Gossip by Edward Graves'. The first prototype models did not carry the 'BAL' prefix.

44 WF, 3 October 1953, p. 22.

45 Brown, *Ultimate Juke Box*, p. 53.

46 Letter to A. Horn, 25 April 2001, from George A. Whittaker of the Blackpool Machine Co.

47 Norman Ditchburn understood that there was a lack of capital in the catering trade and built up his operating business on this assumption.

48 Krivine, *Juke Box Saturday*, p. 131.

49 Record manufacturers Columbia and HMV manufactured for Europe solely on the 78-rpm disc until 1952 and Columbia did not discontinue the 78 until April 1958. See WF, 12 April 1958, p. 1; Krivine, *Juke Box Saturday*, p. 297.

50 WF, 29 August 1953, p. 23.

51 Derek Heathcoat Amory 1899–1981, Conservative minister at the Board of Trade 1953–4; Chancellor of the Exchequer 1958–60.

52 WF, 17 July 1954, 'ACA Clippings', p. 26. Post-war calls for a lifting of import restrictions were confounded in 1947 when the Chancellor imposed severe restraints to imports of machines from the US; WF, 5 July 1947.

53 WF, 26 March 1955, p. 29, 'Juke Jingles by Coingram'. In a phone conversation with George Whittaker, 8 April 2002, Mr Whittaker claimed that he imported them from Belgium and casts some doubt on the assumption that they were made there. He suggests that it was possible that they were imported from America to Belgium and then re-exported to Britain with a Belgian certificate of origin issued from the Belgian Chamber of Commerce.

54 WF, 26 November 1955.

55 WF, 21 January 1956, p. 30.

56 WF, 24 March 1956, p. 32.
57 WF, 16 February 1957, p. 32.
58 WF, 25 January 1958 p. 33, 'Juke box Firm's New Policy is "Sell' Now"'.
59 Ditchburn, *Employees Handbook*.
60 Ditchburn advertising material circa late 1950s – courtesy John Crompton.
61 Chris Pearce, *Jukebox Art* (London: Blossom, 1991), p. 100.
62 Ditchburn, *Employees Handbook*.
63 Tony Holmes writing in Brown et al., *Ultimate Jukebox*, pp. 59–60.
64 WF, 6 June 1959, p. 4.
65 WF, 6 June 1959, p. 4.
66 WF, 6 June 1959, p. 4.
67 Paul Fuller, designer with Wurlitzer from 1936 to 1948. For information on Fuller's juke box designs see Pearce, *Jukebox Art*; Adams, *Wurlitzer*.

3

American music, juke boxes and cultural resistance

Chapter 2 explained and illustrated how American designs in the juke box industry had, for the most part, been excluded from Britain between 1945 and 1959 through economic, social and cultural factors. This chapter examines a more orchestrated mediation process that filtered American popular music. It finds that juke boxes aided the dissemination of American music in a raw form by bypassing the BBC's near-monopoly broadcasting position. BBC radio was broadly resistant to musical forms that did not conform to its ideals of public education. Juke boxes in Britain, by evading the BBC's restrictions, played a remarkably similar role to those in pre-war America, where they avoided restrictions imposed by white-owned radio stations. There were general 'Establishment' concerns over perceived subversive ideological effects inherent in American popular music imports but these were not as pronounced as some contemporary media sources might lead us to believe.

Dating from the second half of the nineteenth century the British ruling classes perceived music dissemination as a moral and ideological issue, and in the late 1940s and 1950s residual Victorian values in the area of popular culture still retained force within 'Establishment' bodies like the BBC. In the Victorian period the upper and middle classes became concerned with educating the populace by directing their energies toward 'rational recreations': musical education was a part of this process.[1] In the second half of the nineteenth and the early twentieth century there was a widely held opinion that attitudes and beliefs could be, and were, shaped by music – that music carried an ideological message.[2] From the period of the creation of the BBC in 1922[3] to the end of World War II middle-class concern, with regard to broadcasting, was to 'educate the people and to promote social harmony by weaning "the horny handed sons of toil" away from "vicious indulgences!" toward more rational, moral and peaceable forms of recreation and leisure'.[4] Ideological factors were still key considerations for BBC radio both during and in the aftermath of World War II.

The BBC's perception of its ideological role can be divided into two main strands: firstly, an intention to bring people together in a common cause, which was as important in the post-war economic reconstruction as it was during hostilities; and, secondly, a portrayal of and identification with 'national values'.[5] After the war the BBC still felt an obligation to uphold wartime and pre-war notions of 'respectability' or, at least, not to spread 'unrespectability'. Moreover, the BBC believed its role was to inform and educate the public in what it perceived as 'good music'.

In an intellectual climate that was wary of juke boxes (see chapter 1) and believed in a link between amusement machines and delinquency, it is unsurprising that the BBC was antagonistic to the world of coin-operated amusements. For example, a TV *Special Enquiry* documentary broadcast in January 1950 highlighted the disdain in parts of the BBC for mass-cultural entertainments. The programme was referred to as grounds for refusing fourteen applications for music licences for juke boxes in Manchester later in that year:

> Then there are 5 Manchester businessmen I knew years ago. They used to meet once or twice a week in the studio of a music shop and spend their lunch hour playing quintets. Get enough people like that around the place and naturally you'll have your Halle[6] orchestras and a great tradition of culture which enriches the life of the whole community. But once we lose sight of this fact, then *we as a nation will drift more rapidly into an aimless, brainless spivery in which £10,000,000 a year can be taken in pennies from the slot machines of the amusement arcades.*[7] That's the true figure you know today; ten millions a year. So what about it? Just have a look round to see what you can do.[8]

In the immediate post-war era the BBC, though in the throes of change, was still wedded to the pre-war ideals of public service associated with Lord Reith.[9] In this period the BBC were 'broadcasters who held constantly in mind the image of a family audience, seated around the fireside at home',[10] what Barnard describes as 'cosiness, conservatism and insularity'.[11] The argument was that the BBC should support family life as an ideal and as an alternative to 'public houses, *thés dansants* and cabarets'.[12] Before World War II the target audience was 'middle class suburban' or 'inhabitants of the rural cottage', and although the Corporation tried to give more representation to working-class tastes after the war its old attitudes were hard to shift and a somewhat patronising rhetoric persisted.[13]

Nonetheless, there were differences of approach towards music within the Corporation. Its music department, directed by Adrian Boult from 1930, kept 'serious' and 'popular' musical forms segregated. Before Boult, '[d]ance bands, the cinema organ, operetta and musical reviews were never officially classified as music', instead they were termed 'variety'. The BBC's music department 'maintained a consistent and resolutely hostile attitude to low brow music'.[14]

A 1953 report from a Manchester court case provides an example of the influence of the BBC in forming public opinion. It also puts the other side of the case by 'light-heartedly' questioning the cultural dominance of the Hallé Orchestra and perhaps even raising the views of an emergent musical culture.[15] It made implicit reference to the aforementioned *Special Enquiry* documentary:

No Music in Milk Bars:
Proprietors of fourteen snack and milk bars in the City of Manchester who wanted to operate 'electronically controlled gramophone recorders', which they installed on their premises received a setback when the Licensing Justices refused to grant the necessary licences ...

Counsel and Arcades:
In submitting this case the counsel said the instruments had been described as 'juke boxes' but that was an epithet springing from an unaccountable public prejudice ... '*The public associates these instruments with pin-tables and spivs squandering money in amusement arcades run by vultures who take a tremendous amount of money from unsuspecting juveniles.*' ...

Light Hearted References to Halle:
This legal advocate went on to say that it was a curious thing when applications were made to the Manchester City Council each year for a subsidy involving thousands of pounds for an orchestra it was considered ungentlemanly or even unpatriotic to oppose them. Why, he asked, should there be opposition to the kind of music relayed in these bars? But when the Chairman of the Justices said the question of the Halle Orchestra was entirely outside the province of the bench's consideration. In relation to the applicant's premises, Mr. Curtis observed he had introduced the comparison 'in a purely light-hearted manner.'[16]

In 1945 BBC radio introduced the Light Programme in order to attract a wider, more working-class, audience and it immediately became Britain's most popular radio channel. But even the Light Programme presented classical music in lunchtime concerts and afternoon symphony performances.[17]

Through this they remained true to Director General William Hayley's diktat that 'while satisfying the legitimate demand for recreation and entertainment the BBC must never lose sight of its cultural mission'.[18]

The BBC had two wings to its music policy: firstly, it pursued 'excellent' standards, meaning great classical pieces; and secondly, it endeavoured to 'raise the level of the general public's taste for, and appreciation of, "good music"'.[19] The BBC's musical history shows that it had a clear idea of what was, and what was not, 'good' music and regarded itself as having a duty to promote the classical. The Corporation's pre-war attitude was that 'pop music has to be broadcast but tastes would soon be "lifted"' because once the listeners 'had heard classical music … they would realise its superiority to popular tunes'.[20] Christopher Stone (BBC Radio's first disc jockey in 1924) championed the 'middle-brow' but still made a point of not playing 'hot American dance music'.[21] There was a deliberate attempt within the BBC 'to make classical music popular and popular music classical'.[22] Moreover, organisers and staff in BBC radio may well have had little knowledge of popular culture and tastes.

Views similar to the BBC's can be seen as pervasive in British Magistrates' Courts. In the following application for music licences for juke boxes both the machines and the music they provided were regarded as a problem. Here there is an evident consensus within the court that the perceived 'unrespectable' aspect of the amusement machine industry is unwelcome. This prejudice was part of the British cultural attitude of the period that was broadly opposed to Americanisation and so-called mass-cultural values. It might be reasonable to assume, then, that if the juke boxes relayed orchestral music then opposition to the licence would be reduced:

> **No at Doncaster too:**
> At Doncaster too, the magistrates have refused applications for music licences for juke boxes. There were six applications and each was turned down.

> **Police Objections:**
> A police inspector in the Doncaster cases said the records were generally speaking of the same type – 'loud and noisy – the hot Jazz type' they 'attracted youngsters – teenagers of the Be-Bop type'. … The café proprietors have denied that their juke box customers were predominantly 'Be-Boppers'.[23]

The 'Be-Bop type' is a reference to those who enjoy 'hot' American music and who are clearly unwelcome by the police inspector. In its defence, claiming that their patrons were not 'predominantly "Be-Boppers"', the defence tacitly accepted this premise.

Class distinctions in Britain affected attitudes towards popular musical forms like jazz and rock 'n' roll. On the basis of empirical research conducted in France, Pierre Bourdieu has argued that 'nothing more clearly affirms one's class than tastes in music'.[24] In Britain in the late 1940s and throughout the 1950s popular American music was generally associated with mass-tastes, and we see repeatedly how institutions like the BBC perceived popular music as uneducated and lacking the professed artistic intensity of classical music. Bourdieu argues ironically that an inability to appreciate classical music 'doubtless represents a particularly unavowable form of material coarseness'.[25] Bourdieu's model is relevant for post-war Britain because it parallels contemporary debates on culture in which the middle classes were seen as valuing music for its artistic merit but deriding it if it seemed commercial. These contemporary attitudes were amongst the ways that American influences were resisted. The defenders of middle- and upper-class 'standards', the BBC, local magistrates and schools, for example, were concerned with what they saw as a negative educational effect that came from American music and influenced formative and impressionable young minds.[26]

Bourdieu isolates three levels of taste, each corresponding directly with social class: 1. employers and professionals, 2. the middle classes and 3. the working classes. Employers and professionals, he maintains, 'indicate their distance from ordinary songs by rejecting with disgust the most popular and most "vulgar" singers'. He stresses that it is the 'middle classes who find in song … an opportunity to manifest their artistic pretensions by refusing the favourite singers of the working classes'.[27] This was broadly the attitude of the upper and middle classes in Britain towards popularly received American music such as 'hot' jazz, and rock 'n' roll.

Following Bourdieu's arguments, the situation where popular music is either subject to derision by the upper and middle classes or classified as insubstantial can be altered. An art form may cross over from low to high culture, from the popular to the serious. This was the case with certain types of jazz that became 'high-brow' forms and were broadcast on the BBC Third Programme. The limited acceptance by the BBC was a signal that some jazz was capable of being enjoyed by cultured people. When crossovers of this nature occur Bourdieu suggests that the qualities of *enjoyment* and *entertainment* are replaced by those of *appreciation* and *instruction*. Upwardly mobile people, then, might signify their aspired status by openly rejecting the popular and commercial and acquiring the 'cultural capital' of serious musical appreciation.

Bourdieu concludes that 'the more strongly a singer is preferred by the less cultivated, the more he or she is refused by the most cultivated'.[28] 'Cultivated' taste in this instance is expressed through rejections of the popular and this is characterised by using 'pitying or indignant remarks': the comments of local magistrates like those in 1957 in Leigh, Greater Manchester, for instance, when they commented that 'there was a "wave of demand" for music in these days, not only for "Rock 'n' Roll" but for good music'[29] support Bourdieu's findings.

The area of jazz in post-war Britain and its relationship with the BBC requires some clarification because it is not straightforward. Jazz had established itself within the domain of a cultured elite, and this can be seen in the BBC schedules where jazz programmes by this time were included in the Third Programme – a seemingly contradictory inclusion for a minority 'high-brow' channel.[30] Within the jazz community, however, there was a definite split between jazz 'revivalists', who attempted to recreate Dixieland or 'Trad' jazz, and jazz 'progressives' who enjoyed the bohemian nature of more improvised musicianship. Strictly speaking, be-bop fell into the latter category, though this was not the common usage of the term be-bop, which was a more general term meaning 'jazzy' American dance music. The Light Programme, the BBC's mainstream radio station, supported the revivalists at the expense of the progressives: an internal memo prohibited 'noisy, advanced jazz' citing Stan Kenton as an example.[31] In 1948 Harman Grisewood, acting controller of the Third Programme explained that 'our interest in jazz must be limited to the strictly musical. We are not … interested in modern modifications of the original impulses that gave rise to the jazz style, believing this mostly to arise from what might be called commercial motives.'[32] Stephen Barnard writes of the BBC's 'arbitrators' of the time:

> Programme producers like Jon Foreman, responsible for *Jazz Club* from 1950 onwards, acted as arbitrators, though he for one came out firmly on the side of the revivalists. Foreman told the *Melody Maker* that he would not feature 'bop' or 'progressive music' on the programme (which was an offshoot of the wartime *Rhythm Club*), citing practical considerations: genuine be-bop could only be heard on disc, not 'recreated' (a reactionary notion, anyway, in the progressive view) by British jazz musicians in BBC studios, so why should precious needle-time be used up on something of such limited appeal and so obviously 'unsuited' to domestic dissemination?[33]

The authorities frowned upon youthful associations with be-bop in its wider meaning. For example, the *Daily Mirror* in 1956 reported that 'police swoop on girls in bebop bus'[34] and a Mass-Observation report from 1949 published an interview with an eighteen-year-old clerical worker who explained the prominence of be-bop in her life:

> I go to the jazz club, dancing, tennis, swimming and listening to gramophone records. On Saturday I went to the Bebop Club in the evening ... I packed up my boyfriend because he didn't like me going to Bop clubs ... .
> I don't disagree with my parents except about 'Bop'. That's the only thing: Mother can't stand that, but I like it. ... What do I want out of life? Just a nice husband, a baby, a house and 'bop' records.[35]

In a study of Huddersfield's youth, Brian Jackson noted police resistance to jazz and its 'detrimental' influence on the young in the 1950s.[36] A jazz club that opened in 1952 had to move premises every few months over the following ten years. One interviewee explained that 'the police were always ready to move the group on' and that 'they could usually do this by invoking the fire regulations and claiming the premises were unsafe'; and, as with juke boxes, a music licence was necessary and often difficult to obtain from local magistrates.

There were cases when the police assumed the role of defenders of moral values, especially when concerning the young, and interpreted the law accordingly. Jackson's interviewee recounted one incident:

> Once a policeman called at 6.30 a.m. and discovered six boys and two girls, all very sleepy – waiting for first bus time so that they could go home and go to bed. It was the fag-end of a jazz-playing, long-talking night. 'He came in and said "What's this? What's going on? We can't have this!" and went to fetch the sergeant. When he came back we'd all gone, except Si. They took Si to the police station and told him "Get out or we'll boot you out".' The next evening there were headlines in the paper 'Six Men and Two Girls Found in Club', and much talk in Huddersfield.[37]

Incidences of local police attitudes to the perceived ideological effect of American-style music were reported in *World's Fair*, where elements in the police hierarchy found the style of juke box music disturbing. In 1957 an officer voiced widely shared concerns:

> For the police Superintendent N. G. Brown said that the sound of the peculiar and eccentric music thumped out on juke boxes might be a trial to elderly or mature people living in the vicinity.
> 'To be quite frank' said Superintendent Brown 'nice young people do not go to these places after 8 p.m. It is my experience that where these licences are granted after eight o'clock nothing but trouble can arise for the people who manage these places and for the police who try to maintain order.'[38]

A distinction can be made, however, between a provincial town like Huddersfield and metropolitan centres. Interviewee Harry Isaacs recalls the more cosmopolitan Manchester jazz club scene taking off in 1951 and 1952 and stresses that these were definitely not youth venues, though teenagers like Isaacs might be tolerated if they sat down, kept quiet and steered clear of alcohol.[39] Because these Manchester jazz clubs were held on licensed premises there would have been few under the age of eighteen. Isaacs estimates the age range of the clientele at between seventeen and thirty, and suggests that males and females attended for different reasons: 'the lads tended to be interested in jazz and the girls were there because the lads were there'. Jazz clubs were different from other musical venues, such as dance halls, in that audiences, according to Isaacs, were typically better educated, probably coming from grammar schools or Manchester's colleges and university.

Sunday observance conventions were another cause for concern for both the BBC and local magistrates responsible for issuing music licences. The BBC adhered to 'respectable' conventions and lost many of their Sunday morning radio listeners to the commercial stations of Luxembourg and Normandie: a listener research unit set up in 1936 found that on Sunday mornings 82 per cent of the BBC's regular listeners tuned into commercial stations to avoid religious programming.[40]

An interview with Jim Cheetham, who grew up on an amusement park in Cheshire, elicited recollections of Sunday observance in the years immediately preceding the war. Cheetham remembers generational frictions where his parents retained 'Victorian morals' and a 'what would the neighbours think?' attitude: 'I can remember about 1938 and we had a Majestic, an American radio which would pick up Luxembourg, but we had to have it turned down on a Sunday because mother would have thought it was absolutely disgusting if the neighbours knew we were listening to dance music on a Sunday.'

Cheetham also provides details of a working compromise that avoided conflict with local churchgoers, and allowed his family to play fairground music on the Sabbath:

> Once we bought a steam-driven roundabout with a fairground organ. ... Then we started to get complaints from the vicar of Great Budland, the local church, if the wind was in his direction, it was interfering with the service. So then we didn't play any music until 2 o'clock on a Sunday afternoon, and finished about 5 o'clock so it didn't interfere with his evening service.[41]

Concerns about music and Sunday observance continued after the war, and strong views about the propriety of popular music were expressed in contemporary debates. Magistrates in Morecambe, for example, maintained that with public relaying of music, the music, if played at all, should not be of a frivolous nature.[42] This notion of frivolity certainly included popular, be-bop, dance and American-style music. Coverage in *World's Fair* of a 1951 challenge to Sunday juke box playing in a Morecambe licence application highlighted concern about the lack of 'appropriate' Sunday music:

> The Clerk said the conditions applying to Sunday musical entertainments would also apply to the juke box and the Police Superintendent explained the two of the fixed conditions applying to Sunday musical licences granted were, firstly, that the music should be of 'a high order suitable for the Sabbath'. And, secondly, that the music should be of the light orchestral type and not 'dance music of a broadly humorous nature'.
>
> A learned debate ensued, in which the police expressed the opinion that juke boxes did not provide light orchestral music, and the operators' solicitor replied that dance music could be of various types – the Ambrose style and the Spike Jones type. In the end an uneasy truce was proclaimed, for the magistrates granted the licences subject to the usual conditions.[43]

In this instance the juke box operators won the day. The applications, however, were made for amusement arcades. In cafés or snack bars, the outcome might well have been different as cafés and snack bars in this region did not yet have a tradition of playing recorded music. The seaside town of Morecambe was dependent for its livelihood to some extent on the revenue generated from amusement arcades. If licences were to be granted, then, they would more likely be approved in a town like Morecambe.

The *World's Fair* continued its commentary suggesting that a long battle against their opponents' prejudices would be required. The humour of the situation was not lost on them:

> This is yet another situation in which amusement caterers, operators more or less on sufferance, will have to gang wearily, for, one may be sure, now the matter has been aired in the local press, that our opponents will be on the alert for assaults on their puritan consciences.
>
> In fact, we prophesy a considerable fall in church attendances, for on Sundays the righteous will haunt the local arcades, making sure that the music provided is of that 'high order suitable for the Sabbath.' A situation, we venture to suggest, of high entertainment value.[44]

In some areas where the film *Rock Around The Clock*[45] was screened it was banned on Sundays, though not always for reasons of religious observance.

In 1956 the *Daily Mirror* reported that

'Rock Around The Clock' which has led to Sunday riots among rhythm-crazy youths will be released to Gaumont cinemas in South London.

The Gaumont circuit, to prevent trouble which broke out when the film was shown in North and East London, has told its managers that the film must not be shown on Sunday night.

The film will now open on Monday when the circuit hopes there will be fewer bored youths around.[46]

'Creeping commercialism' was another issue that caused concern among those bodies that attempted to stem the tide of mass culture. As a public service broadcaster the BBC resisted commercialism on cultural grounds and saw opposition to commercialisation as part of its remit. In the decade after World War II it was also thought that references to commercial products might raise unrealistic expectations within the population of improving their material conditions at a time when the government's message was austerity. There was, however, a contradiction in its remit because the BBC also had a responsibility to the mass-audience who provided its finance via a licence fee. In the case of the Light Programme the BBC tried to cater for what it perceived as working-class tastes, whilst attempting to avoid commercial pressures and keeping true to its culturally educative mission. The commercial broadcasting styles of stations like Radio Luxembourg were rejected.[47]

American music was not necessarily seen as bad by the BBC but was certainly regarded with caution and to be played only in moderation. The Corporation produced its own versions of swing by using predominantly live British dance bands that necessarily mediated the sound. With records, as the 1950s progressed, the BBC preferred to broadcast British cover versions of American songs but did not systematically ban the American versions unless they made reference to commercial products.[48] American artists like Jo Stafford, Frankie Laine and Guy Mitchell, for instance, did get extensive airing.[49]

Much of the high culture/mass culture debate that was being conducted in Britain in the 1950s centred on American popular music and perceived American popular cultural imports like juke boxes.[50] On the side of high culture were, typically, the magistrates, the police and the BBC. On the other side, fighting for popular culture in the form of juke boxes and the music they produced, were existing juke box operators, in the shape of café or snack bar proprietors as well as their teenage customers. The Amusement

Caterer's Association (ACA) and later in the decade the Phonograph Operator's Association (POA) provided legal support for juke box operators. Limited self-support in the form of petitions as well as some positive press coverage supported the predominantly teenage audiences.[51]

Applications for music licences provided clear evidence that the musical selection that juke boxes offered was not seen as 'real' music of cultural value. Juke box music was perceived as phoney and ersatz even before the advent of rock 'n' roll. The Magistrates' comments in a 1951 report from Margate illustrate some dominant opinions about juke boxes:

Music Licence Refused for a Juke Box:
Magistrates at Margate Court on Wednesday of last week refused an application for a juke box at a Northdown Road café … Mr Grove said that the juke box had been used for some time, and there was a question of doubt as to whether a music licence was required. He commented: '*I think we must regard the suppressed noise coming from the instrument – if a juke box can be called that – as music.*'[52]

While a limited amount of American and American-styled music was available in the late 1940s and into the 1950s through BBC radio, and recorded music via Radio Luxembourg, such music was not necessarily readily available to teenagers. A typical family home would have only one radio, and decisions on programme choice and volume control would normally lie with the older generation. Reception for Luxembourg, depending on your location and the quality of your radio, was frequently poor. Those who were in their teens at the time vividly remember these restrictions.

Laura Dowding grew up in the Nelson area of Lancashire and explains that her family had

a little brown box on the wall with Light and Home Service, and in the next road somebody had a great big thing with dials and they could get Radio Luxembourg. … We had the Relay … providing 9 o'clock theatre on Saturday night when my father had read whether it was suitable – and this was at 17 years old – we could stop up and listen to that …

Luckier teenagers might have their own radio: asked if she listened to Radio Luxembourg, Laura replied: 'Very occasionally if you went in somebody's house who had it. But because you didn't have a continuity of following it, it always seemed a bit alien, so I can't say I was a regular Radio Luxembourg listener.'[53]

Valerie Tome remembers:

We had one radio, a cabinet, and my father claimed that tuning it into Radio Luxembourg would seriously distort the mechanism and ruin the membranes and blow up the tubes and … no one was allowed to put it on Radio Luxembourg. But Rita, who had everything, was bought a portable radio, and I can remember us lying on the floor in her bedroom and screaming to Radio Luxembourg. I would scream when Frankie Vaughan came on and Rita would scream when Dickie Valentine came on.[54]

Terry Mitchell, growing up in Prestwich, Lancashire recollects:

I was very fortunate in the early fifties, one Christmas I was given a portable radio, and when I heard people talking [about] the Top 20 and … I discovered using this portable radio with a great deal of difficulty I could pick up Radio Luxembourg. That was the only place to hear modern music. And again in some sense you listened to the music to talk about … had you heard so and so. … We didn't attend musical evenings of any sort or musical groupings. There were no real places to go that we would have dreamed of going. Manchester was somewhere where, all other things being equal, we didn't go, even though it was probably only about five miles down the road.[55]

Mitchell raises the important point that opportunities to listen to popular American music communally, with other youths, were limited. Until juke boxes became accessible in the high street the most likely place to hear these sounds would have been at fairground, seaside or amusement arcade venues.

Popular music had a fairground/seaside resort tradition in the first half of the twentieth century and oral testimony regularly states the first recognition of pop music by youths was in these venues, accompanying the rides.[56] As a youth in the early 1950s John Farmery worked at a funfair in Cleveleys, Lancashire. He explains how American music was disseminated:

And of course the music at the time was being played over the loudspeakers at the fairground and a lot of that was at that time just coming in from America – Les Paul, Mary Ford, Frankie Laine, Guy Mitchell that sort of thing.

A.H.: And did you hear any of this music anywhere else – on the radio?

J.F.: Not so much I don't think at that time. The radio was very stiff and starchy, very much BBC and that sort of thing, so really this was something different, this was what people called fairground music. It hadn't been accepted as general over here.[57]

Key reasons for mediation of American popular music through British influences were protectionist agreements with the Musicians' Union, copyright bodies and the record industry dating from the 1920s. These had the effect of stifling the dissemination of new, emergent, popular and often American forms of music that appealed to a youth market. The conditions of the Musicians' Union agreement meant that the BBC allotted only twenty-two hours per week for broadcasting recorded music or 'needle time'. Moreover, of this 'needle time' only one in every three records could contain vocals. As a consequence, light orchestral music predominated and the taste for this was reinforced by a record industry that promoted its characteristically sedate style mainly because this was the only kind of music that would have any realistic chance of airplay.[58] These restrictions not only worked against rock 'n' roll but also against 'trad' jazz and 'skiffle',[59] all of which had little chance of airing.[60]

A strong contrast to the sedate background music that came from the BBC occurred when rock 'n' roll hit Britain with Bill Haley's (*We're Gonna*) *Rock Around the Clock*,[61] which sold over a million copies. Without quite knowing what it was, the 'Establishment' reacted against the new musical form of rock 'n' roll, any discussion of which cannot be separated from the 1950s youth style of the Teddy Boy and connotations of social disturbance (see chapter 5). The introduction of rock 'n' roll to Britain caused public concern, and a key reason for this was a perceived link between rock 'n' roll and juvenile delinquency that was thought already to exist in the USA. This 'link' was reinforced in both America and Europe by Hollywood in 1955 with the release of the film *The Blackboard Jungle*,[62] which screened images of 'wild, untamed rebel youth'.[63] The soundtrack to the credit sequence was Haley's *Rock Around the Clock* and the film provoked further negative associations between rock 'n' roll music and immoral and criminal behaviour.

One of the biggest and most culturally significant effects of Haley's music, though, was the public reaction to the film *Rock Around the Clock*[64] when it was released in Britain. The film became a rallying point for rebellious youth: Nik Cohn, noted that in 'one shot it crystallised the entire rock rebellion'. For the first time

> the concept of Teenager was used as news, as a major selling point and, in no time, everyone else was up on the bandwagon. Churchmen offered spiritual comfort, psychologists explained, magistrates got tough, parents panicked, businessmen became rich and rock exploded into a central issue.
>
> … And the papers hollered harder, the panic got greater, the circle kept spinning and suddenly the generation war was open fact.[65]

This marked the beginning of a 'moral panic'[66] whose flames were fuelled by an eager press. Cinema owners and managers responded to hostile media reports of wholesale rioting in cinemas and incidents of dancing in the aisles by eventually banning screenings altogether. 'Sociologists had to visit the movie twice: the first time to watch the movie, the second time to watch the audience.'[67] It is probable that press reports of rioting preceded the actuality, and that reports concerning the film's effects were exaggerated. Whitcombe's report, which sheds light on the construction of a moral panic, is worth quoting at length:

> [T]he picture played 300 cinemas scattered around the country (including such tough cities as Glasgow and Sheffield) without any trouble. Then, after a performance at the Trocadero in South London, there was some good natured larking: a few hundred boys and girls danced and chanted 'Mambo Rock' on Tower Bridge, holding up traffic. Some cups and saucers were thrown too. Later there were a few ten-shilling fines. One boy was fined £1 for accidentally kicking a policeman.
>
> But the newspapers splashed the story as a riot: 2,000 were on the streets, claimed the *Daily Express*. More stories followed, and young people appeared and acted out the drama. At a Croydon cinema there was jiving in front of the screen, and when the manager (in evening dress) protested he was squirted point blank by a youth armed with a fire extinguisher. A mob at Lewisham sang 'Nine little policemen hanging on the wall'. The Rank Organization banned the showing of the picture on Sundays. The King of the Teddy-Boys (Desmond Turrell of Reading) was gaoled. Everybody got involved: Fabian of the Yard and Promenade Concert conductor Malcolm Sargent commented; the *Evening News* film critic was baffled by the picture and went in search of a double brandy, reciting Gray's 'Elegy'; but the communist *Daily Worker* found it was a 'direct and refreshing' film, adding that 'the music isn't obscene but the relentless commercialism is'. The manager of the Gaumont, Shepherd's Bush was warned by a young customer: 'Just wait for Friday, mate. We've got the boys from Notting Hill coming, and the boys from White City and Acton. We're gonna tear the place apart.' The Queen, in Scotland, cancelled her screening of *The Caine Mutiny* and commanded a *Clock* print to be sent up by fast train.[68]

Not all press coverage, however, was negative: for example, on 1 September 1956, following reports of disturbances at screenings of *Rock Around the Clock*, the *Daily Mirror* held an experimental 'Rock 'n' Roll Party' to test the effects of the music. Among those present were 'a well known psychologist', 'a parson from an East End parish', 'three young typists' and 'four teenage boys who had nowhere to go'. Following the experimental party the psychologist said, 'It is a perfectly good outlet for the exuberance of youth. But the impact depends on the person. A boy liable to smash a cinema seat could be aroused by many circumstances.' The Reverend John Hornby commented, 'I think rock 'n' roll is an exciting rhythm and enormous fun. It is a red herring to blame it for the bad behaviour of Teddy Boys. It is not fair to brand the music out of hand'. The editorial verdict was: 'It's rhythm for young people. It gets them on their feet. And it can be fun. But musically it is unendearing and monotonous. The danger is that it is a ready-made fuse for youngsters who are liable to make trouble.'[69] Headlines from the inner pages through September 1956 reported on the 'trouble' at screenings of *Rock Around the Clock* but the shock reporting was short lived. Negative reporting in the *Daily Mirror* started on 3 September with 'Rock 'n' Roll Riot Girls Boo Police' and continued with 'Rock 'n' Roll Film Barred on Sundays' on the 6th; '1,000 Rioters Take Manchester by Storm' on the 10th; and on the 12th 'Rock 'n' Roll Film Barred in 2 Towns'[70] where the Watch Committees barred the film because of the trouble it had caused in other towns.[71]

Given the scale of media reaction to rock 'n' roll it is unsurprising that Magistrates' courts reflected contemporary fears. Comments made in Walsall, Staffordshire by Licensing Justices in an application by a transport café proprietor for a music licence for a juke box identified some of the concerns: 'When he granted the application, the Chairman Aid, W.R. Wheway, said: "Let us hope it does not produce any results of Rocking and Rolling"'.[72] And at a Temperance Bar in Leigh, Manchester 'the proprietors of [the] premises wished to install a juke box in order to cater for the needs of their customers. There was a "wave of demand" for music in these days, not only for "Rock 'n' Roll" but for good music.'[73] It is unfortunate that what is meant by 'good music' is not stated. In this case the application for a licence was refused.

It is difficult to assess the size of the youth market in Britain for popular records in the period 1945 to 1960. Gramophone records were not included in the UK's industrial or cultural statistics, and in general assessments of record sales were combined with record players, motorcycles, cinema attendances and 'other entertainments'.[74] We do know, however, that the British record business was worth around £6,000,000 in 1953 and by 1958 this had risen to £27,000,000, that this was approximately 2.5 per cent of all consumer spending and that the industry was dominated by EMI and Decca.[75] As with the juke box business, it was the late 1950s that experienced a massive period of growth. The year 1957 saw a major peak in sales: in 1955 around 50 million singles were sold; in 1956 this was 54 million; in 1957, 64.5 million; in 1958, 56 million; in 1959, 51 million; and in 1960, 55 million.[76]

Wurlitzer 24 of 1938, courtesy Rich Leatham – Always Jukin'

2 The Music Maker
Mark II of 1946,
courtesy of Music Hire
Group, Leeds

3 The Filben Maestro
of 1946,
courtesy Rich Leatham –
Always Jukin'

The Wurlitzer 1015 of 1946, courtesy Rich Leatham – Always Jukin' **4**

AMI's colourful juke box selection **5**

EMBERRED CHARCOAL

SUNBURST YELLOW

FIRECRACKER RED

TAHITIAN BROWN

ATOLL CORAL

PADDY'S GREEN

6
The 40-selection BAL-AMI Junior
from 1956 manufactured by Balfour
Engineering Co., Ilford, Essex, UK,
courtesy Terry Lovell,
The Jukebox Co.

7
The BAL-AMI G80
from 1954 manufactured by Balfour
Engineering Co., Ilford, Essex, UK,
courtesy Terry Lovell,
The Jukebox Co.

As we have seen in chapter 2, the British were reluctant to change over from the 10-inch 78-rpm shellac disc to the 7-inch 45-rpm vinyl micro-groove record that had been available in the US since 1948. This was not because 45s were more expensive to buy (when available) but because a new record player would be needed to play them. Single records were relatively expensive at around 5 shillings each, which included 50 per cent purchase tax.[77] In 1955 46,000,000 78s were sold as opposed to 4,587,000 45s and it was not until 1959 that 45s outsold 78s.[78] This caused juke box opera-tors some problems in trying to source 45s from music shops for their machines: '45 speed records are the main cogs in Britain's juke box money spinning business.'[79] The last 78-rpm pop single was Brenda Lee's *Sweet Nuthins* of 1960, and 78s were still being pressed up till 1970.[80]

One of the reasons why the single record (both 45-rpm and 78-rpm) did not take off in the UK until the second half of the 1950s was that the industry did not really target the teenage market until rock 'n' roll became popular with young people after the second release of *Rock Around the Clock* in 1956. Whereas sales of 300,000 would make a big hit around 1950, *Rock Around the Clock* became Britain's first million-selling record and the music industry became aware that big profits could be made by addressing teenage tastes.[81]

A look at the Hit Single Charts, started by the *New Musical Express* in 1952, graphically shows the changeover from 'easy listening' music, which was intended by the industry to appeal to the widest possible age range, to the then teenage-specific music of rock 'n' roll. Number 1 in November 1952 was *Here in My Heart*[82] by Al Martino and the artist with most weeks in the chart that year was Vera Lynn; in 1953 and 1954 Frankie Laine spent most weeks in the charts, and in 1955 it was Ruby Murray. We may view these years as the immediate pre-rock-'n'-roll period – before the big change came. In 1956 Bill Haley and His Comets topped the charts, in 1957 and 1958 it was Elvis Presley, and in 1960 Cliff Richard.[83]

The American rock 'n' roll artists Bill Haley, Elvis Presley, Little Richard, Chuck Berry and Jerry Lee Lewis had a massive influence on teenagers and the music industry in the latter half of the 1950s. They demonstrated that there was a large audience for rock 'n' roll in the UK and that there was a gap in the market for a home-grown hero. Of all the American rock 'n' roll stars, though, Elvis Presley's influence was the most extensive and he was subsequently widely imitated. None of the imitators, however, could match his star quality, charisma or vocal abilities. The two most notable of Presley's British imitators, and there were many,[84] were Tommy Steele and Cliff Richard, and neither could replicate his talent, sexual presence or record sales. Steele, who was 'discovered' in Soho's legendary coffee bar the 2is, was too homely a personality to emulate the raw rebellious aggression of early American rock 'n' roll. Richard was popular then, and continues to be so, but had nothing of the rebel about him. He would be the first to admit that he was not a serious contender to the crown of 'King of Rock 'n' Roll' and has often paid homage to Elvis. Richard drew directly from the Elvis look with quiff, sideburns and gyrating pelvic movements when performing. He spoke of the situation in which he started to play: 'The climate was absolutely perfect for someone like me to come in and be the Elvis of Great Britain; not that I personally wanted to be, although I was totally influenced by him originally, you know, but there it was: there was this gap and I filled it.'[85] Steele and Richard were leading British artists involved in the castration of rock 'n' roll; part of the familiar twentieth-century pattern of mediating American popular culture.

Television was partly responsible for the surge in the teenage market for single records in 1957. Before this date pop music received an insignificant amount of attention on television, but in 1957 the show *6.5 Special*[86] was first broadcast by the BBC, which presented contemporary music to a live teenage audience drawn from the London area.[87] The BBC TV panel game *Juke Box Jury* was first broadcast on 1 June 1959 and continued until 1967. It was a programme for the mainstream audience 'in which "celebrities" – out of work actors, professional pundits, and assorted media hangers-on – gave their notably jaded and uninformed views on a carefully selected series of single records'.[88] *Juke Box Jury* could not be said to have captured the teenage imagination, though it may have affected record sales.

Juke boxes played a key role in the dissemination of American popular music, particularly rock 'n' roll, and there is a parallel between the role of juke boxes in the UK, where they bypassed BBC radio to disseminate musical forms that were frowned on by the broadcasting authorities, and the situation in the USA. Here a similar process happened, but in the American case white-owned radio stations resisted black music.

Rock 'n' roll had its roots in American 1940s urban blues as well as country music. It was, from the outset, closely associated with rebellion and became attractive to a rebellious white teenage audience in the USA and with working-class youths in the UK. Juke boxes were relatively uncensored and allowed rock 'n' roll to spread in both countries. Radio stations in America relied on advertising revenue and were open to influences from local pressure groups, which left juke boxes 'as the sole public source of the "new" music'.[89] In America rock 'n' roll was resisted because of its black associations, whereas in Britain it was resisted for its American and mass-cultural associations.

In Britain BBC radio opposed popular American music, particularly rock 'n' roll. Their attitude was not an unambiguously racist one in the same way as it was with American radio, but the rhythmical music associated with jazz was not, the Third Programme notwithstanding, perceived to be of the same aesthetically cultured standard as classical music.[90] Some argue, however, that a more intentional resistance to rock 'n' roll was at work within the BBC:

> rock 'n' roll was deliberately ignored and resisted by the BBC radio networks. British balladeers and cabaret-style singers were systematically favoured and in 1956, the year when Elvis Presley's 'Heartbreak Hotel' [HMV, 1956] was released, not one rock 'n' roll record was featured in the annual review of popular songs.[91]

In 1920s and 1930s America black musical forms were moderated to suit white-owned radio stations in much same way that the BBC moderated American musical forms in Britain.[92] White musicians in America 'covered' black originals but these copies were so watered down that they never really reproduced the 'feel' of the black originals in much the same way as British bands could not reproduce the 'feel' or spontaneity of American swing and progressive jazz. By the time the USA joined World War II in December 1941, however, a national infrastructure of juke boxes was in place in the USA which allowed music to be marketed nationally, bypassing radio.[93] This enabled specialist and emergent musical forms like rhythm and blues, country and western, jazz, blues, and gospel to spread uncensored across the country. In Britain the point of a nationwide juke box infrastructure had been reached, to a lesser extent than in America, around 1958 when there were an estimated 13,000 juke boxes increasing at 400 per month.[94]

The growing popularity in the USA of black and rock 'n' roll styles can be traced through the pages of the music publication *Billboard*. It charted the industry by publishing three separate popularity charts: the Hit Parade or Top Twenty, which listed the best-selling records of the previous week; a list of the records played most frequently by top disc jockeys; and a third list, which showed the records most often played on juke boxes. From 'a comparison of the lists, it is possible to trace the development of Rock 'n' Roll out of the previously entrenched musical forms – and to see the defensive tactics of the major music publishers, record companies and radio networks as they sought to resist it'.[95] *Billboard* provided the evidence that it was possible to have a 'juke box hit'; and in Britain a similar, though less detailed, function was carried out by *World's Fair*, which advised the coin-operated industry on 'juke box hits'. Juke box owners were typically unaware of which records would attract teenage customers. The lists of Top Twenty Hits that were published in the British weekly paper *New Musical Express*, for example, would not necessarily indicate a demand in juke box locations because they were based on average sales across the counter. *World's Fair* provided regular reviews of possible juke box hits and made distinctions between different sites and types of customer. For example, more sophisticated venues, referred to as 'posh', were listed as a separate category; but most importantly it published 'Britain's first-ever Top 100 Records', 'compiled each week from detailed, cross-checked juke-box statistics, and augmented by disc jockey returns'. This was aimed specifically at juke box operators. For example, the Top 10 for week ending 1 February 1958 showed seven distinct rock 'n' roll numbers.

Many black and early rock 'n' roll artists in America achieved recognition from the exposure they received from juke boxes long before they became recognised by network radio because commercially operated radio stations were always restricted in what they played by advertisers who wanted to project a clean or 'high cultured' image. In consequence, they were inherently conservative and they 'played safe'. For example, jazzman Earl Bostic's fame was largely due to his popularity on juke boxes.[96] Sam Phillips, owner of Sun Records in Memphis, used local juke boxes to test demand for his artists: indeed, he did this with Elvis Presley's first record *That's All Right*.[97] Philips understood that Elvis' voice had a 'black' sound to it and that he would, as a result, face resistance from radio stations. Consequently, Philips popularised Elvis' records on local juke boxes in tandem with local radio and intended to broaden the singer's popularity through these methods. Radio stations, DJs and retailers alike keenly watched the juke box charts in *Billboard* and based their decisions on whether or not to 'go' for a record on its juke box popularity. Independent record companies were able to test the 'appeal' of a record or of an artist through local juke boxes, because if a record was played regularly and proved to be popular locally, the record company would have more confidence in risking the huge expense of a national launch. Local juke boxes provided a vital testing ground for untried musicians and new styles.

The evidence that juke boxes bypassed entrenched resistance to black music on white-owned radio is compelling. Both the Chess and Duke-Peacock record companies reported experiences similar to Sun's.[98] Juke boxes gave them an entrée into a white youth market that was sympathetic to rock 'n' roll and rhythm and blues. In Britain, once the teenage audience became apparent, juke box distributors and owners began putting rock 'n' roll records in juke boxes and its popularity spread unhindered by the BBC's regulations.

American popular music was mediated in Britain in the post-war period and the BBC played prominent role in the process. Juke boxes bypassed cultural mediation to deliver American popular music, particularly rock 'n' roll, in an undiluted form. Chapter 4 now turns attention to the British 'users' of juke boxes and the 'new' concept of 'teenage culture'.

Notes

1 See for example Hugh Cunningham, 'Class and Leisure in Mid-Victorian England' in *Popular Culture: Past and Present*, ed. by B. Waites et al. (London: Croom Helm, 1982), pp. 66–91; Paddy Scannell, 'Music for the Multitude', *Media, Culture and Society*, 3 (1981), pp. 243–60.
2 Dave Russell, *Popular Music in England 1840–1914: A Social History*, 2nd edition (Manchester: Manchester University Press, 1997), p. 57.
3 Known as the British Broadcasting Company from 1922 to 1927, when it was renamed The British Broadcasting Corporation.
4 Scannell, 'Music for the Multitude', p. 244.
5 Stephen Barnard, *On The Radio: Music Radio in Britain* (Milton Keynes: Open University Press, 1989), p. 17.
6 'The Halle, founded in 1857, ... drew heavily upon the native resources of Lancashire, making particular use of local brass musicians, although reed and string players sometimes gained positions.' Russell, *Popular Music*, p. 280.
7 The concept of 'spivery' is an interesting one that I shall discuss in some detail in chapter 5.
8 BBC, *Special Enquiry* no. 5: A Report for Television on Issues of National Importance. 5. Leisure. 30 January 1953, commentator Robert Reid. Transcript from BBC Archives, Caversham Park, Reading, ref: T21–D421–17-218. My emphasis.
9 Director General of the BBC from 1927 to 1938.
10 David Cardiff, 'The serious and the popular: aspects of the evolution of style in the radio talk 1928–1939', in *Media, Culture and Society*, ed. by R. Collins

et al. (London: SAGE, 1986), pp. 228–46, p. 229.

11 Barnard, *On the Radio*, p. 17.

12 Cardiff, 'The serious and the popular', p. 229.

13 See Asa Briggs, *The BBC: The First Fifty Years* (Oxford: Oxford University Press, 1985), chapter V.

14 Scannell, 'Music for the Multitude', p. 243.

15 For a full discussion of emergent and dominant cultural values see Raymond Williams, 'Base and Superstructure in Marxist Cultural Theory', *New Left Review*, 82 (1973), pp. 1–16.

16 WF, 14 March 1953, p. 22, 'Automatic Gossip by Edward Graves'. My emphasis. The issue of juke box licensing is examined in chapter 7.

17 Briggs, *The BBC*, pp. 247–8.

18 Quoted in Briggs, *The BBC*, p. 245.

19 Scannell, 'Music for the Multitude', p. 243.

20 Simon Frith, 'The Industrialization of Music', in *Music for Pleasure: Essays in the Sociology of Pop* (Oxford: Blackwell, 1988), p. 30.

21 Simon Frith, 'The Making of the British Record Industry 1920–64', in *Impacts and Influences: Essays on Media Power in the Twentieth Century*, ed. by J. Curran et al. (London: Methuen, 1987), pp. 278–90, p. 285.

22 Ronald Pearsall, *Popular Music of the 1920s* (Newton Abbot: David & Charles, 1976), chapter 1, quoted in Frith, 'The Making of the British Record Industry', p. 285.

23 WF, 14 March 1953, p. 22, 'Automatic Gossip by Edward Graves'.

24 Pierre Bourdieu, *Distinction: A Social Critique of the Judgement of Taste*, translated by Richard Nice (London: Routledge & Kegan Paul, 1984), p. 18.

25 Bourdieu, *Distinction*, p. 19.

26 See the discussions addressed in Stuart Hall and Paddy Whannel, 'The Young Audience', in *The Popular Arts* (London: Hutchinson, 1964).

27 Bourdieu, *Distinction*, p. 60.

28 Bourdieu, *Distinction*, p. 61.

29 WF, 29 April 1957, 'No Juke Boxes Here'.

30 Barnard, *On The Radio*, p. 30.

31 Barnard, *On The Radio*, p. 25.

32 Harman Grisewood, quoted in Humphrey Carpenter, *The Envy of the World: Fifty Years of the BBC Third Programme and Radio 3, 1946–1996* (London: Phoenix, 1997), p. 88.

33 Barnard, *On The Radio*, pp. 30–1. 'Needle-time' was a restriction placed on the playing of pre-recorded music by agreement between the BBC, Musician's Union and Phonographic Performance Limited. Barnard, *On The Radio*, p. 26; Peter Wicke, *Rock Music: Culture, Aesthetics and Sociology* (Cambridge: Cambridge University Press, 1990), pp. 55–6.

34 *Daily Mail* (DM), 30 January 1956, p. 3.

35 Mass-Observation, 'A Report on Teenage Girls', 1949, File Report 3150. Quoted in W.J. Osgerby, *One for the Money, Two for the Show: Youth, Consump-*

tion and hegemony in Britain in 1945–70, PhD dissertation, Sussex University, 1992.

36 B. Jackson, *Working Class Community* (London: Routledge & Kegan Paul, 1968): chapter 8, pp. 120–31.

37 Jackson, *Working Class Community*, pp. 120–2.

38 WF, 5 October 1957, p. 33 'Juke Box on Trial – (Chipping Norton, Regent Cinema Snack Bar)'.

39 Harry Isaacs, b. 1934, interviewed 27 July 2001, tape ref: T.02.

40 Scannell, 'Music for the Multitude', p. 252; Barnard, *On The Radio*, p. 19.

41 Interview with Jim Cheetham, b. 1929, 2 November 2001, Hale, Cheshire, tape ref: T.05.

42 WF, 17 November 1951, p. 18.

43 WF, 17 November 1951, p. 18, 'ACA Clippings'. Unfortunately the original court records in this case are untraceable (Lancashire Records Office 27 February 2001). Albert Ambrose 1897–1971: English. 'Ambrose was the leader of one of the most famous and longest-serving British dance bands. Known for its high level of musicianship'; Lindley Murray Jones, 1911–65: American. 'Spike Jones and his City Slickers were the best known comedy band of the forties and fifties.' Hardy and Laing, *Faber Companion*, pp. 13 and 419.

44 WF, 17 November 1951, p. 18.

45 Sam Katzman (Columbia, 1956).

46 DM, 6 September 1956, p. 9.

47 Barnard, *On The Radio*, p. 29. The Beveridge committee of 1950 cited American operators in arguments against the possibility of advertising or sponsorship within the BBC. Beveridge Report, V., xxvii, cmd. 8291, HMSO, 1951.

48 Chuck Berry records were to all intents and purposes banned from the BBC because of their repeated reference to consumer products: for example, his first single *Maybelline* (Chess, 1955) was banned because it mentions Cadillacs.

49 Barnard, *On The Radio*, pp. 29–30.

50 Technically there were no official imports of luxury goods from the USA between 1939 and 1959; see chapter 2.

51 WF, 11 January 1958, p. 32, 'Young Folk Petition For Juke Box'. A temperance bar in Leigh, Greater Manchester submitted a petition signed by 247 customers asking for a music licence to be granted, and a snack bar in the same town presented a similar petition signed by 100 customers to local magistrates. WF, 20 April 1957.

52 WF, 13 October 1951, p. 18, 'Automatic Gossip by Edward Graves', my emphasis.

53 Laura Dowding, b. 1939, interviewed 18 November 2001, Padiham, Lancashire, tape ref: T.07.

54 'Trouble at the Copper Kettle', BBC Radio North, Produced by Amanda Mares, 1994.

55 Terry Mitchell, b. 1940, interviewed 2 November 2002, Mobley, Cheshire, tape ref: T.06.

56 Conversation with Tony Holmes, 11 January 1999; Krivine, *Juke Box Saturday*, p. 128.
57 John Farmery, b. 1939, interviewed 29 October 2001, Longridge, Lancashire, tape ref: T.04.
58 Peter Wicke, *Rock Music*, pp. 55–6.
59 For descriptions of both 'Trad Jazz' and 'Skiffle', see for example George Melly, *Revolt Into Style* (Harmondsworth: Penguin, 1970), section 1.
60 Barnard, *On The Radio*, p. 17.
61 Brunswick, 1954.
62 Richard Brooks (MGM, 1955).
63 Ian Whitcomb, *After the Ball: Pop Music from Rag to Rock* (New York: Proscetium, 1986), p. 226.
64 Sam Katzman (Columbia, 1956).
65 Nik Cohn, *Awopbopaloobop Alopbamboom: Pop from the Beginning* (London: Mandarin, 1996), pp. 11–12. First published in 1969.
66 See Stan Cohen, *Folk Devils and Moral Panics: The Creation of the Mods and Rockers* (New York: St Martins Press, 1980).
67 Whitcomb, *After the Ball*, p. 226.
68 Whitcomb, *After the Ball*, pp. 226–7.
69 DM, 1 September 1956, p. 9.
70 DM, 3, 6, 10, 12 September 1956, pp. 8, 9, 5, 7.
71 After the spate of critical reporting in September 1956 the DM returned to a more balanced coverage.
72 WF, 15 September 1956, p. 29.
73 WF, 29 April 1957, 'No Juke Boxes Here' (Temperance and Snack Bar, Leigh, Greater Manchester).
74 Pekka Gronow, 'The Record Industry: The Growth of a Mass Medium', *Popular Music*, Vol. 3, Producers and Markets (1983), pp. 53–75, p. 73; Dave Harker, *One for the Money: Politics and Popular Song* (London: Hutchinson, 1980), p. 97; Mark Abrams, *The Teenage Consumer* (London Press Exchange, 1959), p. 11.
75 Harker, *One for the Money*, p. 82; Simon Frith, *The Sociology of Rock* (London: Constable, 1978), p. 99.
76 Frith, *Sociology of Rock*, p. 102.
77 Purchase tax was raised to 60 per cent for records in 1955: WF, 29 October 1955.
78 Frith, *Sociology of Rock*, p. 102.
79 WF, 6 July 1957, p. 34, 'These 45 Discs – Are They A Flop?'.
80 *Sweet Nuthins* (Brunswick, 1960); Harker, *One for the Money*, p. 82.
81 Harker, *One for the Money*, p. 68.
82 *Here in My Heart* (Capitol, 1952).
83 Paul Gambaccini, Tim Rice and Jonathan Rice, *British Hit Singles*, 8th edition (Guinness, 1991), pp. 371, 381–3; Dave McAleer, *The Ultimate Hit Singles Book* (Bristol: Siena, 1998).

84 See Melly, *Revolt*, pp. 47–58.
85 Cliff Richard quoted in Peter Everett, *You'll Never Be 16 Again: An Illustrated History of the British Teenager* (London: BBC, 1986), p. 28.
86 Jack Good, BBC, 1957.
87 Harker, *One for the Money*, p. 71; Spencer Leigh, 'Coal in the Bunker, Burning Up Bright', www.spencerleigh.demon.co.uk/Feature_6.5Special (accessed on 23 April 2007).
88 Harker, *One for the Money*, pp. 71–2.
89 Chris Pearce, *Vintage Jukeboxes* (London: Apple, 1988), p. 91.
90 Bill Haley was the first rock 'n' roll star in Britain, followed by Elvis Presley. I have found no evidence that the blackness of Chuck Berry, Little Richard, Bo Diddley and Fats Domino (other major American rock 'n' roll stars) was an issue for resistance in Britain – simply that they were American, mass cultural and not 'good' music.
91 Dick Hebdige, 'Towards a Cartography of Taste, 1935–1962', in *Hiding The Light* (London: Routledge, 1988), pp. 45–77, p. 55. Elvis Presley, *Heartbreak Hotel* (HMV, 1956).
92 For the American story the process of 'sanitisation' is widely reported: see for example LeRoi Jones, *Blues People* (Edinburgh: Payback Press, 1995); Nelson George, *The Death of Rhythm and Blues* (New York: Omnibus, 1988).
93 Roland Gelatt, *The Fabulous Phonograph 1877–1977* (London: Cassell, 1977) estimates that by '1939 there were 225,000 of them, and it took 13,000,000 discs a year to nourish them', p. 272.
94 See WF, 6 December 1958.
95 Charlie Gillett, *Sound of the City: The Rise of Rock and Roll* (London: Souvenir Press, 1971), p. ix.
96 Tony Cummings, *The Sound of Philadelphia* (London: Methuen, 1975), p. 35.
97 Sun, 1954.
98 George, *The Death of Rythmn and Blues*, p. 34.

4

British teenagers

The description 'teenager' in the post-war period was a term, or concept, that attracted considerable attention. This chapter attempts to recapture the dominant view of teenagers in the late 1940s and 1950s by creating a profile of juke box users, which includes jobs, education, social class, spending money, crime levels and military conscription. It also considers the question of whether there was anything particularly new about the post-war condition that led to a unique expression of youth culture. It begins with an extensive view of teenager definitions and youth culture in the British context. It then looks at some of the sociological and 'bio-psychological' theories that have surrounded periods of adolescence, as well as debates about the history of British youth culture, the 'affluent' teenager, and changes in education and class perceptions.

Teenagers were not invented in the 1950s:[1] and the term 'teenager' was in use in Britain before Talcott Parsons' coinage of the term 'youth culture' in 1942.[2] This contests the notion that teenagers were part of an American cultural influence.[3] There is compelling evidence to suggest that youth culture, as a stylistic, economic and social entity, had existed in Britain for a very long time. John Springhall, for example, cites several cases of British youth 'subcultures' dating from the seventeenth century and before, which contain many of the elements associated with twentieth-century youth cultures. It is unlikely, however, that a distinctly teenage economic market came about until the 1950s.[4] Mark Abrams' groundbreaking economic research of 1959 indicated that to an economist 'the teenager as a purchaser is infinitely more important than the teenager as a person'.[5] He defined teenagers as 'those young people who have reached the age of fifteen but are not yet twenty-five years of age and are unmarried'.[6] His definition, though, is narrow and misleading because the age band of fifteen to twenty-five covers a range of widely differing incomes, expenditures and physical maturities.

Teenagers have also been described as 'people between the onset of puberty and marriage' or as persons 'casting off the dependence of childhood without having assumed the responsibilities of an adult'.[7] Although general, these descriptions broadly describe the age range of juke box audiences in the UK, especially in the 1950s. Moreover, the definition of teenager is sometimes expanded to include young people from the age of eleven or twelve at one end of the spectrum and into the first years of marriage at the other. 'Many who marry young are less emotionally mature and stable in the first year or so of marriage than they were before'[8]: teenagers, therefore, might not want to 'grow up' right away at the point of marriage; rather they might wish to continue enjoying the lifestyle more typical of younger people. Indeed, some couples in this period may only have started to behave economically as teenagers and buy records, makeup and have listened to juke boxes after they had 'tied the knot', because marriage gave some young people the first opportunity to break away from parental authority. Consequently, these couples may well have behaved economically as teenagers throughout their twenties. Laurie's circular definition of teenagers, though, is most suitable for this study:

> All definitions are in the end tautologies; perhaps it is best to go straight there, and say that a teenager is someone of any age who behaves in a teenage way. The distinctive fact about teenagers' behaviour is economic: they spend a lot of money on clothes, records, concerts, make-up, magazines all things that give immediate pleasure and little lasting use.[9]

The term 'teens and twenties' seems to describe British juke box users well enough and this was the juke box trade's view.[10] There would be yet further variations, however, even within economic and cultural definitions: *World's Fair*, for example, in the later part of the 1950s, reported on 'sophisticated sites' for juke boxes. These 'up-market' venues, though, were confined to the cosmopolitan settings of the larger cities. A 1957 report highlights a general broadening of appeal:

> As I travel around I find that on more and more café-style locations, the average age and average income group of box players is rising and widening. There are purely teen spots, of course, and teen-and-twenty ones are still way out ahead in numbers. But the twenty-and-thirty group café locations are on the increase, as are the young business people, student, deb, and sophisticated ones.[11]

Abrams' research was the most complete guide to teenage economic behaviour since the war, not least because it was the first time that anyone had 'set out to describe comprehensively the phenomenon of the teenager as a buyer of goods'.[12] For Abrams 'teenager' described a style of consumption. Abrams estimated that in 1958 there were 6,450,000 teenagers between fifteen and twenty-five years of age, and that these represented 13 per cent of the population over fifteen; but he discounted one million from this total because they were married and reassessed the figure at five million: 400,000 of these were at school or college and a further 400,000 serving in the armed forces. Their combined income was around £1,480 million annually, or roughly 8.5 per cent of all personal income in the UK.[13] Abrams calculated that there were 2.75 million male teenagers and that 2,200,000 of these were in jobs that paid around £8 per week, and that out of 2.25 million female teenagers 2 million were working and receiving average wages of £5. 10s. per week.[14] After deducting board payments, which he calculated at 35s. for males and 25s. for females,[15] he was left with a total of 4,200,000 teenagers in receipt of roughly £17 million per week of spending money. If pocket money is added from the 800,000 unwaged then 'a grand total of £900 millions a year [is] to be spent by teenagers at their own discretion'.[16]

Abrams observed that 'the spending is concentrated on clothing, footwear, drink and tobacco, sweets, soft drinks, meals and snacks, pop records, gramophones, romantic magazines, paperbacks, visits to the cinema and dance hall'.[17] For Abrams, the way money was spent by young people was 'distinctive teenage spending for distinctive teenage ends in a distinctive teenage world' and he analysed how this money was spent.[18] Around a quarter went on clothing and footwear, 14 per cent on alcohol and tobacco and 12 per cent on confectionery, snacks and soft drinks in cafés and restaurants. Teenage expenditure was so significant for these markets that the spending 'bulks so large that it almost determines the character and prosperity of the trade'.[19] Without itemising the whole of the report, it is significant that teenage spending was claimed to account for a quarter of all consumer expenditure on record players, records, cinema tickets and 'other entertainments'.[20] The recognition of the teenager as a significant economic entity was arguably an economic enfranchisement of Britain's young people.

Abrams' report, however, relies on general descriptions of economic behaviour, and his references to 'total expenditure' and 'average earnings' conceal major disparities.[21] It is probably 'unfair to subject Abrams' data to rigorous scrutiny since it was never produced with the intention of being a thoroughgoing piece of academic investigation'. However, because Abrams' work is regularly cited uncritically and because his figures 'clearly distorted and exaggerated the scale of young people's economic power', it needs to be properly assessed.[22]

Abrams neglected to draw attention to marked regional variations in earnings and spending.[23] Pearl Jephcott, for instance, found in her Scottish survey that over half of those aged fifteen to seventeen-and-a-half had less than £1 per week to spend, and over 80 per cent of those aged seventeen-and-a-half to nineteen spent less than £3. This led Jephcott to note: 'The popular image of today's adolescent was certainly not true of the great majority of these Scottish boys and girls.' Even with overtime and bonuses, take home-pay was less than £5 for 41 per cent, and only 7 per cent earned over £9.[24] A report into teenage boys in Glasgow between 1947 and 1950 found that over 80 per cent of seventeen-year-olds in skilled occupations were earning around £4 per week and that for 'the lower grades of workers, whether manual or non-manual' wages were marginally higher.[25] And a study of teenagers in Bury, Lancashire in 1966 found that of the fifteen-to eighteen-year-olds only 5.5 per cent spent over £2 a week and, like Jephcott, concluded that the 'popular picture of affluent teenagers grossly simplifies the very real differences in income among them'.[26]

It has been proposed, not least by Abrams, that youths in the 1950s had more expendable income than previous generations and that their increased spending power led to a stronger cultural influence. Writing in 1957 the novelist and essayist Colin MacInnes noted that

> Today, youth has money, and teenagers have become a power. In their struggle to impose their wills upon the adult world, young men and women have always been blessed with energy but never, until now, with wealth. After handing a pound or two over to Mum, they are left with more 'spending money' than most of their elders, crushed by adult obligations.[27]

Observations like these from MacInnes and Abrams are too general to be taken as an overall picture of Britain, however, and this is primarily because economic differences would have existed both regionally and with respect to gender, and because much influential commentary is written from the perspective of southeast England.[28] The wealthy teenagers to whom he refers need not have been confined to this date. In Britain most young people left school and started full-time work at fourteen years or under before World War II and fifteen years after 1947, and, although in receipt of lower wages than adults, they would not necessarily have been an economic drain on their families.

It was standard practice for young people in paid employment to give a proportion of their income to their parents for board. Abrams took these payments into account and made a general calculation that the payments were 35s. for males and 25s. for females. Unfortunately, he neglected to draw attention to the very real regional differences and age dispersal in the actual amount of these outgoings.[29] These payments were obligations that Rowntree observed in 1930s York.[30] Here, the proportion of board payments changed with age and it was often the case that the under-sixteens handed over the whole of their wage packet to their parents, receiving pocket money in return, but this was only common for the youngest wage earners. After they became sixteen the youths frequently retained half of their earnings. Fowler explains that

> Age, it seems, was the most important determinant of disposable income. As revealed in the studies of Rowntree and other social investigators, while 14- and 15-year-olds might hand over their wage packets to their mothers and receive only a few coppers back, those of 16 and older insisted on keeping much more of their earnings.[31]

Ethnographic work observed that girls in the north of England were more likely to hand over their entire wage packet to their mothers throughout their teenage years.[32] Indeed, Pearl Jephcott's 1938 study of *Girls Growing Up* uncovered a keen sense of responsibility among girls from the age of fourteen to contribute to the family budget. One respondent said, '[n]ow I am fourteen I must go out and work for my own living instead of depending on my mother for everything'; and another said that 'you can hardly wait for the future when you leave school, so that you can bring your wages in to Mother'.[33] Jephcott explains that

> The child herself is conscious of this obligation to her family. She can at last begin to earn her 10/- or her 16/- a week, and she is also very properly concerned to acquire some pocket money, 3/6 or 5/-, for herself. It is this urgent consideration which binds down the child to the first job that offers her a chance to start earning quickly.[34]

Even if they brought home similar wages, all the girls would have been given some pocket money but the amount varied, depending on factors like home circumstances.

A further study from Jephcott in 1945, in which she interviewed the over-twenty age group, drew attention to regional differences which placed girls from the 'North Country' at an economic disadvantage. It is probable that there was more parental pressure on wage-earning girls in the north of England to contribute to the family budget:

> some of the London girls had entire control of their earnings since they were 14 or 15. From the first week that she goes 'on board' and contributes to the weekly house-keeping, a girl's saving or not saving, her spending on essentials or luxuries, is her own affair. In money matters she is finally responsible to no one but herself. [In London] [m]any a girl's mother has no idea what she earns.[35]

Whereas 'North Country girls even at 18 and 19 still give their pay packet to their mother, who controls all the important spending'.[36] A 1950 report on Birmingham adolescents established, as in the late 1930s and early 1940s, that all of the respondents had some spending money and that there were wide variations in the amount received, but with both boys and girls this pocket money increased at each birthday.[37]

Certainly there was a public perception of youthful affluence in the 1940s. A letter in the *Daily Mail* from 1949 claimed: 'Teenagers are pampered with high wages, first-class working conditions and excellent conditions in education.'[38] Public perceptions, however, are not evidence; indeed, most available sources point to the opposite view. Jephcott was clear that '[t]alk of extravagant war-time wages for young people was certainly untrue as far as these [North Country] girls were concerned',[39] and that the reported 'high-wages-racket of certain sections of the press is largely based on exceptional circumstances'.[40]

The type of employment that young workers might have engaged in bears direct relevance to their income levels and social class and highlights gender differences. Another Jephcott survey from 1954 indicated that in the work place, with both genders, young people were not separated from adult workers. Teenage boys' jobs 'were mostly plebeian ones. They were plumbers, painters, machinists, tool-makers, filing-clerks, packers, butcher boys and so on', whereas the 'girls were employed in less skilled jobs and a narrower range of work than their brothers'; in Nottingham and London girls were routinely employed in manual factory jobs.[41] These 'plebeian' occupations were still the primary youth occupations in 1950.[42] Abrams, though, had observed a change by 1959 in youth occupations since the 1930s:

> [Teenage] occupational pattern is strikingly different from what it used to be. In 1931, it would appear from the census, a high proportion of adolescents

were engaged in menial and often dead-end occupations – errand boys, tea makers, van boys, farm servants, messengers, and, of course, domestic servants.[43]

What made post-war youth economically distinctive from previous generations of teenagers was that in general they were comparatively more affluent. Teenage affluence came about through changes in working-class employment structures and labour markets, and increased teenage spending was confined mainly to the working classes.[44] Increased demands for youth labour in the post-war period led to a rise in young people's earnings, and working-class youths from this period typically left school at fifteen and went into manual jobs that were relatively well paid. In the early 1950s the highest-paid work for young people was unskilled.[45]

Arguments like Abrams' that propose an affluent teenage consumer in the 1950s with a high disposable income, and that support MacInnes' statement that '[t]oday, youth has money',[46] rely on two basic premises: firstly, that there was an improvement in real earnings over previous decades and secondly that there was a reduction in unemployment over the same period. Fowler argues that the conditions for teenage consumers were in place before World War II and questions this premise, because although (according to Abrams' statistics) teenage earnings had increased by 400 per cent since the 1930s similar large increases had occurred in the 1930s and these were offset by inflation (Figures 4.1 and 4.2).[47]

Social surveys on poverty connected within the inter-war period indicate that the years between starting work and getting married were 'the one point during the life-cycle when a person was least likely to be experiencing poverty'.[48] Rowntree reported that the wage of boys and girls 'may be, and often is, higher than that of [the] rest of the family'[49] and a higher proportion of the under-twenties and twenty- to twenty-four-year-olds were single in the 1920s and 1930s than in the 1950s. Moreover, in the inter-war years there were more fifteen- to twenty-four-year olds in the population than in the 1950s and 1960s.[50] The situation before World War II shows that teenagers had disposable income and were often the most affluent members of their families.

Fowler concludes that an affluent teenage consumer existed in Britain in the 1920s and 1930s when 'the economic and demographic conditions for a youth market to emerge were extremely favourable'.[51] Conclusions like Reed's, however, that by 'all the standards of earlier generations [teenagers] certainly have a great deal of money to spend',[52] Osgerby's that 'although

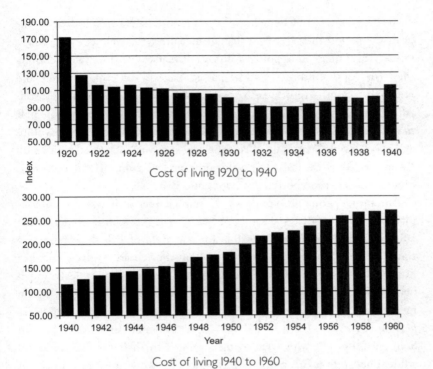

Cost of living 1920 to 1940   **4.1**

Cost of living 1940 to 1960   **4.2**

Source: A. H. Halsey (ed.), *Trends in British Society Since 1900: A Guide to the Changing Social Structure of Britain* (London: Macmillan, 1972), Table 4.11, p. 122.

not bulging, the wage packets of young workers in post-war Britain were proportionally more replete than those of earlier generations',[53] and Jephcott's, where compared to the nineteenth century 'the economic stresses that used to affect every aspect of the life of the working-class youngster have been erased'[54] are more convincing.

There is general agreement that, although not rich by later benchmarks, on the whole teenagers of the 1950s were more affluent than previous generations in most of Britain's regions.[55] In the inter-war years young, single people were more affluent compared to the other members of their family than after the war, but post-war teenagers, allowing for regional variations, still had more money to spend in real terms. There was a prevalent 'primary poverty' that was observed in the 1930s that had been practically eliminated by 1961, when only 3 per cent of English people were living in poverty and most of these were old people.[56] Parental dependence on their children for long-term security was also diminished following the introduction of the Welfare State in 1945.[57]

Teenagers cannot be defined simply as economic entities. Indeed, in the post-war period they were considered in cultural as well as in economic terms. The American sociologist Talcott Parsons is credited with coining the term 'youth culture',[58] and he passed over youth's economic role and noted that 'youth culture has a strong tendency to develop in directions which are either on the borderline of parental approval or beyond the pale in such matters as sex behaviour, drinking and various forms of frivolous and irresponsible behaviour'.[59] Parsons, however, was concerned with youth culture in America and there were pronounced cultural and economic differences between youths in America and Britain.

Amongst Britons in World War II (see chapter 1) it was a commonplace observation that visiting Americans were more affluent than their British hosts. Had it been possible for a sample of British teenagers to travel to the US in the period 1945 to 1960 they could not have failed to notice that, in general, white American teenagers were economically much better off than they were. In the author's own experience of growing up in Harrow, Middlesex in the late 1950s and 1960s, American Air Force personnel employed at a local USAF (United States Air Force)[60] base in South Ruislip and who were living locally with their families appeared affluent beyond the dreams of local children, for whom to see an American car was an awesome experience. Striking examples of their wealth were the use of seemingly exotic foodstuffs in their ordinary diet such as potato salad and 'dips', as well as Coca-Cola, 7up and ice cream that we Britons might otherwise only see on occasions like Christmas and birthdays. The American children introduced us to previously unknown commodities as diverse as Marvel comics and felt-tip pens. This relative affluence allowed cars, for example, to play a central role in white-American youth culture but not in British. The differences in young people's economic and social behaviour between the USA and the UK allowed different interpretations of the same popular cultural influences in each country.

Socialising is a consistent theme in teenagers' lives and is reflected by their economic behaviour. Listening to juke boxes and buying clothes and make-up, for example, were all channels of communication or, to be more precise, channels of non-verbal communication for the post-war generation. Teenage communication is of a characteristically non-verbal nature and has a high emotional content that is expressed naturally in music, dancing, dress styles and in 'certain habits of walking, standing, in certain facial expressions and "looks" of an idiomatic slang'.[61] 'The things they buy appear to be personal indulgencies, but in fact they are all commodities of social contact'.[62] Teenagers 'more than any other section of the community are looking for goods and services that are highly charged emotionally',[63] and these commodities were used as badges of peer group belonging.

'Bio-psychological' views of the adolescent period had been developing from the early twentieth century and were aired after World War II. This was a time when there was a growing public perception that adolescence was an inevitable consequence of 'bio-psychological' developments that occurred before reaching the age of adult responsibility. These approaches concerned themselves with physical, behavioural and emotional changes occurring at a time of hormonal change and sexual awakenings.[64] This period of teenage development has been described as 'unavoidably traumatic – a period of storm, stress and turmoil for young people and anyone who shares their company'.[65] Although these views on adolescence were later contested,[66] under their presumptions society had the comfort of believing that adolescent troubles were simply an inevitable life phase and a natural part of growing up. If these 'growing pains' were more visible after World War II this could have been the result of increased affluence reflected in a new and more visual and aural teenage market in tandem with increasing media coverage.

Following World War II sociological views on youth began to gain popular credence, and these evolved from ethnographic work conducted earlier in the century. For instance, the anthropologist Margaret Mead, from the 1920s, suggested that adolescent troubles were not a universal phenomenon but a socially constructed product of the industrialised world.[67] Here, the argument goes, in industrial societies the adult world is not fully open to adolescents because most adult occupations are conducted behind closed doors, in factories, offices, and so on. Moreover, in industrial societies the childhood period has been 'idealised' and it was expected that adolescents reflected values that were not observed by adults in practice; a world in which adults accept individual responsibility and independence while '[c]hildhood is an "unreal" world of tolerated parasitism, legitimate dependence, submission and irresponsibility'.[68] Since within the period 1945 to 1960 most British youth began their working lives in an adult environment at the age of fifteen, when they contributed to the family budget with the widespread practice of 'board' payments, these views of 'parasitism' and 'dependence' seem, in hindsight, to be ill-observed for the British experience.

Mead suggested that transmitting culture through parents may work smoothly in slowly changing societies but in the industrialised world where 'the child is expected to take the parent as a model for his own life style ... [t]he child will never be, as an adult, a member of the same culture of which the father stands as the representative'.[69] By the 1960s Mead's views were not universally accepted, as British youth, in general, did not appear to be ideological rebels. British empirical work observed that generational conflict in values was 'virtually non-existent'.[70]

The period 1945 to 1960 was a time of great social and economic change that provided a contrast with life both before and during the war, creating a larger than normal 'generation gap'. The devastating effects of World War I, the inter-war years of economic slump and residual Victorian values were preoccupations of parents but not of post-war youth. Oral testimony supports this view. When asked if he was aware of a generation gap when he was a teenager, interviewee John Farmery emphasised musical differences: 'Oh yes, definitely, even more so than there is today. Because the wartime people were brought up on band music and, as I say, this light-hearted sort of thing, and then rock and roll came in and it was so vastly different that a lot of the older generation couldn't or wouldn't take to it at all.'[71] There has been little evidence, however, of severe or sustained generational frictions, and assertions of a general generation gap are contested: 'Studies of "young rebels" indicate that, while there is a certain degree of child-parent tension, the major thrust of youthful discontent is directed not at family but outward, at social, political, and academic institutions that are only indirectly identified with the older generation.'[72]

In his study of young people's economic and social behaviour in the inter-war period Fowler talks of this group as *The First Teenagers* and concludes that young working-class wage-earners were 'principal benefici-aries' of commercial leisure provision, and that their lifestyles and spending patterns were similar to those of 1950s teenagers. Similar establishments to 1950s youth entertainment and meeting places, namely cinemas, dance halls and milk bars, were in place and widely frequented before the war. This view is persuasive and can be supported by primary research into amusement arcades, pin tables and youth gangs.[73] For Fowler, youth in this period 'were as preoccupied with clothes and fashion, and spent their disposable income on similar products (clothes, cosmetics, magazines, motorcycles and soft drinks)'. The 'phenomenon market researchers claimed they discovered in the late 1950s was already visible in Britain's towns and cities by the 1930s'.[74] In the inter-war period, young wage earners benefited from cultural, economic and social opportunities in much the same way as 1950s youth, and the 'moral guardians' of the time were just as 'outraged' by affluent young people producing their own youth culture as were the post-war 'Establishment'.

There were class, educational and gender barriers to youths mixing freely in the late 1940s and 1950s but these were probably less pronounced than for previous generations. In the field of juke box reception those youths who were in paid employment were in a position to spend their money more freely in the increasing number of youth venues that were emerging (see chapter 7).

Education was an important factor in constructing a distinctive post-war youth culture because improvements in secondary education provision shaped a separate teenage identity that in itself was split on the basis of the kind of school attended. The 1944 Education Act was passed to set up a tripartite system for state-funded secondary education (grammar, secondary modern and technical schools).[75] In its implementation, in the majority of regions, however, it became a bipartite system (grammar and secondary modern): 10 per cent of over-elevens were educated outside the state system.[76] The minimum school-leaving age was raised from fourteen to fifteen years in 1947, extending the period of parental dependence by holding back young people from the adult sphere of employment by another year. It may also, in a small way, have helped to further 'identify youth as a distinct social category and [give] substance to notions of a newly emerging "culture of youth" during the fifties and sixties'.[77] The changes between the years 1931, 1951 and 1961 meant that 'a second rung had been added to the educational ladder on which ... nearly all children can place their feet'.[78] This was a very different position to 1931 and it shows that over the 1950s around one-third of pupils in state-funded secondary education attended grammar schools, which was a significant minority. Despite these increases, in the 1950s around 80 per cent of children left school at the minimum age of fifteen, and further educational opportunities were unequally distributed across the social classes. Entry to a university education was extremely limited as most children, even in the grammar schools, left school to enter paid employment.

There were undoubtedly significant regional variations within this overall picture. Unfortunately, few regional statistics are available except for those that indicate comparisons between England and Wales. Here they show a

consistently higher percentage of grammar school pupils in Wales continuing education compared to England. In 1951, 17 per cent of grammar
school boys and 27 per cent of grammar school girls left school to 'attend
university, training college or further education' in England; the figures for
Wales were 23 and 34 per cent respectively.[79] In this instance the Welsh
figures were higher. Entrances to universities based on the British regions
for this period are unknown.[80] It is probable, however, that further research
would uncover evidence of wide regional differences within Britain and this
would be an important area for further study.

It has been posited that youth may have become a class in its own
right.[81] Hall and Whannel, for example, observe that youth behaves as
if it was a distinct class,[82] and Mark Abrams' work has been important
in developing this idea. He wrote generally of class that 'in the post war
world class barriers have tended to lose their clarity' and under 'conditions
of general prosperity the social study of society in class terms is less and less
illuminating. And its place is taken by differences related to age'.[83] This line
of argument has been referred to as 'embourgeoisement' and is contested
because of the 'continuing centrality of class inequalities in structuring
both the life styles and life chances of adolescents'.[84]

Embourgeoisement theories depend upon an assumption that the determining factor of class is living standards and spending power but this over
simplifies the British class system. Definitions of class remain unsettled: 'the
fundamental problem of determining the criteria which distinguish one class
from another is still unresolved, and it would be difficult to find a definition
and form of measurement which would be universally acceptable.'[85]

With juvenile workers, income groups do not identify social class because
some jobs have a relatively high social prestige but attract comparatively
low incomes.[86] It was young workers, unencumbered by family responsibilities, that had, since at least the inter-war years, relatively high spending
power, and it was the manual and mundane occupations in manufacturing
that paid the most money. Abrams noted in 1959 that the youth market
was almost entirely working class and wrote:

> Its middle class members are either still at school and college or else only
> just beginning on their careers; in either case they dispose of much smaller
> incomes than their working class contemporaries and it is highly probable,
> therefore, that not far short of 90 per cent of all teenage spending is condi-
> tioned by working class tastes and values. The aesthetic of the teenage market
> is essentially a working class aesthetic ...[87]

Particularly in the case of youth it is improbable that spending power denoted higher social status; indeed, the opposite is more likely.

Broadly there was a connection between education and social class. Children educated privately and at grammar schools generally stayed on at school for longer and, when they did start work, were paid less money. Moreover, as some high-status occupations required particular types of education, entrance to training for these occupations was limited to those who attended schools where this kind of learning was provided.[88] Middle-class youths in the post-war period were slower to break from parental control, leave school, take on full-time jobs and marry, and these economic factors may well have contributed to existing class divisions rather than creating a classless youth.[89] Terry Mitchell, who attended a Manchester grammar school in the 1950s, described the disruptive effect that selective secondary education had on childhood relationships:

> When we were little, pre teens, we were all friendly, we all went to each other's birthday parties, but once we got to the teen … secondary school, everybody went off to different schools, and we either went to boys' schools or girls' schools or grammar schools or secondary modern. … We lost touch despite the fact that you could almost be living next door; we all had different friends presumably based on the schools we went to.[90]

Brian Jackson's observations of Huddersfield's grammar school girls revealed clear class divisions. Respondent Rosemary Lundman explained the difficulties involved with socialising in the public sphere where 'most of the dance halls are of a low class', and 'the coffee bars and cafés are of the low class type'. Jackson observed that 'again and again many of them write as if all other teenagers in Huddersfield were hooligans or "scruffs": the teddy boy stereotype expands to cover most of the ex-secondary modern population'.[91] There seemed to be a class barrier that some of grammar school girls were reluctant to cross: 'Many of the older girls … would have delighted in a kind of superior coffee bar life, but not for anything would they have turned off into the "Santa Maria"', where working teenagers mixed.[92]

The issue of class and perceived respectability, however, can be confused because class barriers were not as rigid as they are sometimes portrayed, especially within age groups, and this is perhaps a departure from the pre-war situation. Venues where groups of 'teens and twenties' congregated were criticised for being 'low class' but this was not necessarily a criticism of occupation or standard of living; it was, though, a criticism of perceived respectability or the lack of it. People and establishments viewed as 'rough' were warned against or prohibited by parents of all social classes.

Parental authority was the deciding factor in what was considered respectable or not in the case of Laura Dowding:

> My father: his word was law, and if he said I wouldn't go in the Sunbeck Café, I certainly wouldn't go in the Sunbeck Café because they had a juke box and formica top tables and catered for what my father would have called 'the wrong sort'.[93]

Barry Stott describes how, although both he and his friends were 'free', he thought that 'respectable' parents would want their children to avoid amusement arcades and coffee bars:

> In those days we were free to go wherever we wanted to. So I would go off on my bicycle with my mates and we would spend the whole night in the arcades on the Golden Mile. There was no – there was not the slightest threat of violence in those days. There were no muggings. You could walk anywhere at any time day and night in Blackpool and not feel threatened in the 50s and early 60s. ... But, you know, if you had professional parents, they wouldn't want their children going off to the Golden Mile or the town centre for the evening, and maybe sitting in coffee bars all night was considered a bit rebellious. But it was no problem for us because we made our own rules.[94]

Parents instilled notions of 'respectability' and class into their children and this 'accepted wisdom' of the older generation was consequently part of the period's teenage consciousness. Teenagers, however, regularly ignored these social parameters when it came to the social setting of the amusement arcade, snack or milk bar.

The 'most enduring negative image of youth has been its association with crime'.[95] In the late 1950s reports of hooligan behaviour became 'innumerable' and were 'national preoccupations'. Official and public fears about a 'crime wave' perpetrated by juvenile delinquents in the years following World War II increased throughout the 1950s, and at face value the available statistics support these concerns. Official figures (see Table 4.1) show a steady rise in convictions of male offenders between the years 1955 and 1961 in the age groups fourteen to seventeen, and seventeen to twenty-one. One of the official 'Establishment' responses to this youth 'crime wave' was to introduce harsh disciplinarian regimes in Borstals and detention centres and, as a consequence, the Borstal population went up from 2,800 in 1956 to over 5,000 by the end of 1960.[96]

There was a general and widely held belief that the juvenile 'crime wave'

Table 4.1 Male offenders convicted of an indictable offence in England and Wales

Year	Age 14–7	Age 17–21
1938	11,645	10,131
1955	13,517	11,269
1956	15,029	13,425
1957	18,149	16,962
1958	21,628	21,232
1959	23,059	22,342
1960	24,749	25,068
1961	28,244	27,667

Source: T.R. Fyvel, *The Insecure Offenders: Rebellious Youth in the Welfare State* (Harmondsworth: Penguin, 1963), p. 15.

was the inevitable result of the social upheavals that occurred in the war. The perception was that those who had been termed 'war babies' were, because of fathers being absent and mothers working away from home, more likely to become problem adolescents. A Home Office report, concluded, however, that although the war conditions were primarily responsible for the generation born between 1935 and 1942, they could not be the only reasons for juvenile delinquency's statistical increase.[97]

It would, however, be difficult to argue that there was a correlation between juvenile crime and social deprivation. Fyvel makes the point that the rising levels of recorded crime occurred at the same time as increased prosperity and welfare reforms:

> British juvenile-crime figures have certainly shown one of the steepest increases of all, and the chief point is that they have risen against a background of steadily rising welfare services. ... A generation ago it was still widely held that even if poverty was only one among the main causes, the delinquency figures would at least roughly follow the curve of economic dislocation and unemployment. Today this link has clearly been severed.
>
> Economically the years from 1953 to 1960 were a phase of distinct progress. They were years of full employment, higher wages, and rising mass consumption, especially on the part of the young. ...Yet the figures of juvenile crime did not go down in these years as had been hopefully predicted earlier, at the end of the wartime hangover.[98]

Concerns that the teenager may be the weaker for being affluent were certainly raised but this was not a new perception. The detrimental effects of affluence have been consistently raised over the centuries as a primary cause for hooliganism.[99]

After the war, youth crime was a 'dominant preoccupation', but the fear of crime was far from the reality. In official opinion and responses to the behaviour and cultural orientations of the young they were consistently caricatured, overstated and generally misrepresented.[100] Statistical data supporting the impression of a post-war 'crime wave' are also open to other interpretations. Since the beginning of the twentieth century crime statistics point to youth as primary contributors but, as there were proportionately more adolescents, more of these were brought before the courts.[101] Due to the unreliability of statistical information it would be impossible to assume that an increase in juvenile crime figures necessarily meant a corresponding rise in actual youth crime:

> Whether the number of persons found guilty of offences of all kinds can be taken as a measure of the incidence of crime in the community as a whole is by no means certain. ... Until a great deal more is known about the incidence and pattern of crime in the community it would be unwise to suggest that there has been any marked increase or decrease in modern times.[102]

As measures of criminal activity, criminal statistics are notoriously unreliable because they are influenced by factors other than crime levels:

> The growing size of the police force and its supporting apparatus is the most obvious and general factor [in statistical crime increases]. Changes in the routines of law enforcement, the increased mobility of the police, changes in what the law counts as crime, fluctuations in the vigour with which the law is applied, and shifts in public attitudes and tolerance – these must all be counted within the hidden dimensions of the manufacture of crime figures.[103]

Over the twentieth century the way in which criminal information was collected and stored underwent so much change that it is questionable whether one period can usefully be compared with another. Moreover, crime statistics do not take into account increases in police efficiency, willingness or reluctance to give evidence, enthusiasm or not to prosecute and changes in what the law defines as crime.[104] Crime figures may also be observed in an historical context: 'The fact that young people are over-represented in the criminal statistics is repeatedly rediscovered in each successive wave of concern as a particularly "new" and shocking feature of the problem.'[105]

It would be unrealistic to compare the pre-war period with the post-war and suggest that the former was a time of less actual youth crime: 'there is nothing in the history of the 1920s and 1930s to justify the cosy nostalgia that is now cloaked around the pre-war years':[106]

It may well be that the intense public interest in 'juvenile delinquency' during and after the Second World War was in part responsible for more sustained efforts to detect and prosecute young offenders who in earlier years might have been subject to no more than a serious talking-to by the local constable and would not therefore have been shown in the criminal statistics.[107]

Some of the statistical crime increases could also be accounted for by police procedural 'formalisations' and restructuring of the organisation and scope of law enforcement.[108] The overwhelming problem for the crime historian is that very little is known about the criminal because over half of crimes are unsolved. This means that the statistics are based on those who get caught, and it is unlikely that those who are caught are representative of all criminals. Being a teenager may be a significant factor in getting caught as it seems probable that teenagers in general are relatively easier for the police to detect than their more experienced adult counterparts. Contemporary concerns about an apparent increase in 'violent' crime may have come about through a misinterpretation of the word 'violent', which in its legal sense does not necessarily refer to physical violence. Marsh makes the point that violence 'may consist of nothing more than opening a door! The legal meaning of violence is highly complex and technical'.[109] It is reasonable to conclude that delinquent behaviour in the period 1945 to 1960 was comparatively rare as there is no age category where conviction rates are over 3 per cent of the total. According to criminal statistics, over 97 per cent of teenagers were not recorded as committing delinquent acts.[110]

One of the cultural peculiarities that affected Britain's young men following World War II was military conscription. The National Service Act of 1948 introduced compulsory military service for young males of eighteen, and this disrupted the working and social lives of over two million young men between 1948 and 1960. Continuing education and apprenticeships were grounds for deferment but not exemption, which could be obtained for medical reasons and which accounted for approximately 16 per cent per annum of those who would otherwise be eligible for conscription.[111]

National Service had two apparent effects on the youth scene. Firstly, what was known as the 'call-up' contributed to the perception of a 'youth problem' because there was a three-year gap between the usual school leaving age and military service that left young men in a state of limbo. Understandably, employers were reluctant to invest in training and educating young men in work skills when they would soon be 'called up' and might not return to their jobs. Youths in this interim period found themselves excluded from jobs and careers. A young man interviewed in 1957 expressed the general feeling about the gap between leaving school and being 'called up':

> Well, there's no need to think too far ahead, is there? When I get in the Army I suppose most of my ideas will change anyway. There'll be time enough to think about a job when I come out. ... Between now and the time I'm eighteen I've got to 'do the lot'. Ave a good time, I say, before I get called up, blown up or married.[112]

And the *Evening Argus* in 1954 observed that

> The period prior to National Service is unsettling even for the best behaved youth. Too many lads, especially those from indifferent homes, adopt a don't-care attitude. Why should they not do as they like in civilian life when they are faced with two years of military discipline? [...] there is no question that conscription temporarily disrupts a lad in his civilian life and job. The year or so preceding service is a dangerous and frustrating period.[113]

The Reverend Douglas Griffiths came to similar conclusions: 'Many of the lads I have met feel that life ends at eighteen when they will be called up. They want to cram as much as possible into life first.'[114]

Moreover, a 'generational consciousness' may have developed as a direct consequence of military service because a two-year split from their home environment allowed young men to socialise in an almost exclusively teenage setting where shared recreational, leisure and style interests could be experienced. In their commonly rural camps, 1950s youth culture, music and styles would be disseminated as urban youths mixed with their fellow rural and suburban conscriptees in an environment which, although closed, allowed them leave to fraternise with local populations and spread the new styles further. Ted Webb describes the situation:

> You had these big camps of thousands of teenagers – eighteen, nineteen – all crammed together in bloody [sic] some places [that were] total wildernesses ... National Service broke up a lot of things. It took so many young people away from home, away into a wilderness quite often, and you were with thousands of like-minded characters. And you just went to pubs and dance halls.[115]

The impact of National Service on youth culture, spending patterns, social activities, being away from home and so on are all subjects that have been under researched and are certainly areas of cultural history that would prove productive for further investigation.

Post-war youth were not the first generation of teenagers, though they may have received more comment and media attention than previous generations. They were shaped by the cultural, economic and social influences around them. Most girls and boys left school at fifteen years when they entered the adult world of plebeian employment that was often regional in nature. Certainly, in the 1950s they had more expendable income than pre-war teenagers and the extension of the school leaving age and improvements to secondary education meant that they were a more distinctive group than previous generations.

Chapter 5 now assesses the influence of 'rebellious' male dress codes over the same period and argues that rebellious style meanings in, for example, Teddy Boy regalia were soon watered down and absorbed into the mainstream.

Notes

1 David Fowler argues that the inter-war period gave rise to the 'First Teenagers', and research by Chris Brader, into London during World War I, has uncovered references by women police officers to young women as 'highly painted teenagers': David Fowler, *The First Teenagers: The Lifestyle of Young Wage-earners in Interwar Britain* (London: Woburn Press, 1995). Christopher Brader, *Timbertown Girls: Gretna Female Munitions workers in World War 1*, PhD dissertation, Warwick University, 2001.

2 Talcott Parsons, 'Age and Sex in the Social Structure of the United States (1942)' in *Essays in Sociological Theory*, ed. by Talcott Parsons (New York: The Free Press, 1964), pp. 89–103.

3 Fowler's search of the *Oxford English Dictionary* uncovers a reference to 'teens' from a 1693 dancing magazine: 'Your poor things, when they are once in their teens, they think they shall never be married.' Fowler, *The First Teenagers*, p. 3.

4 John Springhall, 'Adolescence in historical perspective', in *Coming of Age: Adolescence in Britain 1860–1960* (Dublin: Gill & Macmillan, 1986), pp. 13–37. See also Geoffrey Pearson, *Hooligan: A History of Respectable Fears* (New York: Schocken, 1983).

5 Peter Laurie, *The Teenage Revolution* (London: Anthony Blond, 1965), p. 133.

6 Mark Abrams, *Teenage Consumer Spending in 1959 (part II): Middle Class and Working Class Boys and Girls* (London: London Press Exchange, 1961), p. 3.

7 Laurie, *Teenage Revolution*, p. 9.

8 Laurie, *Teenage Revolution*, p. 9.

9 Laurie, *Teenage Revolution*, p. 9.

10 The term 'Teens and Twenties' is regularly used by the *World's Fair* columnist Bingo Beaufort to describe juke box audiences.

11 WF, 19 October 1957, 'You Need The Right Discs For … You Can't Fool a Juke-Box audience', p. 31.

12 Editorial in Mark Abrams, *The Teenage Consumer* (London: London Press Exchange, 1959), p. 1.

13 Abrams, *Teenage Consumer*, pp. 5–7.

14 Abrams, *Teenage Consumer*, p. 9.

15 Mark Abrams, *Teenage Consumer Spending in 1959* (part II) (London: London Press Exchange, 1961).

16 Abrams, *Teenage Consumer*, p. 9.

17 Abrams, *Teenage Consumer Spending in 1959 (part II)*, p. 5.

18 Abrams, *Teenage Consumer*, p. 10.

19 Abrams, *Teenage Consumer Spending in 1959 (part II)*, p. 4.

20 Abrams, *Teenage Consumer*, p. 11.

21 W.J. Osgerby, *One for the Money, Two for the Show: Youth, Consumption and Hegemony in Britain in 1945–70, with special reference to a south east coastal town*, PhD dissertation, Sussex University, 42-2586, A9F, 1992.

22 Bill Osgerby, *Youth in Britain Since 1945* (Oxford: Blackwell, 1998), pp. 25–6.

23 There are little official data on this. David Metcalf explained about regional earnings that 'The only data available are those published six-monthly since April 1960 on wage earnings.' David Metcalf, 'The Determinants of Earnings Changes: A Regional Analysis for the UK, 1960–68', *International Economic Review*, 12/2 (June 1971).

24 Pearl Jephcott, *Time of One's Own* (London: Oliver & Boyd, 1967), p. 55.

25 T. Fergusson and J. Cunnison, *The Young Wage Earner* (London: Oxford University Press, 1951), pp. 100–1.

26 Cyril Smith in Osgerby, *Youth in Britain*, p. 25.

27 Colin MacInnes, 'Young England, Half English: The Pied Piper from Bermondsey', *Encounter* (December 1957), in *England, Half English* (London: Macgibbon & Kee, 1961), pp. 11–18, p. 11.

28 For example, MacInnes, 'Young England'; T.R. Fyvel, *The Insecure Offenders: Rebellious Youth in the Welfare State* (Harmondsworth: Penguin, 1963); Melly, *Revolt Into Style*.

29 Abrams, *Teenage Consumer Spending in 1959 (part II)*, p. 3.

30 B.S. Rowntree, *Poverty and Progress: A Second Social Survey of York* (London: Longmans, 1941).

31 Fowler, *First Teenagers*, p. 98.

32 Elizabeth Roberts, 'Woman's Place' in *The Working Class in England, 1875–1914* ed. by J. Benson (London: Croom Helm, 1985), pp. 1–35. Extensive interviews conducted by Elizabeth Roberts covering the period 1890–1940 in Lancaster, Preston and Barrow found that 'it would be unusual to find much real independence, still less youthful rebellion'. She found it normal for youths to hand over the whole wage packet to their mother. In Lancaster, for example, the mother would allocate pocket money at the rate of 1s to £1. For further discussion see Fowler, *First Teenagers*, p. 98.

33 Pearl Jephcott, *Girls Growing Up* (London: Faber & Faber, 1942), p. 69.

34 Jephcott, *Girls Growing Up*, p. 74.

35 Pearl Jephcott, *Rising Twenty* (London: Faber & Faber, 1948), pp. 126–7.

36 Jephcott, *Rising Twenty*, p. 139.

37 Bryan H. Reed (director) *Eighty Thousand Adolescents: A study of young people in the city of Birmingham by the staff and students of Westhill Training College for the Edward Cadbury Charitable Trust* (London: Allen & Unwin, 1950).

38 DM, October 1949, in Laurie, *Teenage Revolution*, p. 18. The perception of the overpaid youngster was not confined to the post-war period. Osgerby, for example, uncovered continuing correspondences in *The Times* from 1941 concerned with 'excessive earnings' amongst young people that include suggestions that youth wages might be capped. *The Times*, 1 December 1941; *The Times Educational Supplement*, 31 January 1942, in Osgerby PhD, p. 183.

39 Jephcott, *Rising Twenty*, p. 138.

40 Jephcott, *Girls Growing Up*, p. 93. See also P. Kerrigan, 'Wages and War Effort', *Labour Monthly* (January 1942); 'High Wages for Juveniles', *The Economist* (31 January 1942).

41 Jephcott, *Some Young People*, p. 82.

42 Reed, *Eighty Thousand Adolescents*, p. 24.

43 Abrams, *Teenage Consumer*, p. 11.

44 Osgerby, PhD, p. 193.

45 See for example Abrams, *Teenage Consumer*, p. 13; Fergusson and Cunnison, *The Young Wage Earner*.

46 MacInnes, 'Young England', p. 11.

47 Abrams' figures are from: Ministry of Education, *The Youth Service in England and Wales*, report of the Committee Appointed by the Minister of Education in November, 1958, Cmnd 929 (London, 1960), pp. 23, 24; Fowler, *First Teenagers*, p. 93, statistics from R. Stone and D.A. Rowe, *The Measurement of Consumers' Expenditure and Behaviour in the United Kingdom 1929–1938*, Vol. II (Cambridge: 1960), Table 40, p. 93; A.H. Halsey (ed.), *Trends in British Society Since 1900: A Guide to the Changing Social Structure of Britain* (London: Macmillan, 1972), Table 4.11 'The Cost of Living in the United Kingdom, 1900–1968', p. 122.

48 Fowler, *First Teenagers*, p. 94. See also Manchester University Settlement, *Ancoats: A Study of a Clearance Area, Report of a Survey Made in 1937–8* (Manchester, 1945); H. Tout, *The Standard of Living in Bristol* (Bristol: Arrowsmith, 1938); M. W. Hogg, *Has Poverty Diminished?* (London: 1925).

49 Rowntree, *Poverty and Progress*, p. 125.

50 Fowler, *First Teenagers*, p. 94.

51 Fowler, *First Teenagers*, p. 94.

52 Reed, *Eighty Thousand Adolescents*, p. 38 '[t]he average pocket money of fifteen-, sixteen- and seventeen-year-old girls and boys is about four shillings a week'.

53 Osgerby PhD, p. 191.

54 Jephcott, *Some Young People*, p. 154.

55   Osgerby, PhD, chapter 4 on 'Socio-Economic change and the cultural visibility of post-war youth'.

56   Rowntree, *Poverty and Progress*, in Gillis, *Youth and History*, p. 136.

57   Gillis, *Youth and History*, p. 192.

58   Parsons, 'Age and Sex', p. 93.

59   Parsons, 'Age and Sex', p. 93. See also Graham Murdock and Robin McCron, 'Youth and Class: The Career of a Confusion' in *Working Class Youth Culture*, ed. by G. Mungham and G. Pearson (London: Routledge & Kegan Paul, 1976), pp. 10–26, pp. 11–12.

60   My family exchanged Christmas cards with American friends that they met in those years until very recently.

61   Stuart Hall and Paddy Whannel, from 'The Young Audience' in *The Popular Arts* (London: Hutchinson, 1964), quoted in *Cultural Theory and Popular Culture: A Reader*, ed. by John Storey (London: Prentice Hall, 1994), pp. 61–77, p. 65.

62   Laurie, *Teenage Revolution*, p. 12.

63   Abrams, *Teenage Consumer*, p. 19.

64   See G.S. Hall, *Adolescence* (New York: Appleton, 1916).

65   Kenneth Roberts, *Leisure and Recreation Studies 3: Youth and Leisure* (London: George Allen & Unwin, 1983), p. 33.

66   For an examination of these arguments see John Springhall's conclusion 'The myth of the adolescent "storm and stress" syndrome' in *Coming of Age*, pp. 224–36.

67   Margaret Mead, *Coming of Age in Samoa: A Study of Adolescence and Sex in Primitive Societies* (London, 1928) and *Sex and Temperament in Three Primitive Societies* (London: Routledge & Kegan Paul, 1935). See also Murdock and McRon, 'Youth and Class', p. 11.

68   Roberts, *Leisure*, p. 34.

69   Margaret Mead, 'Social Change and Cultural Surrogates' in *Personality in Nature, Society and Culture*, ed. by C. Kluckhohm and H.A. Murray (New York: Alfred A. Knopf, 1948), quoted in Frank Musgrove, 'The Problem of Youth and the Social Structure of Society in England', *Youth and Society*, 1/1 (1966), pp. 38–58, p. 40.

70   Musgrove, 'Problem of Youth' pp. 39–40; D.S. Wright, 'A Comparative Study of the Adolescent's Concepts of His Parents and Teachers', *Educational Review*, 14 (1962); A. Hancock and J. Wakeford, 'The Young Technicians', *New Society*, 5 (1965).

71   John Farmery, b. 1939, interviewed 29 October 2001. Tape ref: T.04.

72   John R. Gillis, *Youth and History: Tradition and Changes in European Age Relations, 1770–present* (London: Academic Press, 1981), p. 205. Gillis extends this argument to cover the 1960s and 1970s.

73   See chapter 1; see also Robert Roberts, *The Classic Slum: Salford Life in the First Quarter of the Century* (Manchester: University of Manchester Press, 1971); Paul Wild, 'Recreation in Rochdale, 1900–40' in *Working Class Youth Cultures*, ed. by John Clarke and Tony Jefferson (London: Hutchinson, 1979), pp. 140–5.

74 Fowler, *First Teenagers*, pp. 169–70.

75 There were also a small number of comprehensive and 'special' schools. For a fuller examination see David C. Marsh, 'Social Classes and Educational Opportunities', chapter 7 in *The Changing Social Structure of England and Wales 1871–1961* (London: Routledge, 1965), especially pp. 208–9.

76 Marsh indicates that in the 1920s, 1930s and 1940s approximately 90 per cent of children were educated in state-aided elementary and secondary schools and that the situation changed only slightly over the 1950s – in 1951, 88 per cent attended state schools rising to 91 per cent in 1961.

77 Osgerby, PhD, p. 172.

78 Marsh, *Changing Social Structure*, p. 210. In 1931 less than 20 per cent of eleven- to fourteen-year-olds received secondary education; this rose to 38 per cent in 1938 and had risen, to all intents and purposes, to 100 per cent by 1962. In 1951, 912,000 over-elevens attended state secondary moderns and 284,000 attended grammar schools. There was only a marginal increase in the proportion of grammar school entrants over the decade but higher overall numbers. In 1961, out of a total of 2,322,000, the figures were 1,373,000 and 385,000 respectively.

79 Marsh, *Changing Social Structure*, p. 215.

80 Marsh, *Changing Social Structure*, p. 217.

81 See Frank Musgrove, 'The Problem of Youth and the Social Structure of Society in England', *Youth and Society* 1/1 (1966), pp. 38–58.

82 Hall and Whannel, *The Young Audience*, p. 62.

83 Mark Abrams, *The Newspaper Reading Public of Tomorrow* (London: Oldhams, 1964), pp. 13–14; Mungham and Pearson identify this perceived 'classlessness' of youth and indicate that arguments have been taken further to include the concept of a 'nationless' youth – 'Introduction: Troubled Youth' in *Working Class Youth Culture*, ed. by G. Mungham and G. Pearson (London: Routledge & Kegan Paul, 1976), pp. 1–9, p. 3.

84 Murdock and McCron, 'Youth and Class', p. 10.

85 Marsh, *Changing Social Structure*, p. 195.

86 Marsh, *Changing Social Structure*, pp. 205 and 196.

87 Abrams, *Teenage Consumer*, p. 13.

88 There were certainly moves in secondary education to retain more students after the minimum school leaving age throughout the 1950s. In 1951, for example, 15 per cent of both sexes between the age of 15 and 19 were 'students in educational establishments' and this had risen to approximately 25 per cent by 1961. On this evidence there is a strong case for arguing that a process of educational embourgeoisement had begun in the 1950s through increased educational opportunities. But university entrance, although increasing after the war, was still small and not the usual path even for the middle classes; in 1961 around 4 per cent of British youths entered university. Marsh, *Changing Social Structure*, pp. 221, 207 and 218.

89 Roberts, *Leisure*, p. 127.

90 Terry Mitchell, b. 1940, interviewed 2 November 2001. Tape ref: T.06.
91 Brian Jackson, *Working Class Community* (London: Routledge & Kegan Paul, 1968), pp. 142–3.
92 Jackson, *Working Class Community*, p. 139: see chapter 5, p. 190.
93 Laura Dowding, b. 1939, interviewed 18 November 2001. Tape ref: T.07.
94 Barry Stott, b. 1941, interviewed, 11 July 2001. Tape ref: T.01.
95 Osgerby, PhD, p. 96. Research into Brighton's press in the post-war period uncovered extensive reporting of vandalism and violence by teenagers and 'louts': Osgerby, PhD, pp. 97–9.
96 Fyvel, *The Insecure Offenders*, p. 17.
97 Leslie T. Wilkins, *Delinquent Generations* (London: Home Office, 1960), p. 9. Wilkins also noted a connection with youth dress styles when he proposed, without being specific, that the 'crime wave among young males has been associated with certain forms of dress and other social phenomena'.
98 Fyvel, *The Insecure Offenders*, pp. 14–15.
99 Geoffrey Pearson, *Hooligan: A History of Respectable Fears* (London: Macmillan, 1983), pp. 208–9.
100 Osgerby, PhD, p. 112.
101 Terence Morris, 'The Teenage Criminal', *New Society*, 1/28 (1963), pp. 13–16, p. 13.
102 Marsh, *Changing Social Structure*, p. 253.
103 Pearson, *Hooligan*, p. 213.
104 Pearson, *Hooligan*, pp. 214–16.
105 Pearson, *Hooligan*, p. 209.
106 Pearson, *Hooligan*, p. 38.
107 Marsh, *Changing Social Structure*, p. 259.
108 Pearson, *Hooligan*, part 4; Osgerby, PhD, p. 113.
109 Marsh, *Changing Social Structure*, p. 243.
110 Morris, 'Teenage Criminal', p. 14; Marsh, *Changing Social Structure*, p. 260.
111 See introduction to B.S. Johnson (ed.), *All Bull: The National Servicemen* (London: Quartet, 1973), pp. 1–16; Osgerby, PhD, p. 176. The forces would not take young men under eighteen despite government pressure.
112 T. Philpot, 'The World at Their Feet', in *Picture Post*, 8 April 1957, in Osgerby, PhD, p. 177.
113 *Evening Argus*, 4 May 1954, in Osgerby, PhD, p. 178.
114 Springhall, *Coming of Age*, p. 211.
115 T. Webb, Oral Testimony, in Osgerby, PhD, p. 179. Tape Ref: 14: A: i.

5

Spivs and Teds:
changing meanings of
'rebellious' male dress styles

Teddy Boys, the distinctive and flamboyant male youth 'subculture' of the mid-1950s, were not original expressions of youth culture but part of a continuum of male display whose origins can be traced back to earlier fashions and youth 'subcultures'. Indeed, Teddy Boy fashions are a further example of mediated cultural expression that is by no means straightforward. The following discussion identifies style-dissemination, in the male youth world of the mid-1950s, as being negotiated regionally as it spread across Britain in a movement that was influenced, and in part constructed by, exaggerated press coverage. The typically rebellious male youth styles and style-meanings, of the Teddy Boy, were adapted locally to become part of mainstream youth culture.

In England's north the full 'dandified' Teddy Boy regalia was never widespread. Nik Cohn suggested that 'on the streets of Manchester, Glasgow or Leeds, the move towards peacockery has been slow and scattered often to the point of near invisibility'. Cohn made a 'liberal' estimate of the take-up of fashion in the British menswear market of 5 per cent.[1] How much less that may have been in northern towns in the post-war period can only be speculation. However, since before the 1950s northern males were 'too busy surviving to give fashion a thought', it is unlikely to have been more than Cohn's 5 per cent.[2]

A 'Teddy Boy' style developed in London in the years 1952 and 1953 and it appears to have followed a familiar pattern whereby style innovations that originated in the capital were then picked up in the provinces 'one, five or even ten years later'.[3] The outfits of Edwardian jackets, waistcoats and crêpe-soled shoes embodied rebellious codes and messages that would become synonymous with the 1950s. As Simon Frith explains:

Teddy Boys were Britain's first visual symbols of the fearful possibilities of the teenager, and, if it was not their delinquency that was new but their aggressive and exclusive sense of youthful style, the effect was still to identify style with trouble – 'teenager' and 'delinquent' became associated terms.[4]

The origins and meanings of Teddy Boy clothes have been the subject of discussion. There is a body of opinion that suggests that the Teddy Boy jacket was born out of the drape suit that was the favoured dress of the post-war London 'Spiv'. Spivs and Teddy Boys were 'folk devils' in the late 1940s and 1950s and both were easily identifiable through their distinctive and somewhat similar dress styles.

These suits took on social meanings. Stuart Cosgrove has argued that the first meanings were racial and originated in 1930s America where ethnic minorities adopted zoot suits as visually stylistic symbols of resistance to subservience in white America.[5] Style meanings change, though, and the original adherents may drop a style because its meanings have metamorphosed and been adopted by other groups. Zoot suits were subsequently adopted by white Americans in the 1940s. This white adoption diluted the zoot suit's strength of meaning, which meant that it was no longer seen as a powerful symbol of racial resistance. White American youth, however, adopted the zoot or drape suit as a symbol of their identity and generational resistance. At this point zoot/drape suits became 'an integral part of the birth of the teenager as a social category'. The suits signified youthful rebellion and were associated with teenage concerns like 'hedonism, narcissism, faddism, star idolatry and conformity to subcultural codes'.[6] By 1948, however, when the International Association of Clothing Designers launched 'squarer shouldered, longer, draped jackets with fuller chests to give an aggressive look to the American male', the style moved into mainstream male fashion.[7]

For the British the drape suit was an American style-import that 'took on' in the late 1940s and predated the Edwardian look of the early 1950s. The zoot or drape suit would have first been seen in Britain in Hollywood films and also by some in the flesh when worn by black GIs in Britain after 1942 and, as Figure 5.1 indicates, by West Indian immigrants following the landing of the ship the *Empire Windrush* in 1948. In post-war Britain, though, the drape suit was a shocking piece of clothing because it was regarded as American, was associated with gangster films, was flamboyant, and because it took up more cloth than was necessary at a time of restrictions and rationing.

Zoot suits, 22 June 1948. Three Jamaican immigrants (left to right): John Hazel, a 21-year-old boxer, Harold Wilmot, 32, and John Roberts, a 22-year-old carpenter, arriving at Tilbury onboard the ex-troopship Empire Windrush, smartly dressed in zoot suits and trilby hats   **5.1**

A Mass-Observation report from 1949 described a London dance hall where there were approximately one hundred and fifty people, four-fifths of whom were aged between seventeen and nineteen and where there was an equal split between male and female. The dancers are described as 'jiving' 'jitterbugging' and 'doing an ordinary quickstep'. The report drew attention to '[s]ix black males in [US] Air Force uniform' who 'are jiving whenever they get the opportunity'. There was competition among the girls to 'dance with the Blacks [sic], the reason being ... their superb sense of rhythm, and their natural ease of keeping in time with the music'. It also noted that there was 'not the slightest suggestion of colour distinction'.[8] Apparently the young women saw the black American Airforcemen as glamorous, even exotic, and this is one reason why some resident British males emulated American dress styles like the drape suit. The Spiv, in these descriptions, appeared elaborate, even dandified. Later the Mass-

5.2   Artist's impression of Cecil Gee's American Look

Observation report drew attention to single males arriving late who wore suits in the 'American film star style ... with heavily padded shoulders ... flamboyant shirts and large knotted ties'.[9] When worn by the young British male American zoot suits still signified rebelliousness, but this had been nuanced by British social conditions. Styles would have varied in their detail because cloth was rationed and suits could not be made-up legally without clothing coupons. New meanings, then, included extravagance and flouting officialdom's message of austerity.

Around 1946 Cecil Gee, a men's outfitter of London's Charing Cross Road, developed an 'American look'. This was a re-vamped American style from ten years earlier. The zoot/drape suit and Gee's American Look both had visual connections to Hollywood gangster suits (Figure 5.2). Gee's American Look was a clear break from the demob suit and 'based on double-breasted, wide-shouldered jackets, rather like the ones Cary Grant and Clarke Gable had worn in thirties' films. They were often pinstriped, with wide lapels and big drapes.'[10] Among an array of American-style clothes Gee also sold 'hand painted ties with pictures of cowboys and Indians or airplanes on them.' The overall look was 'masculine, very confident, a bit rakish' and one of the reasons why the look never became widespread in the country as a whole was because it was ignored by the national press.[11] Nonetheless, the zoot suit and Gee's American Look spread within London. The American Look was taken up by the post-war Spiv: 'The zoot was a wild exaggeration of Gee's own look, with jackets halfway down to the kneecap and shoulders padded like American football pros. It had already caught on in the states and, when it was introduced to Britain, it became the standard uniform of the spiv.' Like the zoot suit the American style had 'grown delinquent implications' and 'instead of Cowboys and Indians, the ties had nudes on them, and there were champagne bottle tiepins ... and watch straps that winked in the dark'.[12] To all intents and purposes the zoot suit and the American Look developed in parallel and eventually fused. Toward the end of World War II the drape suit or 'zooter' was relabelled as 'spiv', 'a handle which referred less to the style of dress than to the characteristic occupation of the wearer' – a black marketeer.

Some have argued that, before this time, the British working-class male youth 'had no tradition of flamboyant dress',[13] but this is contentious. Geoffrey Pearson, for example, has written extensively on the 'hooligan' styles of Victorian Boys, and his research places the Spiv style in a historical continuum of young, urban, working-class style rebellion.[14]

Spivs loitering in London's Notting Hill area, *Picture Post*, 1954

London Spivs *Picture Post*, January 1954   **5.4**

The general public perception of the Spiv, though, was of a man clearly identifiable by his dress: a rogue dealing in restricted goods and ration coupons who was the public face of crime. There does seem to have been some confusion in the media, though, as to whether a Spiv was a youth dressed in a drape suit or an older black marketeer. Images originally published in the *Picture Post* indicate the uncertainty between Spiv and Teddy Boy. In Figures 5.3 and 5.4 the *Picture Post* refers to the young men as 'spivs'; however, although they are not wearing velvet collars, they appear to fit the dress style of the Teddy Boy and 1954 is a time when Teddy Boys had been in existence for at least a year.

Contemporary photographs may reveal an average age-range for Spivs. Few actual photographs of Spivs have come to light, however, and those that have surfaced are primarily from London, which may suggest that 'Spivs' were not common in the regions. Although evidence from the north of England has been particularly elusive the *Blackpool Gazette and Herald* ran a small article in 1950 and this made no connection between Spivs and youth culture. The report defined Spivs as 'the illicit sands and street traders' and explained that '[d]uring the war this type of trader got a strong hold in Blackpool'. Spivs are referred to as a 'fraternity who came to Blackpool during the season for what they think are easy pickings from the visitors'. They were said to trade in 'ice-cream, rock, rubber bladders, sunglasses and other things'.[15] It can be assumed, therefore, that although youths may have worn Spiv-style clothes, Spivs were not specifically a youth phenomenon.

An interview with Harry Isaacs shed some light on the popularity and style of the drape suit in Manchester, which was a centre for the clothing trade. Isaacs remembers drape jackets especially well because his father was a tailor and he came from a family that worked in the clothing industry. He recalls that around 1949 to 1950 'you had a full drape jacket, double breasted with a rolled front. You pressed it so that you could roll it over. [I] was about fourteen when I first got one of those – drape back and rolled front.'[16]

The many shortages and restrictions following World War II set the conditions for the Spiv to develop as a rogue trader with an ambiguous function. Ambiguous because on the one hand he was technically criminal but, on the other, he supplied much sought-after goods. The Spiv image needed to be stylish in order to advertise a contrast to the prevailing conditions of drab austerity. His hair was shaped like a duck's tail at the back, a style that would be referred to in the vernacular as the 'duck's arse' and was influenced by American film stars – the Spiv, to suggest abundance, emulated Hollywood styles.[17]

Despite the scarcity of Spiv photographs plenty of cartoon depictions are in circulation and Chibnall describes them as 'figures in trilbys with beaks like birds of prey and camel hair overcoats with shoulders like coat hangers'.[18] Stock characters from British films and television have reinforced the stereotype: for example, George Cole as Flash Harry in the *St Trinian* films and James Beck as Private Walker in *Dad's Army*, neither of which could be described as youths. The public perception of the Spiv has been born as much out of the comic types as out of the reality.[19]

The Spiv may have been originally associated with the London 'wide boy' but the drape suit symbolised American affluence and was a snub to an 'old-fashioned' and upper-class 'Establishment'. The fashion was 'a symbol of fundamental disrespect for the old class modes and manners – a disrespect born of a romance with an alien culture', that is to say, America.[20] The Spiv style and the American Look were not specifically associated with youth whereas the Teddy Boy outfit was. The drape suit with its American connotations was 'the embryonic teenage culture and style and full five years before its discovery by pressmen and academics in the Teddy Boy panic', it was 'a sartorial cipher for the codes of the new teen style'.[21] This is the style observed by Richard Hoggart in his description of the Juke-Box Boys as 'aged between fifteen and twenty, with drape suits, picture ties and an American slouch'. Here Hoggart draws attention to a body language typical of the 1930s Hollywood gangster.[22]

Christopher Breward identifies an emergent Teddy Boy style, and argues that 'though it doesn't name him as such, the figure of the Teddy Boy was rapidly emerging as a particular working-class London type'.[23] Breward tries to pinpoint the definitive difference between Spivs and Teddy Boys and suggests that it lies in the greater narcissism of the Teddy Boy: 'whilst the spiv adopted the sleek glamour of the Latin crooner in front of his bathroom mirror (good looks aiding his professional role as a swindler), the teddy boy called on a more extensive battery of styling techniques that placed his prouder narcissism firmly in the public sphere.'[24] Youth, though, is most probably the determining factor because Teddy Boys were almost exclusively teenagers.

The drape-suit style was established in the country in the 1940s where it was roundly derided by authority figures and much of the press. Therefore teenagers adopting this style were entering into an established set of signs with an established set of popular prejudices against them. They kept some of the meanings, lost some and added others.

Some have argued that the Teddy Boys, as the name implies, usurped a style from the upper-class suit of the 'New Edwardian' and reversed its meanings.[25] The situation, however, was more complex because Teddy Boy styles and mannerisms were a stage in a tradition of working-class youth that followed on from the Spiv. Their dress and appearance was influenced by America and, as the style spread to Britain's regions, meanings and actual style lines were modified and mediated.

Stan Cohen states that Teddy Boys 'were the first group whose style was self-created' and that the style, taken from the upper-class 'Edwardian dandy', was then exaggerated and ritualised.[26] Chris Steele-Perkins and

Richard Smith identify this 'Edwardian dandy' style as 'a style developed in homosexual circles, half-collars of velvet on long Edwardian jackets'.[27] Cohn's account, though, appears to be more authoritative. He contends that in the late 1940s a 'New Edwardian' style was advanced by guard officers wearing 'ornate brocade waistcoats, in the style of the 1890s'. This style really caught on around 1948 when guardsmen

> began to appear in long and narrow, single-breasted jackets and narrow trousers; turned-back velvet cuffs and velvet collars on overcoats; carnations, patterned waistcoats and silver-topped canes.
>
> It caught on. Naturally, it wasn't always worn in such an extreme form but the basic narrowness of line spread into the homosexual world, and then into the would-be smart middle class and, by 1950, the Edwardian Look had become the dominant London fashion.[28]

Its uptake by homosexuals 'helped to finish it off as an ordinary middle-class fashion'. The Edwardian Look, however, held on until around 1954 'by which time it had been taken up and caricatured by the Teddy Boys, who made it so disreputable that even homosexuals were embarrassed to wear it'.[29] So, for Cohn, the Teddy Boy style was a mix of upper-class English plus black and/or white American criminal with homosexual overtones.

The Teddy Boy attire consisted of drape coats, which contained elements of the zoot and the Edwardian suit, with 'tight drainpipe jeans, tapered to the ankle, and luminous yellow socks; creepers, large crêpe-soled shoes like boats; brass rings on several fingers, worn both for ornament and for destruction; riverboat gambler's bootlace ties; and often, in the back jeans pocket, a flick-knife.'[30] Moreover, the outfit was expensive. At a time when the average weekly wage was £5. 2s. 5d.,[31] 'a proper Ted suit would cost between £15 and £20, hand-made by a back-street tailor, and all the accessories would double that. If you wished to make a top Ted, you had to be prepared to stroll into a dance hall with £50 on your back.'[32]

T.R. Fyvel's *The Insecure Offenders* includes a potted history of the Teddy Boy phenomenon in London.[33] Here he notes that the hairstyles were distinctive and American-influenced: 'The most common consisted of aggressive sideboards, with masses of hair at the back and a fuzzy shock of it above the brow. Other styles favoured were the jutting Tony Curtis, the Boston, the fiercely shaved Mohican.'[34] The 'Tony Curtis' and 'Boston Slash Back' were both styles that Spivs had been observed to wear, indicating a style continuity, and both are clearly North American influences with the Mohican originating from a Native Canadian tribe. Steel-Perkins and Smith are clear that the Teds originally adopted their hairstyles from American models. Concurring with Fyvel they argue that

> The Teds were in the forefront of the Fifties hairstyle experiments, styles which contrasted sharply with the short-back-and-sides of National Service. There was the crew-cut of the U.S. Marines and Ted versions at the crew-cut: the Spikey-Top and the Silver-Dollar. These were long and short crew-cuts, respectively, but the hair was kept full at the sides and greased back. There was the Mohawk, derived from early T.V. show Canadian Indians: the head was shaved except for a central strip of hair. There was the full, curly head of Tony Curtis. There was the greased-straight-back of the dedicated drinker. At the back, the hair was greased in from the sides to meet the hair coming down. This was the Duck's Arse, the D.A., or, more politely, the Duck Tail. In contrast to the D.A., there was the Square-neck or Boston: the hair was chopped straight in a fringe at the neck.[35]

Paul Rock and Stan Cohen date the crossover from upper-class fashion to working-class youth style at 1953 and they comment that the new Edwardians were 'lumpenproletarian "creepers"' and not of the 'respectable working class'.[36] Fyvel's account explains that the Edwardian fashion was usurped by working-class youths in 1953 after it had been 'launched from Savile Row ... as an answer to American styles'. It was bold and rebellious in its own right before its usurpation by Teddy Boys because it was an extravagant upper-class snub to the post-war Labour Government and its message of austerity. Fyvel claims that, in this form, the fashion was short-lived because, having started in Mayfair, it soon vanished from London and entered the suburbs.[37] In the meantime it was transported and transformed to the South London working-class areas of Elephant and Castle, Vauxhall and Southwark, where it retained its meaning of social revolt but in a new context, that of petty crime and swank, with clear connections to earlier groups like Spivs.

There are differing accounts of where in London the Teddy Boy style actually started and the ensuing pattern of geographical expansion. Cohn, for example, maintains that

> The first Teds emerged in the East End and in North London, around Tottenham and Highbury, and from there they spread southwards, to Streatham and Battersea and Purley, and westwards, to Shepherds Bush and Fulham, and then down to the seaside towns, and up into the Midlands until, by 1956, they had taken root all over Britain.[38]

The metamorphosed style has been described as 'a grotesque parody of American gangsters and Jermyn Street Edwardiana'.[39] Fyvel's view is that 'in terms of age-groups, they still had their links with the older cloth-capped gangs which in earlier periods had dominated areas like the Elephant, keeping the police on the run and razors in their pockets.' He quotes the views of a social worker from the Elephant and Castle area to illustrate their wayward nature: 'the local Teddy-boy fashion in its first bloom had few law-abiding members. It was definitely the submerged tenth who popularise the new clothes. They were the groups who were not respectable, not socially acceptable.'[40]

For Pearson the Teddy Boys were not a new phenomenon and their American influences have been overstated. He does not, however, stress the sartorial element

> What was and is totally submerged in the conventional understanding of the Teddy Boys was that their style and demeanour was by no means unprecedented. Their rough fighting, territorial edginess, for example, is better understood as a continuation of earlier forms of gang-life in working-class neighbourhoods – rather than a sudden departure from tradition. So, too, the Teds had borrowed large parts of their supposedly unprecedented cultural equipment from earlier youth cultures.
>
> … It is clear that the conventional picture of the sudden and unrivalled appearance of the 'affluent' and Americanised Teddy Boys … must be seen as a gross distortion of the actual events.[41]

For some the Teddy Boy style was a consumerist release from a downtrodden position in the class system: 'the trappings of working-class dandyism, though spectacular in their expense and visual effects symbolised little more than a naïve trust in the power of consumerism to transform humdrum realities.'[42]

Teddy Boys paraded a catalogue of American influences and adapted them to suit their own needs: the display of sideburns (or sideboards) described as 'their greatest glory',[43] for example, was named after the American General Burneside. The Teddy Boy image 'owed less allegiance to Edward VII: more to the western gunfighter' as portrayed by Hollywood. The drape jackets were similar to 'the frock coat of the saloon shoot-out' and after initial use of narrow ties 'the gambler's bootstring became the convention'.[44] This was no doubt influenced by the prolific and popular American Western Films, 'where it was worn, most prevalently … by the slick city gambler whose social status was, grudgingly, high because of his ability to live *by his wits*.'[45] The bootstring tie was held together with silver medallions in the shape of 'death heads, cross-bones skulls, eagles, dollars and other symbols of America, miniature boots or holsters … the little cow's head, based on the skulls of long-dead Texas longhorns.'[46]

Fyvel describes the Ted's eye-catching flamboyance: 'Among the clothes the jacket of the suit, long and fully draped with flaps and velvet collar, came nearest to true "Edwardian". With it went knitted ties, plain or flowery waistcoats, tight-fitting trousers or "strides", and – incongruously at first – blunt shoes with enormous crêpe soles.'[47] Of one particular Teddy Boy group (the Ploughboys) Tony Parker says that

> They were smart, these boys, and, being smartly dressed, were there to see and be seen. Long hair pouring in an often-combed wave over the forehead, sideblinds down the cheek.[48] And their suits: long jackets fully draped at the back, deep layers sometimes of velvet; tapered trousers without turn-ups, drainpipes crinkling down to heavy black shoes with thick crêpe soles.[49]

From these descriptions, and from photographic evidence (Figures 5.5 and 5.6), the 'original' London Teddy Boys can be seen as visually flamboyant and rebellious toward the 'Establishment'. Moreover, this visual defiance was extended toward respectable adult members of their own class who were hostile to any male 'dandyism' that might suggest effeminacy.

On the question of lawlessness George Melly stresses the criminality of the original London Teds and argues that it was of a different nature to that of earlier deviant characters like Spivs: 'the Teds were a kind of new criminal for whom violence was an end in itself and "crime" in the traditional sense neither obligatory nor even necessary'.[50] This is a point with which Cohn concurs: the Teds 'didn't break laws for profit, or not primarily – the attraction lay in the excitement, the sense of action. The word "kicks" was used a lot and it meant something, anything that made time pass'.[51]

The public became acutely aware of Teddy Boy violence through media coverage of a brutal murder, and this media coverage spread the Ted's 'bad boy' image to the rest of the country. The murder occurred from a 'gang' stabbing on Clapham Common, London in July 1953 and became symbolic of what the population thought they might expect from the Teddy Boys – violence, aggression and murder. It marked for the nation the beginning of the Teddy Boy era and set the tone of the media response. Parker in *The Plough Boy* made a detailed and illuminating account of the trial proceedings, concluding that the young man judged guilty of the murder, Michael Davies, found himself in the predicament of a condemned murderer because the 'Establishment' and the country as a whole needed to find someone responsible, a Teddy Boy to fit the bill. Parker explains:

A Teddy Boy in a London Street, *Picture Post*, 1954

Cool Ted – A Teddy Boy gets admiring glances from his friends   **5.6**

Michael Davies is by no means the first person to have been sentenced to death not so much for what he might have done, as for being a symbol of something which the contemporary public found abhorrent and threatening to their stable way of life. In his case it was the Teddy Boy – of which, in fact, he was not a very good example, if clothing and hair-style are considered. But he was for a jury representation of the public, near enough.[52]

Before the summer of 1953 Teddy Boys were sources of amusement: 'by those who thought they were better-class they were laughed at, derided, called "Teddy Boys". But not with much more than mild amusement, not with hostility in those days, or contempt, or fear, that would come later.'[53]

The public fear of Teddy Boys following the Clapham Common murder, however, appears to have eased by the mid-1950s and the 'mild amusement' that Parker noted before the killing returned. This was a time when juke boxes and youth cafés were increasing in numbers and geographical distribution, and were becoming part of mainstream popular culture.

From an examination of the mass-market tabloid the *Daily Mirror* for the years 1955 and 1956 and the weekly *Picture Post* for 1955, for example, it is evident that Teddy Boys were seen, even at these dates, as not so much as a threat but as more of a colourful distraction. In June 1955, for example, under the heading 'The Duke and the Teddy Boys' the Duke of Edinburgh was reported to be involved with 'sporting' answers to the 'Teddy Boy problem'.[54] The papers' tone was consistently light-hearted with reports like 'Teddy Boys on Parade' where the show business celebrities Danny Kaye, Laurence Olivier and John Mills dressed up as Teddy Boys for a charity show at the London Palladium.[55] A 'Live Letter' from August 1955 ran 'My Dad, a retired schoolteacher aged eighty two wouldn't dream of wearing his trousers wider than seventeen inches. Does this make him a Teddy Boy too?'[56] In November 1955 a headline ran 'Those Two Teddy Boys Stole the Show' and reported that

> Mike and Pat, two Teddy Boys from the Elephant and Castle devastated the 'peasants' – their slang for the non-Teddies...
>
> They took part in the BBC 'Special Enquiry' into teenagers and walked away with the show. Their dress, their hairstyles, their experiences were something to see.[57]

Fyvel estimates that in 1953–54 there were a 'few thousand' Teds, that they roamed the streets in gangs and that they were territorial and occasionally violent towards other Teddy Boy gangs.[58] 'Gang', however, is a word that means different things to different people; gangs are a matter of perception. Parker's interviewee (1) in *The Plough Boy* explained that there was little or no organisation involved in his group of youths:

> You just went around with a group of fellers you knew, that was all there was to it. But there you were, that was it, in the eyes of other people you was a gang. Personally, I don't think we was ever organised enough or, what's the word, cohesive enough. We were just a bunch of lads with nothing much to do, nothing much to think about, and we knocked around most times together because we all lived around the same area. If we were off our own manor, people might say 'There's the Plough boys', you know – but it wasn't nothing you had a membership card for, you weren't elected to the gang, nothing like that.[59]

The period 1953–54 was probably the most spectacular for a London Teddy Boy, when there were some large-scale fights and some police baiting.

Male display in youth culture, however, was rarely universally spectacular and a realistic picture of Teddy Boy life would probably be more mundane. Teenagers, especially boys, spent time going to amusement arcades, youth cafés and gathering round juke boxes. One of the first East London Teds was asked where they 'hung' out. And his reply that

> They used to collect at Arcades or in a caff. The pictures, too. They were always going in there. In the afternoons they'd bump their way in without paying; evenings too, and Sundays. Then they'd go back to a café and sit there till closing time.

suggests a dull reality. In reply to the question, 'And what happened to the original Teds?' he answered,

> Some were put away. Borstal, quite a lot went to. What happened to most of the others was exactly what happened to ordinary people in ordinary life – mixing with the opposite sex and sooner or later they'd go steady and they'd end up pushing a pram. [60]

Before World War II youth cultures like the Teds would have remained local; however, following the war, with an increase in media coverage and subsequent public interest and concern, these 'subcultures' spread to other regions. In the case of the Teddy Boys the original style-meanings would have fused with other local codes, the original territorial loyalties forgotten and the London meanings diffused. An example of this fusion with regional styles was the 'ratter' or working man's cloth cap, which was 'modified by some Teds and taken on as a vital part of the uniform'.[61] This 'stripped Ratter, or Cheesecutter cap' was an integral part of the Ted look in some areas as was another improvised Teddy Boy style development – the duffle coat.[62] A gang from 1956 'wore Ted clothes but, instead of the drape, black duffle coats'. By 1956 Ted styles were 'no longer a minority cult, their style had gained wide acceptance and, as the style spread, Ted violence waned'.[63]

For Fyvel there seem to have been relatively few original London Teddy Boys, and he estimates their numbers in 1953–54 as a 'few thousand'. Gangs of delinquent youths are a rarity in Britain and 'even in 1956, the zenith of the Teddy Boy "movement", they were insignificant'.[64] Moreover, official figures that point to a juvenile 'crime wave' are open to other interpretations (see chapter 4). Even so, despite the localised and compact nature of the original movement, both the fashion and the delinquent reputation of the Teds spread across Britain. The argument that the media, and most particularly the press, was responsible for this dissemination of style and reputation is compelling and several commentators state that this was indeed the case. Melly, for instance, points out that Teds were a 'small minority, a fact it would be difficult to realise from the newspaper files of the period which tended, as always, to inflate the phenomenon in such a way as to suggest it was all pervasive.'[65] For Melly, however, the original 'nihilist' Teddy Boy spirit, after its original reportings, was watered down in both fashion and outlook as a consequence of its dissemination. The media were key in disseminating style and attitude and 'the trajectory of the teddy boy was as much a process of journalistic misrepresentation, as it was a sequence of commercial and social transactions'.[66]

The way the Teddy Boy style and attitude spread appears to fit the classic model of a moral panic as outlined by Stan Cohen in his seminal work *Folk Devils and Moral Panics*. Although Cohen's main focus in here is not style-dissemination, style is inextricably tied up within the same media-amplified process.[67] The Teddy Boys are his first example of 'folk devil' and he says of them: 'In the gallery of types that society erects to show its members which roles should be avoided and which should be emulated, these groups have occupied a constant position of folk devils: visible reminders of what we should not be.'[68]

Perhaps the Teddy Boys would have been forgotten and fallen into obscurity like the Victorian 'hooligans' if, in reporting the phenomenon, the media had not played a key part in their creation. Sarah Thornton suggests that '[c]ommunications media create subcultures in the process of naming them and draw boundaries around them in the act of describing them'.[69] Teds 'had created the outrage: outrage had created the Teds'.[70] With 'deviant' Teddy Boy behaviour 'societal reaction to deviance (and certainly that of the mass media), increases its incidence, but similarly de-emphasise[s] the original behaviour'.[71] Media amplification dilutes the original styles and messages.

As we have seen with the zoot suit, in the course of the dispersal of meaning-laden dress styles, the process of dissemination inevitably changed the original meanings. As the Teddy Boy culture spread beyond its original London haunts, 'most of the new converts stopped half-way. They didn't bother with the full uniform, down to the boot-lace ties and luminous socks, but contented themselves with a pair of tight blue jeans and a duck's arse haircut, just to give the general impression.'[72]

Undoubtedly there was some kind of moral panic surrounding the Teds but this has been overemphasised as there *was* more neutral reporting. In the *Daily Mirror*[73] for the years 1955 and 1956, for example, Teddy Boy stories never appeared on the front page and the paper took a consistently balanced view. As we have seen, the tone of reporting was light-hearted and viewed Teddy Boys with the faint amusement usually reserved for British eccentrics. For instance, a Teddy Boy club in Bradford was reported as being organised by a Reverend Maurice Bennett where 'he gives them bebop at his club for the velvet collars'.[74] Moreover, in a deliberate policy of balance and neutrality the *Daily Mirror* devoted a full page to a constructed 'Teenage Parliament' where 'Teenagers asked the questions and teenagers gave the answers'. Mark, a labourer of nineteen 'hair in a forehead fringe, double-breasted jacket, drainpipe trousers' said, 'When chaps in Edwardian clothes let off steam it gets into the papers, that's all. Teddy clothes are like red rags to a bull.' On the question of 'thugs' he said, 'The thugs were thugs before they became Teds', to which another youth (Peter, seventeen) added 'They were called Spivs once'.[75]

To test public reaction to Teddy Boy styles *Daily Mirror* reporter Eric Wainwright went 'under cover' in Teddy Boy clothes and discovered that he then became an 'Outcast in a Velvet Collar'. He explained: 'You see, last week a Teddy Boy complained bitterly … that a lad who likes to wear Teddy clothes is regarded as an outcast by the public – just because of the cut of his suit and his hair. And regardless of his conduct. I decided to find out how true that is for myself.' The feature article concludes with the question: 'Is it fair to regard every lad who wears a velvet collar as an anti-social no-good with a bicycle chain up his sleeve?'[76]

In the *Daily Mirror* the reporting flurry only really lasted for about a month and their editorial policy did not dwell on the negative. Indeed, the paper was sympathetic to Teddy Boys and teenagers in general. There were, however, regular reports on Teddy Boys and it seems more likely that the daily reporting of the phenomenon did more to educate new teenagers into the new fashion than the few weeks of negative coverage that surrounded the release of *Rock Around the Clock*.[77]

In the process of 'style-amplification' original meanings are lost or diluted and new ones developed just as the meanings connected with zoot suits regularly altered whilst still retaining some of their original 'rebellious' significance. 'Social types can be seen as the products of the same processes that go into the symbolic collective styles in fashion, dress and social identities.'[78] In the case of Teddy Boys, press reports, for example, of disturbances at screenings of *Rock Around the Clock* set into action an amplifying and circular process: 'The impact (deviance) is followed by a reaction which has the effect of increasing the subsequent warning and impact, setting up a feedback system ... [E]ach event can be seen as creating the potential for a reaction which, among other possible consequences, might cause further acts of deviance.'[79]

Dick Hebdige has argued that within subcultures (in which he includes Teddy Boys) style is the indicator of a 'secret identity' communicating 'forbidden meanings'. He takes an anthropological model of 'bricolage' from Claude Lévi-Strauss and adapts it to British working-class subcultures, taking it to mean a complex system of alternative signifiers and style codes.[80] In 'this way the teddy boy's theft and transformation of the Edwardian style ... can be construed as an act of *bricolage*'.[81] This is certainly an attractive model for Teddy Boys but it does not really address the speed at which the meanings were constructed or changed and assumes an 'authentic' period when the Teddy Boy style was homogenous and fixed. It is unlikely, however, that a fixed state ever occurred because the Ted style was always in a state of flux, absorbing new influences and dropping others, and its evolution developed with different variations in different areas.

Subcultural theory implants into youth styles meanings that are not necessarily recognised by those who wear them and, in looking for group signs and identities, subcultural theorists have ignored the many individual inputs that have introduced change to youth fashions. Subcultural theory plays down the importance of individual experiment and improvisation in developing youth fashion. Frith suggests, for example, that 'in reading youth styles for signs and symbols of collective consciousness, the sub-cultural approach underestimates the individual joy of dressing up, inventing an image, striking poses'.[82] While individual input has been underestimated, group identity, however, *was* a key component of the first London Teddy Boy 'gangs', in that the style was specifically collective.

If Teddy Boys were a subculture in their first expressions in 1952 and 1953 London then this was lost in the next few years. The recorded signifiers of territorial aggression and crime synonymous with the first Teddy Boys, like 'Tony Curtis' haircuts, soon changed their meanings and became part of the timid youthful rebelliousness of the school boy who simply wanted to identify with the energy of American rock 'n' roll in 1956. Although Teddy Boys were originally specific to London they were not a static phenomenon and their perceived secret signs had been diluted along with the style as time moved on and the image spread. Indeed, the Teddy Boy styles were absorbed into and became part of mainstream youth culture.

One of the major criticisms of subcultural theory consolidated in Hall and Jefferson's influential *Resistance Through Rituals* is that it relies on media and secondary sources.[83] Certainly with the Teds, Fyvel's account in *The Insecure Offenders* has been a key text for many retrospective studies. Frith roundly criticises subcultural theory's absence of empirical research maintaining that

> The reading of youth styles in 'Resistance Through Rituals', for example, are based not on direct observation but on media sources – youth styles are analysed according to the ways they've been labelled. This gives the description of style as conflict a certain conviction – the media do set up sub-cultures as 'threats' to society – but it also raises doubts about the real extent of those threats.[84]

Other criticisms have been directed at subcultural definitions because they pay little attention to the labelling process in creating a subculture. Sarah Thornton explains: 'they position the media and its associated processes outside, in opposition to and after the fact of subculture. In doing so, they omit precisely that which clearly delineates a "subculture", for labelling is crucial to the insiders' and outsiders' views of themselves as different.'[85] When Hall and Jefferson say that subcultural groups contain a 'distinctive enough shape and structure to make them identifiably different' because they are 'focused around certain activities, values ... territorial spaces' and are 'either loosely or tightly bonded'[86] this definition could apply to other cultural categories which we could interpret as groups as diverse as car-owner clubs or students.

Subcultural theories can be criticised because they describe 'the rich and resistant meanings of youth music, clothing, rituals and argot in a miraculously media-free moment when an uncontaminated homology could be identified'. On the other hand, 'moral panic' theories 'assume that there is little or nothing prior to the *mass* media labelling'.[87] Indeed, 'derogatory media coverage is not the verdict but the *essence* of their resistance'.[88]

After 1954 Teddy Boys began to be sighted in the provinces and this caused general concern; however, press reports probably exaggerated any actual dangers. Certainly social stability was never seriously threatened. Even recorded delinquency was rare as 97 per cent of teenagers were not recorded as committing delinquent acts (see chapter 4).[89]

From ethnographical research, a consistent picture emerged from a sample of people who were teenagers in England's northwest during the 1950s.[90] The consensus from their retrospective oral testimony is that although Teddy Boys, or male youths who absorbed the Ted style signifiers, were perceived as frightening, in reality there was little actual trouble. For example, Barry Stott, who grew up in Blackpool, recalled that 'Teddy boys were a bit of a threat. I never saw any violence but they were reputed to be ready for a bit of bother. And they used to be around the Pleasure Beach with velvet collars.'[91] John Farmery, who lived in the Lancashire holiday town of Cleveleys and worked on a fun fair as a teenager, remembered of the Teddy Boys that 'one or two were [a menace], a lot of it was bravado, but there wasn't a terrific amount [of violence] – not over here anyway – not a terrific amount of trouble. It was just sort of showing off really.'[92] Jim Cheetham, whose family ran a boating lake and amusement park in Pickmere, Cheshire, when asked whether they had any trouble with Teddy Boys in the 1950s, maintained that 'they were quite well behaved. Let's face it, they spent a fortune buying a suit, the last thing they wanted to do was get involved in some all-in fight and getting it all dirty I should imagine. No we never had any trouble with them.'[93]

Some interviewees voiced opinions on the reasons for the media perceptions of 'Teddy Boy' trouble: 'I mean teenagers and youngsters will be youngsters won't they, whatever's going there's always one or two that spoil it for the others, but there was always a good hard core of decent teenagers.'[94] And Harry Isaacs, growing up in Manchester, volunteered a more analytical view in line with Cohen's media amplification model:

> I think the fighting and the trouble that's associated with them was grossly exaggerated. Old people always say if they see groups of young lads – they did with us – always think that we're up to no good, whereas young lads are just rowdy and noisy and like punching each other and shoving each other around and it's nothing like as fearful as people think. … They're like that, they're exuberant but it must have appeared fearsome maybe to older people who saw a group of lads in these type of outfits. But the press pick up on stories.[95]

Regional oral testimony describes a very different scenario from the descriptions of London Teddy Boys by Fyvel, Melly, and Rock and Cohen. And if these accounts are to be taken at face value, much of the actual Teddy Boy menace appears to have diffused as it spread, along with the style, to the regions. Parts of the Teddy Boy style were adopted by mainstream youth. Interviewee Barry Stott describes how the Ted styles influenced male teenagers both in school and in work. He talks of his brother and his own experiments with bits of the style in school:

> my brother who was in the army in the '50s, he came back with a velvet collar and suit which I borrowed once. I even went to school in it and caused a bit of a rumpus. ...
>
> And I tried to grow sideboards like Elvis, but I had trouble so I used to chalk them in a bit with dark crayon. But also the drainpipe suits, the narrow trousers were very fashionable and if you tried to go to school in even slightly narrow trousers you were in trouble from the headmaster.[96]

Terry Mitchell explains that Ted hairstyles were forbidden at his grammar school and that to achieve a rebellious style boys would resort to hair re-arrangements after school:

> I remember there seemed to be two styles – the Tony Curtis one which was really quite flamboyant and the crew cut which some people went in for, which of course is like the shaven heads now except you did actually have hair about half an inch ... both of which were totally frowned on, you couldn't get away with them at a grammar school. ... You could never get away with a Tony Curtis because that was longer. You could probably re-arrange your hair out of hours to conform to the convoluted wings at the side and the way it came to at the back.[97]

Isaacs recalled the shoes as being an affordable part of the Ted style: 'huge thick brothel creepers, lots of entwined leather on the top and very very thick crepe soles. Now that spread because you get shoes easier than you could get clothes.'[98]

In the mid-fifties sartorial signifiers like 'drain-pipe' trousers may well have identified a Teddy Boy but this would have only been the case within the 'teens and twenties' age bracket. Male teenagers sported certain signs of peer group belonging like the hair, the trousers and the shoes, but the Teddy Boy uniform in its entirety was not widely adopted by the mainstream teenager. Outside of London, few youths adopted the whole of the Ted style, rather they took on only parts of it – the ones that they could get away with if they could afford them, 'there were a lot of the drainpipe trousers and haircuts and things like that'.[99]

The Teddy Boy 'subculture' was predominantly male, teenage and originally working class, and its dress codes developed in London in 1952 and 1953 from a range of sartorial influences: the American zoot/drape suit, Cecil Gee's 'American Look', the Spiv's meaning-laden attire and the upper-class Edwardian style that gave rise to their name. The Ted's visual image was a highly original fusion of predominantly American influences like drape jackets, haircuts and ties, that had been mediated through contact with British social and economic conditions, and home-grown improvisations like the Edwardian jacket, cloth caps and duffle coats. The meanings attached to the look were perceived as essentially rebellious and a threat to authority; but its adoption was probably more symbolic of peer group belonging.

Though teenage culture certainly did exist before the arrival of the Teddy Boy, many see the Teds as the start of a homogenous British youth culture.[100] Cohn, for example, claims that 'In terms of English teenagers, Teddy Boys were the start of everything: rock 'n' roll and coffee bars, clothes and bikes and language, jukeboxes and coffee with froth on it – the whole concept of a private teen life style, separate from the adult world.'[101] Cohn's observations are generally sound but need to be grounded later in the 1950s by which time the fashion had spread and become part of a new, more mainstream, youth culture. As this geographical dissemination increased the original meanings of the Teddy Boy had become so diluted that they no longer posed any real or imagined threat to the established order.

Notes

1 Nik Cohn, *Today There Are No Gentlemen* (London: Weidenfeld & Nicolson, 1971), p. 2.
2 Cohn, *Today*, p. 9.
3 Cohn, *Today*, p. 3. Cohn dates the first Teddy Boys to 1952, p. 29.
4 Simon Frith, *Sound Effects: Youth, Leisure, and the Politics of Rock* (London: Constable & Co. 1983), p. 184.
5 Stuart Cosgrove, 'The Zoot Suit and Style Warfare', *History Workshop Journal*, 18 (Autumn 1984), pp. 77–91.
6 Steve Chibnall, 'Whistle and Zoot: The Changing Meaning of a Suit of Clothes', *History Workshop Journal*, 20 (Autumn 1985) pp. 56–81, p. 57.
7 Chibnall, 'Whistle and Zoot', p. 61.
8 Wilcox, H.D., *Mass-Observation Report on Juvenile Delinquency* (London: Falcon Press, 1949), pp. 47–8.
9 Wilcox, *M.O. Report*, p. 50.
10 Cohn, *Today*, pp. 18–19.
11 Cohn, *Today*, p. 19.
12 Cohn, *Today*, pp. 20–1.
13 Chibnall, 'Whistle and Zoot', p. 65.
14 Geoffrey Pearson, *Hooligan: A History of Respectable Fears* (London: Macmillan, 1983); see also Robert Roberts' description of the 'scuttler' and his 'moll' in

The Classic Slum: Salford Life in the First Quarter of the Century (Manchester: University of Manchester Press, 1971), p. 123.

15 *Blackpool Gazette and Herald*, 15 April 1950.
16 Interview with Harry Isaacs b. 1934, 27 July 2001 tape ref: T.02.
17 Chibnall, 'Whistle and Zoot', p. 66.
18 Chibnall, 'Whistle and Zoot', p. 67. Interestingly David Mellor maintains that these images show exaggerated Semitic features: Plenary address 'Imagination: Visual Culture and Identity in Britain since the 1940s', Conference at Tate Britain, 20 and 21 September 2002.
19 Chibnall, 'Whistle and Zoot', p. 67.
20 Chibnall, 'Whistle and Zoot', p. 69.
21 Chibnall, 'Whistle and Zoot', p. 70.
22 Richard Hoggart, *The Uses of Literacy* (Harmondsworth: Penguin, 1960), p. 248.
23 Christopher Breward, 'Style and Subversion: Postwar Poses and the Neo-Edwardian Suit in Mid-Twentieth Britain', *Gender and History*, 14/3 (November 2002), p. 566.
24 Breward, 'Style and Subversion', p. 571.
25 See Paul Rock and Stan Cohen, 'The Teddy Boy', in *The Age of Affluence 1951–64*, ed. by V. Bogdanor and R. Skidelsky (London: Macmillan, 1970); Stan Cohen, *Folk Devils and Moral Panics: The Creation of the Mods and Rockers* (New York: St Martin's Press, 1980).
26 Cohen, *Folk Devils*, p. 183.
27 Chris Steele-Perkins and Richard Smith, *The Teds* (Stockport: Dewi Lewis, 1979), no page numbers.
28 Cohn, *Today*, pp. 22–3.
29 Cohn, *Today*, p. 27.
30 Cohn, *Today*, p. 29.
31 *The Observer*, 1 June 2003, 'Then and Now', facts and figures from 1953 and 2003.
32 Cohn, *Today*, p. 30.
33 Fyvel, *Insecure Offenders*.
34 Fyvel, *Insecure Offenders*, p. 41.
35 Steele-Perkins and Smith, *The Teds*.
36 Rock and Cohen, 'The Teddy Boy', p. 289.
37 Fyvel, *Insecure Offenders*, p. 39.
38 Cohn, *Today*, p. 29.
39 Peter Laurie, *The Teenage Revolution* (London: Anthony Blond, 1965), p. 15. Jermyn Street adjoins Savile Row in London's West End. Savile Row has been a centre for tailors servicing the wealthy and aristocracy since the mid-eighteenth century.
40 Fyvel, *Insecure Offenders*, p. 40.
41 Pearson, *Hooligan*, p. 22.
42 Breward, 'Style and Subversion', p. 565.

43 Cohn, *Today*, p. 29.
44 Steele-Perkins and Smith, *The Teds*.
45 Tony Jefferson, *The 'Teds': A Political Resurrection* (Centre for Contemporary Cultural Studies, University of Birmingham, April 1973), pp. 3–4, original emphasis.
46 Steele-Perkins and Smith, *The Teds*.
47 Fyvel, *Insecure Offenders*, p. 41.
48 By 'long hair' he probably means the Tony Curtis style.
49 Tony Parker, *The Plough Boy* (London: Hutchinson, 1965), p. 20.
50 Melly, *Revolt Into Style*, p. 34.
51 Cohn, *Today*, p. 29.
52 Parker, *Plough Boy*, p. 235.
53 Parker, *Plough Boy*, pp. 20–1.
54 DM, 9 June 1955, p. 2.
55 DM, 23 June 1955.
56 DM, 4 August 1955, p. 12.
57 DM, 2 November 1955, p. 4.
58 Urban youth 'gangs' had always been territorial and one of the reasons put forward for this is that they, for the most part, lacked transport. This is perhaps one of the reasons why youth culture in Britain developed in different ways from that in America. In Britain it would have been unusual for a teenager to own a motorbike or scooter, let alone a car, before the 1960s.
59 Parker, *Plough Boy*, p. 25.
60 Quoted in Fyvel, *Insecure Offenders*, p. 43–4.
61 Geoff Mungham and Geoff Pearson (eds), *Working Class Youth Culture* (London: Routledge & Kegan Paul, 1976), p. 5. The 'cheesecutter' cap is also reported in the *Daily Mirror*, 27 September 1956, p. 11. In a feature 'Youth Hits Back' interviewee Mark was reported as saying 'People have scared themselves with all their talk … One day a bloke accidentally knocked me down. Then, very frightened, he picked me up, brushed off my lapels and handed me my cheesecutter (cap)'.
62 This improvisation is particularly believable because duffle coats were common at the time could be bought cheaply from Army Surplus stores, which were a feature of the post-war high street. See, for example, Cohn, *Today*, p. 17.
63 Steel-Perkins and Smith, *The Teds*.
64 Rock and Cohen, 'The Teddy Boy', p. 299.
65 Melly, *Revolt Into Style*, p. 34.
66 Breward, 'Style and Subversion', p. 565.
67 Cohen, *Folk Devils*, p. 24.
68 Cohen, *Folk Devils*, pp. 9–10.
69 Sarah Thornton, *Club Cultures: Music, media and subcultural capital* (Cambridge: Polity Press, 1995), p. 164.
70 Steel-Perkins and Smith, *The Teds*.
71 Jefferson, *The 'Teds'*, p. 1.

72 Cohn, *Today*, p. 31.

73 Taking its statistics from a Hulton Press independent report the *Daily Mirror* claimed its readership of 11,220,000 to be the highest on earth. DM, 12 July 1956.

74 DM, 23 February 1956.

75 DM, 27 September 1956, p. 11.

76 DM, 6 October 1956, p. 2.

77 Sam Katzman, *Rock Around The Clock* (Columbia, 1956).

78 Cohen, *Folk Devils*, p. 19.

79 Cohen, *Folk Devils*, p. 24.

80 Claude Lévi-Strauss, *The Savage Mind* (London: Weidenfeld & Nicolson, 1966).

81 Dick Hebdige, *Subculture: The Meaning of Style* (London: Methuen, 1979), pp. 103–4.

82 Frith, *Sociology of Youth*, p. 58.

83 Stuart Hall and Tony Jefferson (eds), *Resistance Through Rituals* (London: Hutchinson, 1976).

84 Frith, *Sociology of Youth*, p. 47.

85 Sarah Thornton, *Club Cultures*, p. 119.

86 Hall and Jefferson, *Resistance*, pp. 13–14, in Thornton, *Club Cultures*, p. 119.

87 Thornton, *Club Cultures*, p. 119.

88 Thornton, *Club Cultures*, p. 137, my emphasis.

89 Terence Morris, 'The Teenage Criminal', *New Society*, 1/28, 1963, pp. 13–16, p. 14; David C. Marsh, *The Changing Social Structure of England and Wales 1871–1961* (London: Routledge, 1965), p. 260.

90 Adrian Horn, *Americanisation and Youth Culture: Juke Boxes and Cultural Fusions, with Special Reference to Northwest England 1945–1960*, PhD, Lancaster University, 2004.

91 Barry Stott, b. 1941, tape ref: T.01.

92 John Farmery, b. 1939, tape ref: T.04.

93 Jim Cheetham, b. 1929, tape ref: T.05.

94 Farmery, tape ref: T.04.

95 Isaacs, tape ref: T.02.

96 Stott, tape ref: T.01.

97 Terry Mitchell, b. 1940, tape ref: T.06.

98 Isaacs, tape ref: T.02.

99 Farmery, tape ref: T.04.

100 See David Fowler, *The First Teenagers: The Lifestyle of Young Wage-earners in Interwar Britain* (London: Woburn Press, 1995).

101 Cohn, *Today*, p. 28. See also Melly, *Revolt into Style*, and Frith, *Sound Effects*.

Cutting your coat according to your cloth: dress styles for young women after World War II

There were no standard dress styles for teenage girls in the late 1940s and 1950s and few direct American influences. A combination of lack of money and import restrictions meant that young women needed to be resourceful and innovative in order to present themselves with novel looks. As sewing and dressmaking were common skills among women at this time, standard dress patterns were adapted and ideas for new styles and style-fusions were taken from magazines and the cinema.

Subcultural styles in young women have not been a widely recorded feature by academics, and the post-war years are a period when teenage girls were largely ignored by social scientists. This may be because there appears to have been nothing to match the flamboyant challenges to the 'Establishment' that were posed, for example, by the Teddy Boys. As a photographic record by Ken Russell testifies, Teddy Girls *were* noticed in the mid-1950s but a moral panic was not attached to them.[1] A counter-cultural style did, however, develop in the late 1950s among the middle class that was influenced by the screen stars Juliette Gréco, Audrey Hepburn and Leslie Caron.

Throughout our period of study, particularly towards the beginning, money, or rather the lack of it, was a major concern for young women buying clothes. Pearl Jephcott noted in 1948 that a proportion of her interviewees had made regular savings since they began earning money and that this was often conducted through clothing clubs into which some girls paid regular amounts of 2s. a week. Although these clubs made purchases proportionately more expensive the girls saw them as a practical way of saving for items of clothing.[2] Hire purchase and catalogue buying were also a way by which families would spread out the cost of buying new clothes.[3]

Fashion-conscious teenagers concentrated their energies on details like hairstyles. Jephcott records the joy of seeing young women making the best of their looks despite low incomes:

> With their gay coats and shining hair they are often by far the most refreshing sights of the mining village or city street which is their background. Some have achieved this result against the odds of dirty work (which is an accepted reason for giving up a job), a squalid home, no long mirrors, seldom a bathroom, and little time for clothes, washing, drying, ironing and mending.[4]

Hairstyles were certainly seen to be of primary concern when attracting young men and could prove expensive:

> Local hair-styles which dictate a combination of nine-pennyworth of peroxide, two-pennyworth of ammonia and a 25/- perm, may give a curiously brazen look to a mild little face below, but normally the girls make relatively few mistakes for the very good reason that, since they were about 14, they have been spending regularly so much thought and time on their appearance, 'You get dates early if you manage to look older.'[5]

Among women in general there was a desire to get away from what was perceived as the drab and austere environment dictated by war-time conditions. Mass-Observation reports revealed women's responses to the prevailing restrictive conditions. Comments like 'after the war is over I would like to scrap all my clothing and get a brand new outfit' were typical and clothing 'occupied a prominent place on women's post-war shopping list'.[6] Gallup polls from 1947, 1949 and 1950 showed that there was a high demand for women's clothes but that high prices were a more important factor in restricting purchases than a shortage of ration coupons.[7]

A 'utility' clothing scheme was started for the best of reasons in 1941, and although the clothes attracted a price control and were exempt from purchase tax they were generally unpopular. This was, perhaps, more so for teenage girls. Utility clothes were, however, widespread, accounting for four-fifths of clothes produced during and after the war, and were available until the scheme was scrapped in 1952.[8]

The period between 1945 and 1960 witnessed a profound change in the availability and cost of women's clothes, and the effects of mass production influenced the market more and more leading up to the 1960s. Although clothes rationing was abolished in May 1949, home dressmaking was widespread throughout this time and there were many improvements in the available clothes patterns after the war.[9] Certainly there was more variety and, 'even couture patterns were available to the general public'.[10] For the inexperienced in sewing skills evening classes in dressmaking were generally accessible, which allowed any woman with limited resources and some spare time to be able to 'run up' their own dresses. Although 'Easy to Make' patterns were widely used the couture patterns needed 'considerable skill' and were far more complex to use; they were not, therefore, commonplace.[11] Home dressmaking, moreover, allowed young women not only to get up to date with the latest fashions but also to adapt dress patterns to make their own versions: they were able to customise, individualise and subvert mainstream styles.[12]

Readily available, recycled materials were also used and home adaptations were made with whatever cloth became available. An interviewee recalls: 'I remember having a skirt my mother made out of some curtain material for me, and I thought this was great. People used to say 'Your skirt's made of curtains and I'd say No it isn't ...'.[13] Reading had been a key influence on dress styles since before World War II, fashion tips coming from a wide range of women's magazines. An increased number of titles after the war, particularly from the mid-1950s, allowed dress styles to be more widely disseminated:

> The only subject on which certain girls ever do any reading for a specific purpose is connected with their personal appearance. They consult with real care the women's magazines which provide up-to-the-minute information on how to be glamorous in the current mode or which can help decide a question that requires an almost religious intensity – what amount of make-up a girl should use at a set age.[14]

Demand for make-up was high and rising in World War II and, as supplies were restricted, cosmetics were sold extensively on the black market.[15] Make-up was important in a teenage girl's life and, although parental control was exercised more strongly over girls than boys, not all make-up was frowned upon by all parents. When asked if her mother and father allowed her to wear make-up to go out interviewee Gwynneth Broadbent, shedding light on the influence of women's magazines, replied:

> Oh yes, they did. I have to say I wasn't a particularly forward sort of girl at all, but I mean ... oh yes we used to read *Woman* and *Woman's Own* and follow all that avidly, all the problems, the agony aunts. You got a lot of your information about that ... about all sorts of things and make-up and things. Yes, they [parents] had no problem with it [make-up]. I think perhaps if I'd plastered it on, they might have said something, but no, I can never remember that.[16]

Fashions spread across the country in diverse ways and there was a differ-ence in consumption patterns between urban and rural settings, the latter tending to lag behind somewhat. Peter Laurie wrote about the different levels of mascara use over time across the country and noted considerable regional differences:

> the way fashion spreads is rather like the growth of an inkblot on a map. ... It is extraordinary how long it can take fashions to spread, even though in theory we are all exposed to them at the same time through the same media: magazines, television, newspapers. Women's cosmetics show this delay well because they are cheap, easy to use, and available everywhere: the only reason for using them or not is a social one. Mascara is an interesting example. This eyelash paint came in early in the 'fifties. By 1955 one in ten London women were using it. By 1960 a quarter of them, and slightly fewer in 1963. In the south of England, a mere fifty miles away, it took until '60 before even one in ten women were using it: although in the North, North-East and West several hundred miles away the number using it lagged only slightly behind London.[17]

Fashion dissemination is geographically complex and regional factors affect the process. Mascara use was 'still increasing in the North, while decreasing in London' and the North was 'an autonomous area for fashion, which, although it might use the same materials as London, thereafter dictated their use itself.' Though it is most likely to be a combination of both, Laurie's expla-nation for the evident 'time lags' between the regions is that fashion spreads not through the mass media 'but by personal contact and example'.[18]

There had been a variety of magazines targeted at the working-class teenage girl between the wars that included *Girl's Cinema* (1920), *Secrets* (1932), *Oracle* (1933) and *Miracle* (1935). After World War II, however, the number of magazine titles directed at young women increased dramatically and were more culturally specific. Examples include *Marilyn* ('The Great All-Picture Love Story Weekly', 1955), *Valentine* ('Brings You Love Stories in Pictures', 1957), *Boyfriend* (1959), *Romeo* (1957) and *Cherie* ('Exciting Love Stories in Pictures', 1960).[19] Moreover, the 1950s were also 'the heyday of women's magazines'. The readership of *Women*, *Women's Own* and *Women's Realm* was in the millions.[20] In this period these mainstream magazines, directed at adult women, absorbed youthful images for their own fashions, which was a process that continued into the 1960s and beyond.

Since, particularly among young women, the cinema became a massively popular entertainment in the interwar years, it was an essential source for fashion tips and American style-influences:

One of the reasons why a girl must go regularly to the pictures, particularly from about 14 to 16 ½, is to study and learn to apply to herself the immaculate coiffure that an admired film star displays. A girl will take exact note of the frock that her star of the moment is wearing, describe it to a dressmaker friend and will appear in a replica in three weeks' time. One begins to realize, when talking to these girls, the amazing extent to which the minutiae of the clothes and hair arrangement of an American actress may affect the spending habits of a child in a mining village in Durham or a girl in a tenement in Central London.[21]

British teenage girls of the 1950s did not wholeheartedly take on board the look of the American college girl that has been the subject of so much retrospective nostalgia as in the film *American Graffiti*[22] and the television series *Happy Days*.[23] The mainstream styles evident in Figure 6.1 are probably more typical. The 'extremes of the "bobbysoxer" fashions, with oversized boy's team jackets and full skirts held out by a mass of petticoats, were ignored by most girls'.[24] American teen styles of the 1950s did, though, present a model for some to aspire to. Imports of American clothes, however, were largely unavailable until the late 1950s and, when they were obtainable, were too expensive for most teenagers and their parents. The American college girl look was by that time out of date, overpriced and perceived as bourgeois.[25]

There was no standard teenage style for the girls of our period. Young women were not and never will be a homogeneous grouping and individual expressions, and varying levels of interest in fashion and personal appearance, are evident in all classes, economic groups and regional levels. Jephcott's survey of *Some Young People* in 1954, observed a range of attitudes to appearance that highlight the importance of individual interpretations:

> Seventeen year-old Eileen 'comes in from work, gets smartened up and goes out apparently to hang around the streets'; June is '[s]weet seventeen at its least hackneyed. Pretty frocks, a piquant face, warm hearted, spontaneous'; fifteen year-old Gladys' 'clothes were grubby and she had nicotined fingers (she came to the door smoking) … She [w]ould like to have more money for the clothes which she so patently does not know how to look after. Had thoughts of going to evening classes for dressmaking but gave up the idea'; and fifteen year-old Esmé is a 'well set, trimly dressed young woman, who looks more like a girl in work than in school.'[26]

Teenage girls may well have epitomised in the public's mind the concept of the post-war teenager. Despite this popular perception, though, teenage girls have been largely overlooked by social researchers. This could be because

Fans wait for Bill Haley at London Airport, 1957   **6.1**

their behaviour was deemed at the time to have been less conspicuous and threatening to the wider society than that of young men. It is certainly possible that young women were a prominent part of street cultures but that they had a less noticeable and media-reported role: more research needs to be directed to this area. 'Youth sociologists have looked mainly at the activities of adolescent boys and young men and their attention has been directed to those areas of experience which have a strongly masculine image.'[27] When retrospective accounts of post-war youth culture have been constructed by academics, for example by the CCCS (Centre for Contemporary Cultural Studies), they have 'been reconstructed in overwhelmingly masculine terms when, in fact, changes in young women's lives were more profound than those affecting young men'.[28] Young women's dress styles did not contain the same meanings of rebelliousness against the 'Establishment' as did, for example, the Teddy Boys styles.[29] This was, perhaps, because aggressive masculinity was part of the Teddy Boy essence. When looking back at the 1940s and 1950s we may observe the lack of recorded subcultural styles among young women and wonder why there was nothing to match the male sartorial expressions of the Spivs and Teds. The methods of subcultural analysis that have been used in discussions of male groups do not work with women because their participation in 'spectacular' subcultures is limited. Women's cultural responses are most often drawn from the mainstream, and this traditionally casts them as 'less culturally "creative" or "oppositional"'. It is better to 'recognise the ways in which young women use the commercial machinery to demarcate their own "cultural space" and contest their subordination'.[30]

In the 1950s working-class women used 'consumer skills' which, when turned towards fashion, enabled them to articulate their position in the social structure in ways that were original and distinctive of the era.[31] Traditionally the working class in our period have been viewed as either on the 'margins' (where they subvert and reject the conventional meanings and values of commodities), or part of the 'mainstream' (where they are perceived as passive consumers): the former are perceived as 'masculine' and the latter 'feminine'. Angela Partington explains that 'While working-class women's activities have been associated with devalued cultural practices, male working-class culture has enjoyed the status of "subversion", on the grounds that the commodity is either refused or creatively "appropriated"'.[32] The 'New Look' of 1947 flaunted extravagance and was perceived as a challenge to the Labour government's post-war ethic of material sacrifice.[33] Working-class women 'improperly' consumed fashions like the New Look because they used style to meet needs that were not intended or assumed by fashion designers and the fashion industry.[34] Partington notes that fashions seen in the 1950s family photographs, for example, show an appropriation, or misappropriation of the New Look.

The New Look was expensive and not widely taken up as a popular fashion by women or teenagers, and it attracted considerable opposition.[35] However, it adapted its appearance to adjust to the needs of the British high street. Incidences of fashion modifications were undoubtedly widespread and are an area of fashion history that is under-researched, particularly in the region of youth styles. Among the reasons for the lack of interest may be that they were not perceived as spectacular nor were they an ideological challenge to dominant cultural values.

There is evidence from Ken Russell's photographic essay of 1955 that Teddy Girls as young as fourteen existed at least in the London working-class areas of Walthamstow, Bethnal Green, Tottenham, Poplar, East Kensington and Plaistow (Figures 6.2, 6.3, 6.4 and 6.5).[36] The girls who posed for Russell sport a creative and imaginative fusion of styles that combine to produce a distinctive and individual look illustrative of the time and place. A feature article titled 'What's Wrong With the Teddy Girls' appeared in the *Picture Post* in 1955 and sheds a little light on the subject. It reports that the Teddy Girls of Russell's essay worked in places like offices, factories and hospitals. There were three main aspects of the Teddy Girl style:

First, Teddy Girls (and their boys) are frequently to be found in admirable, morally unexceptionable, law-abiding clubs, doing exactly the same things as non-Teddies. These girls had been members of this club for five years, and had been Teddies for only one.

Second, female Teddyism has little direct connection with the women's fashions of King Edward VII's reign, but was initially based on an adaptation of male Teddyism.

Third, as a result of this evolution, a Teddy Girl is not so easily classified as a Teddy Boy is. She may wear trousers, she may wear a skirt, she may wear quite ordinary clothes, with Teddy accessories.[37]

The Teddy Girl look was an ingenious and complex adaptation of Teddy Boy styles:

The tight black trousers were taken over and so were the velvet collars. Then followed the variations. There were high-necked, elaborately embroidered blouses, with turn-down collars and cameo broaches. Loose-fitting, many pocketed jackets, mannish waistcoats. Lace-up sandals and coolie [sic] hats ('Teddy' only in the sense of being different or unorthodox). There were striped boater hats and a general preference for black-and-white as the basic colours. The one constant and compulsorily note was provided by the thin, long-handeled umbrella and the long, flat, hand-bag.[38]

6.2   Elsie Henden, aged 16, Jean Rayner, 14, Rose Henden, 16, and Mary Toothy,
January 1955

The Teddy Girl fashions that Russell expertly showcased were unlikely to have been widespread across Britain and there is no suggestion by Mitchell that the style was seen outside of London at this time. It is probable, however, that Teddy Girl styles may have received some limited popularity in other British towns and cities. In Manchester, Harry Isaacs remembers that they used to be called 'Vicky' girls. 'Well you'd got the Teddy Boys, the Edwardians, we used to call the girls the Vicky girls. And … they tended to wear little high collars like that and it was easier maybe for girls to get their clothes.'[39] They were not the subjects of a moral panic and so the unconventional fashion did not spread through media-amplified

Pat Wiles and Iris Thornton, both aged 17, from Plaistow, January 1955   **6.3**

notoriety. Mitchell and Russell's contemporary reports witness an imaginative resourcefulness and style sense among the girls that posed for the photographs. Research in this area may well prove to be fruitful whilst it is still possible to interview the Teddy Girls of the period.

Toward the end of the 1950s some young women, particularly within the middle classes, adopted 'scruffy' clothes and these were perceived as, and were intended to be, a challenge to the 'old guard'. They may have been a reflection of strong anti-commercial and anti-American feelings noted in university students, intellectuals and among left-wing political groups which all had links to the CND (Campaign for Nuclear Disarmament).[40]

6.4   Jean Rayner, aged 14, January 1955

The style confronted established ideals of femininity and cultural subservience. Young women who were deliberately untidy in their appearance demonstrated culturally oppositional meanings and carried them into the public realm. This sartorial method of opposition did not become apparent until the late 1950s and was seen mostly in the middle classes. It was largely restricted to politically aware young women of student age and could not really be seen as a teenage style. It suggested 'an artistic or intellectual calling' that no doubt annoyed parents.[41] Protest movements in the late 1950s epitomised by the CND's Easter rallies, the first of which was from London to Aldermaston in 1958 (Figure 6.6), presented counter-cultural style fusions that 'were *alternative* fashions, assembled to express a critique

Eileen, aged 16, January 1955   **6.5**

of society, or to claim a group's or an individual's right to speak on its own':[42]

> Young women wore thick black, or sometimes dark green or maroon stock-
> ings, and full dirndl skirts that derived both from the Dorelia John fashions
> of prewar Chelsea and from the postwar cult of ballet. They wore items of
> male clothing: check shirts, oiled wool fisherman's jerseys from Norway (or
> men's jerseys from Marks and Spencer), and duffle coats from Millets or
> other army surplus stores. They wore tight 'drainpipe' trousers made of black
> velvet or Black Watch tartan, and were beginning to wear jeans.[43]

These fashions, or counter-fashions, were showcased in the jazz clubs
of urban Britain, particularly in those towns and cities with colleges and

universities. Attitudes of university students in Oxford and Manchester, in 1962, identified an assumed connection between the CND, jazz and 'beat' behaviour. In Oxford respondents commented that jazz is a symbol of revolt against the conventional:

"It is a protest against middle-class values, snobbery, narrow-mindedness, materialism, security and anxiety"; "It is a symbol of despair and nihilism and represents the basic predicament of our age." "The beat phenomenon is interpreted as a protest against the paraphernalia of our technical civilisation, the rejection of everything but art ..." "It is difficult to maintain one's distinct personality. The increasing pressures to conform produce a counter-reaction, and hence the Beat"[44]

There was a connection between the scruffy artistic and intellectual fashions expressed by British students and American Beat and French Bohemian fashions of that same period. Indeed, American expressions could be seen in the Beat look of New York's Greenwich Village and San Francisco's North Beach.[45] The French film star Juliette Gréco (Figure 6.7) was a role model for the young intellectual English woman because she had a 'cool worldly chic', and at the same time the Hollywood film stars

6.6   On the first London to Aldermaston march of Easter 1958, CND supporters wore duffle coats and donkey jackets, which became symbols of nonconformity and protest

June 1956: Juliette Gréco, French actress and singer, at the Festival of Dijon   **6.7**

Belgian-born Audrey Hepburn and the French Leslie Caron (Figures 6.8 and 6.9) were also a significant influence on the British counter-cultural image. They 'popularised a Left Bank *gamine* look as reinterpreted by Hollywood'. Hepburn's 'doe eyes' and short hair became much imitated and the effect of Hepburn, Caron and Gréco's continental origins 'disrupted class-bound British stereotypes of beauty'. The Parisian Hubert de Givenchy designed Hepburn's film and personal wardrobes. Fashionable influences on Britain's young middle-class women, then, were European as mediated by Hollywood.[46] Barbara Hulanichi recalls how the look of Hepburn in the comedy *Sabrina Fair*[47] influenced her and her fellow students:

6.8 October 1953: Belgian-born actor Audrey Hepburn (1929–93) with American actor William Holden on the set of director Billy Wilder's film *Sabrina*. Hepburn wears a black sweater, black Capri pants, hoop earrings, and flats

> *Sabrina Fair* had made a huge impact on us all at college; everyone walked around in black sloppy sweaters, suede low-cut flatties and gold hoop earrings. … Audrey Hepburn and Givenchy were made for each other. His little black dress with shoestring straps in *Sabrina Fair* must have been imprinted on many teenagers' minds forever.[48]

Another interviewee recalls of Juliette Gréco:

> I can remember Juliette Gréco particularly. I rather fancied looking like Juliette Gréco. I had a white fluffy duffle coat which I used to wear until it practically ran away. I mean you wore the same thing day after day. The other thing was black polo-neck sweaters.[49]

1955: French-born actress Leslie Caron in Jean Renoir's *Orvet*, Theatre of the   **6.9**
Renaissance, Paris

Oral testimony sheds light on Hepburn's influence among the young women who frequented 1950s jazz clubs:

> the great influence on them was Audrey Hepburn. So you had Audrey Hepburn look-alikes. … She [Hepburn] was a tall girl so she wore flatty shoes. So they wore what they called ballet shoes, flat shoes, what they now call ski trousers with the elastic underneath and little short white duffle coats and sometimes they used to wear their cardigans back to front so they buttoned up the back.[50]

These actresses of the late 1950s started to make 'slacks', or women's trousers, popular in Britain although they were not a common sight in the

1940s.[51] Jeans in women's sizes were unavailable until the late 1960s and 'until 1968 girls who were attracted to Levi trousers had to buy men's'.[52]

There were clear style fusions between America, Europe and Britain in the 1950s. Though the intention was not to appear bourgeois the influences of these were essentially on middle-class fashions: 'Amid the general conformity then, at a time when Continental was a code word for chic, youth fashions brought about a convergence between French and American style in creative combinations. Left Bank style was a largely middle-class approach to dress …'.[53]

Young women's dress styles from the period 1945 to 1960 is an under-researched area. It is, however, possible to conclude that dress codes were not perceived as a dangerous ideological challenge to the *status quo*. As home dressmaking was commonplace there were limitless individual adaptations of standard fashions that were presented in magazines and of glamorous styles, both American and French, which were shown in the cinema. Direct American influences appear to have been minimal and 'dressing down' was a symbolic ideological challenge adopted by parts of the artistic and politically aware middle classes toward the end of the 1950s.

Notes

1 Ken Russell, *Photo Essay on London Teddy Girls* (copyright: Topfoto/Ken Russell).

2 Pearl Jephcott, *Rising Twenty* (London: Faber & Faber, 1948), p. 127.

3 Elizabeth Wilson and Lou Taylor, *Through the Looking Glass: A History of Dress from 1860 to the Present Day* (London: BBC, 1989), p. 158.

4 Jephcott, *Rising Twenty*, p. 61.

5 Jephcott, *Rising Twenty*, p. 62.

6 Ina Zweiniger-Bargielowska, *Austerity in Britain: Rationing, Controls, and Consumption 1939–1955* (Oxford: Oxford University Press, 2000), p. 93.

7 Zweiniger-Bargielowska, *Austerity in Britain*, p. 93.

8 Zweiniger-Bargielowska, *Austerity in Britain*, pp. 93–5.

9 Zweiniger-Bargielowska, *Austerity in Britain*, p. 184; Pearson Phillips, 'The New Look' in *Age of Austerity 1945–1951*, ed. by M. Sissons and P. French (Harmondsworth: Penguin, 1964), pp. 132–54, p. 141.

10 Wilson and Taylor, *Through the Looking Glass*, p. 167.

11 Wilson and Taylor, *Through the Looking Glass*, p. 167.

12 Angela Partington, 'Popular Fashion and Working Class Affluence' in *Chick Thrills: A Fashion Reader*, ed. by Juliet Ash and Elizabeth Wilson (London: Pandora, 1992), p. 151.

13 Peter Everett, *You'll Never Be 16 Again: An Illustrated History of the British Teenager* (London: BBC, 1986), p. 13.

14 Jephcott, *Rising Twenty*, p. 62.

15 Zweiniger-Bargielowska, *Austerity in Britain*, p. 91.

16 Gwynneth Broadbent, b. 1938, *North West Sound Archive*, tape Ref: 2001.0723a, 15 May 2001.

17 Peter Laurie, *The Teenage Revolution* (London: Anthony Blond, 1965), pp. 51–2.

18 Laurie, *Teenage Revolution*, pp. 51–2.

19 W.J. Osgerby, *One for the Money, Two for the Show: Youth, Consumption and Hegemony in Britain in 1945–70, with special reference to a South East coastal town*, PhD dissertation, Sussex University, 42-2586, A9F, 1992, p. 269.

20 Wilson and Taylor, *Through the Looking Glass*, p. 167.

21 Jephcott, *Rising Twenty*, pp. 62–3.

22 George Lucas, *American Graffiti* (Universal, 1973).

23 *Happy Days* (ABC, 1974–1983, 256 episodes).

24 Clare Rose, *Children's Clothes Since 1750* (London: Batsford, 1989), p. 133.

25 See for example the advertisement by Wallis, January 1960, in *Women's Day*.

26 Pearl Jephcott, *Some Young People* (London: Allen & Unwin, 1954), pp. 39–44.

27 Angela McRobbie, 'Second-hand Dresses and the Role of the Ragmarket' in *Zoot Suits and Second-Hand Dresses*, ed. by Angela McRobbie (London: Macmillan, 1989), pp. 23–49, p. 24.

28 Osgerby, *One for the Money*, p. 258.

29 See chapter 5.

30 Osgerby, *One for the Money*, pp. 255–6.

31 Partington, 'Popular Fashion', p. 145.

32 Partington, 'Popular Fashion', p. 147.

33 The 'New Look' was not in general use until 1948; see Phillips, 'The New Look', p. 141.

34 Noted also by Zweiniger-Bargielowska, *Austerity in Britain*, p. 92.

35 Phillips, 'The New Look', p. 141.

36 This was the subject of a recent exhibition titled 'Bombsite Boudiccas', Spitz Gallery, London, E1, 18–26 June 2005 (www.teddygirl.co.uk). See also Martin Heapy, 'Bombsite Boudiccas' (www.teddygirl.co.uk/essay.htm; accessed 17 June 2008).

37 David Mitchell, 'What's Wrong With the Teddy Girls', *Picture Post* (4 June 1955), pp. 37–40, p. 38.

38 Mitchell, 'Teddy Girls', pp. 38–9.

39 Harry Isaacs, b. 1934, tape ref: T.02.

40 Ferdynand Zweig, *The Student in the Age of Anxiety* (London: Heinemann, 1963); Communist Party of Great Britain. National Cultural Committee Conference 1951, *The American Threat to British Culture* (London: Arena, 1952); Bertrand Russell et al., *The Impact of America on European Culture* (Boston: Beacon Press, 1951); Richard Hoggart, *The Uses of Literacy* (Harmondsworth: Penguin, 1960).

41 Elizabeth Wilson, *Adorned in Dreams: Fashion and Modernity* (London: Virago, 1985), p. 184.

42 Wilson and Taylor, *Through the Looking Glass*, p. 161, original emphasis.

43 Wilson and Taylor, *Through the Looking Glass*, p. 161.

44 Zweig, *Student in the Age of Anxiety*, pp. 60–1.

45 Wilson and Taylor, *Through the Looking Glass*, p. 162.

46 Wilson and Taylor, *Through the Looking Glass*, p. 162–3.

47 Billy Wilder, *Sabrina Fair* (Paramount, 1954).

48 Barbara Hulanichi, *From A to Biba* (London: Hutchinson, 1983), p. 43 in Wilson and Taylor, *Through the Looking Glass*, p. 163.

49 Peter Everett, *You'll Never Be 16 Again*, p. 37.

50 Harry Isaacs, b.1934, tape ref: T.02.

51 Pearl Jephcott, *Girls Growing Up* (London: Faber & Faber, 1942), p. 170. Trousers for women in Britain started to appear and become acceptable in the 1920s. They were originally called pyjamas and were worn for home lounging. Jane Dormer puts the time at which they became known as 'slacks' at around 1936. Jane Dormer, *Fashion: The Changing Shape of Fashion Through the Years* (London: Galley Press, 1979), pp. 67, 73, 75, 76.

52 Dormer, *Fashion*, p. 109.

53 Wilson and Taylor, *Through the Looking Glass*, p. 163.

7

Venues: from arcade to high street

In the fifteen years that followed World War II, casual youth meeting places went through a period of change and 'crossed over', with juke boxes, from amusement arcades into small-scale catering establishments. These were rapidly expanding nationwide both geographically and in actual numbers. This chapter concerns 'unorganised' youth venues as opposed to youth clubs, church organisations and so on.

When milk bars and snack bars began to provide juke boxes in the late 1940s the whole area of music licensing was exposed as confusing and ambiguous. The first section examines the legal implications surrounding the public playing of recorded music and the complex situation concerning juke box use and copyright law. The more culturally revealing *local* licensing of juke box music, which was aired in local Magistrates' Courts, is seen to highlight contemporary discourses on public attitudes toward young people, youth venues, popular music and perceived 'undesirable elements'.

The next section considers the style and type of new youth venues and places post-war commercial youth venues in a regional, social and cultural context by looking at different types of small-scale catering establishments. These include milk, temperance, coffee and snack bars, caffs and cafés, and, for the purposes of this discussion, the general label of 'youth café' is adopted as a collective term. It was around the suitability of these 'new', sometimes cramped and dangerous, premises that the granting of licences often depended. These venues were responsible for the limited import of foreign design influences: in milk bars, for example, décor was influenced by American drug store soda fountains and Australian milk bars,[1] whilst many coffee bars attempted an Italian aesthetic. At the mundane level, however, the youth cafés appeared distinctly British and of the period because the limited imported design influences had been mediated through British social, economic and cultural forces. This meant that when juke boxes did enter the youth cafés they entered into an established set of British design fusions.

The last section examines the social uses of youth venues. Although milk bars had been in existence since the 1930s, after the war new youth cafés opened up spaces where young people could socialise and listen to juke box music. These new youth cafés made room available for young people to mix away from the gaze of parents and well-meaning adults, and provided a counter to the adult male-dominated public house. This section, apart from identifying prominent social uses of youth venues, follows the discourses, both contemporary and retrospective, that surround them.

I: Legal implications

The law concerning music copyright was ambiguous because before 1956 it contained no specific references to relaying music through juke boxes.[2] Legal interpretations were based on the Copyright Act of 1911 that specified gramophone records as being copyright protected for the first time. In this respect it stated that 'copyright'

> means the sole right to produce or reproduce the work or any substantial part thereof …
>
> In the case of a … musical work, to make any record, perforated roll, cinematographic film, or other contrivance by means of which the work might be mechanically performed or delivered.
>
> Copyright in a work shall also be deemed to be infringed by any person who for his private profit permits a … place of entertainment to be used for the performance in public of the work without the consent of the owner of the copyright[3]

Two separate bodies were set up in the mid-1930s to collect copyright royalties: the Phonographic Performance Ltd (PPL), which were to act as agents for the record manufacturers, and the Performing Rights Society Ltd (PRS), which would act, and collect dues, for the performing artists; namely the musicians and singers.

This meant that juke box operators needed two separate licences, and the cost of these added a significant financial burden. The PPL set their fees at 2 guineas per season or 3 guineas per annum, per machine, which was increased to 5 guineas per annum in 1958. For the period 1947 to 1958 the PRS fee stood at 6 guineas for 1d. operated machines and at 10 guineas per

2d. machine.[4] The amounts, though, had remained stable: in the PPL's case for over twenty years and with the PRS for over a decade. In September 1955 the trade paper *World's Fair* printed a clarification:

> Section 19 of the Copyright Act, 1911, protected gramophone records from being copied, but in 1933 a court of law decision interpreted this section as conferring a performing right as well. As a result the gramophone manufacturers formed a company, Phonographic Performance Ltd., to exercise control on their behalf, and nowadays a licence must be obtained from this concern if it is desired to play a gramophone record in public, within the copyright period of the record itself.
>
> That is most important, the copyright period of the record. It is that and not the copyright in the actual music, which is the operative factor in Phonographic Performance Ltd. demands. Copyright in the music itself is the concern of the Performing Rights Society Ltd. from whom also a licence has to be obtained.[5]

A less ambiguous piece of legislation was introduced with the Copyright Act of 1956. Replacing the Act of 1911 it strengthened copyright terms for musical recordings. Mr H.G.S. Gilbert, Secretary of the PPL, said that 'It states simply and specifically that the law requires all who cause sound recordings to be heard in public to be licensed. … And I would like to emphasise that the legal position is that the operator and the site owner are jointly and separately liable.'[6]

The legal situation was convoluted further through local by-laws that licensed music in public places. In Lancashire, for instance, the Blackburn Hundred maintained separate registers for music licensing, singing and dancing, where radio, piano and radiogram were specifically noted, and the Kirkdale Division Petty Sessions music and dancing register 1949–61 refers to 'coin-operated phonograms'.[7] Local licensing did not happen evenly over the country though; instead, interpretations of the law were subject to local and regional peculiarities. In 1956 it was reported that 'There is [a] legal problem – the attitude taken by the local licensing authorities. The Justices view of this music appears to vary from place to place. Some areas hold that a music licence is required for a juke-box, whether it is in a public house or a milk bar.'[8] Applications for music licences 'very often hinged on local bye-laws and the interpretation of these laws, and on the attitude of the local chief constables.'[9]

Attitudes that fixed amusement arcades in the degeneracy bracket were culturally pervasive, and media reports often assumed that these venues were magnets for male 'deviant' youths. This perception was apparent in reported references to 'pin-tables' and deviancy.[10] A Mass-Observation report on delinquency in 1949 commented on arcades having a detrimental effect on youth: 'it seems to me clear that juvenile delinquency is only part of a much deeper and greater problem – the problem of uninspired and unadjusted youth … the endless intoxication of the slot machine in an Oxford Street arcade, reflect[s] something just as grave as breaking a window or pinching a watch.'[11]

Local magistrates were particularly concerned with problems that might arise from attracting these 'undesirable' or 'delinquent' elements and had apprehensions over public safety. Readings of the law were crucial to the juke box market as a whole and, in particular, to would-be commercial operators. In consequence magistrates' decisions received detailed coverage in *World's Fair*. An appeal 'against two fines of 5s. imposed by The Liverpool Stipendiary Magistrate for playing music to the public in a milk-bar' in Smithdown Road, Liverpool in 1950 was seen as a test case by *World's Fair* and provides detail of a specific and influential legal interpretation. The ruling hinged on whether the milk bar in question provided music to the public. The Recorder, Mr H.I. Nelson, ruled that Magistrate's licences were 'needed by café and milk-bar proprietors who have juke-boxes on their premises for the provision of music to the public'.[12] The judgement was made because the juke box returns were stated as between 20s. and 30s. per week. Record plays cost 2d. Therefore, according to the Court, if 'the instrument was used six days a week between the hours of 6-pm and 1pm, music for the public was being provided for approximately one third of that time.' The recorder noted that, 'the consistent playing, night after night, six days a week, of this machine in this milk-bar, for approximately one third of the time, must be described as public music.'[13]

By 1950 the judiciary in many regions were agreed that a music licence was necessary for anyone offering juke box music as a public amenity. As a consequence applications for licences were made to local magistrates. Cases where applications were refused, though, should not be taken out of context because wholesale granting of music licences for juke boxes occurred in the period and most passed without comment.[14] Where applications were contested the cases were frequently reported in *World's Fair*.

Reports suggest that in the minority of cases where licences were contested it was because of perceived connections between juke boxes, amusement arcades and male youth deviancy, and this affected the growth of the new youth venues. The 'old guard' had fixed views on what they saw as the 'seediness' and degeneracy involved with amusement arcades and these were frequently used as arguments within local Magistrates' courts against granting music licences to café and snack bar owners.

The Ditchburn juke box organisation gave a high priority to their social responsibility claiming that by siting their juke boxes, rather than selling them, they could deal with any adverse social consequences that might arise. They provided their leased equipment as an amenity and not as a local 'nuisance'. Occupying the moral high ground, Ditchburn maintained that they would turn down any business that might cause a particular problem or be seen as socially divisive. In this respect the firm was self-regulatory.

A 1958 report on the Ditchburn Company noted problems and resistance to perceived American influences faced since the firm started out in 1947:

> Many difficulties of course were encountered. Prejudice from café owners, prejudice from the public and the Press had to be overcome in many cases. Music licences were required in some districts. Magistrates turned down all applications rather than permit this 'terrible invention from America.'
>
> The Ditchburn organisation while politely and quietly putting forward a reasonable case for this new method of entertainment did not attempt to flout public opinion. In towns where it was made quite clear that machines were not wanted they quietly withdrew and concentrated on other areas, believing that the time would come when public opinion would swing round in favour of the Music Maker.

By taking a 'softly softly' approach to introducing juke boxes and having a stated policy of cooperation with the police and sensitivity to local feelings Ditchburn did not challenge dominant cultural values at the local level: 'In every new area the operating organisation co-operated with the Police, keeping in touch with them and removing immediately machines from any premises which became undesirable.'[15]

In a letter to the *Daily Telegraph* in July 1954 a 'bilateral quota of £10,000 for 12 months ... for the import from Western Germany of automatic coin-operated amusement machines including gramophones and phonographs' was criticised by Mr Norman Ditchburn on the grounds of social irresponsibility. The concerns he raised masked his self-interest, a desire to protect an eroding, near monopoly manufacturing position, but his objections were a lone voice that, if acted upon, would have resisted foreign design influences, in an otherwise overwhelmingly enthusiastic industry:

> Sir,- British manufacturers of coin-operated phonographs ('juke boxes') will be disappointed that a licence is to be issued for the importation of foreign

made machines. There is a social as well as commercial aspect of the matter. 'Juke boxes' in undesirable sites have been known to attract undesirable young people. Some of us who manufacture British coin-operated phonographs (we call them music-makers) are very conscious of this problem and have done our best to collaborate with the police and social workers. This collaboration has taken the form in our case of refusing to allow our music-makers to be installed in any but well-conducted sites, withdrawing them instantly from many sites about which there are complaints or even doubts, and ensuring that the music provided is of high quality. Now this work, gladly undertaken even when financially disadvantageous, is apparently to be rendered useless by a hasty decision of the Board of Trade.[16]

As it became apparent that a lot of money could be made out of juke boxes in manufacture, distribution and at the point of sale, established attitudes softened.

Juke boxes did not receive widespread acceptance in British public houses which catered for, and were patronised by, an older age group. Rochdale Magistrates' refusal to licence 160 pubs for juke boxes as late as 1958 highlights a wariness of juke boxes and their associations by the licensed trade.[17] On 5 September 1958 Rochdale Borough Magistrates renewed music licences for 160 public houses on the condition that, 'juke boxes, automatic gramophones or other similar devices, coin or token operated, shall not be installed in the said premises'. The *World's Fair* headline ran, 'Rochdale Ban On All Forms of Automatic Music: JUKE BOXES ARE "OUT" IN THIS TOWN'.[18]

Rochdale is a satellite textile town of Manchester and in the late 1950s juke boxes had only recently started to intrude into pubs in towns like these.[19] The Rochdale case fixes the pub position into a firm context. Evidence that was raised in the case shows that the relationship between juke boxes, pubs and alcohol that would be significant in the 1960s was a contested area in 1958. The town's Chief Constable (Mr S.J. Harvey) summarised the local position, saying

that there were three public houses with juke boxes, none with an electric organ at the moment, and four with claviolines.

Provision had been made for radio or gramophone music, but only seventeen out of 89 licensees in the central division had taken advantage of this. It was admitted that juke boxes were an attraction to young people and it was agreed that conditions varied considerably from house to house and from district to district; what perhaps was good in one house was not so in another.

The same report also noted current views on breweries: 'It was apparent from what had been said that morning that the majority of licensees did not want juke boxes, and it seemed that the brewery companies did not want any change, for no separate representations on their behalf had been made to the court.' Despite evident support for the right to install juke boxes, the ban went through apparently without strong resistance:

> Mr A. Wright, solicitor on behalf of Harry Vincent Bewley, licensee of the Brownhill Hotel, Heights Lane, Rochdale, said that so far as juke boxes were concerned, his client would not have one installed, but on the other hand he considered that licensees who wanted to do so should be permitted to install them. It was felt that if a juke box brought disorder into a public house the remedy was obvious – have the installation removed.[20]

The Lincoln Inn of Oldham Road, Rochdale had had a juke box installed for the previous eleven months and claimed complete control over its output and wanted, along with forty-eight of their customers, to keep it:

> He [the licensee] was the only person who controlled the playing of the juke box, and the previous day had enquired from his regular customers whether they wanted the juke box to continue. Forty-eight people signed a petition in its favour.
>   It was felt that every case should be considered on its merits and the juke box at the Lincoln Inn had been accepted by the customers there for the last eleven months.[21]

Clearly the massive expansion of the juke box business was not taking place here as only seventeen out of the eighty-nine pubs in Central Rochdale had provision for gramophone or radio.

It would be inaccurate to suggest that local Magistrates were part of a general 'Establishment' resistance to juke boxes and young people. Mr Noel Goldie QC, Recorder in Manchester, for instance, was insistent that he did not wish to stop young people enjoying themselves or that he had any personal problems with juke boxes. Indeed, he found it important to say, before refusing the appeals of twelve tradesmen for juke box music licences, that he wished 'to make it clear that I have no criticism whatso-ever of these machines'. These applications were made by 'proprietors of snack bars, restaurants and milk bars in parts of the city in which electron-ically-operated music machines – "commonly called juke boxes" – had been installed'.[22] In this case Mr Goldie was adamant that the machines in themselves did not lead to 'the assembly of undesirable customers'. Indeed, he commented that 'they add to the amenity of the premise, and in large cafes and restaurants, as distinct from small shops, I can visualise them being of service to customers'. His concern was with the suitability of the premises, public safety and the practical problems of attracting crowds into small and inadequate spaces. Although he was not a culturally authoritarian figure attempting to halt the influence of American popular culture, his refusal to grant licences would have had this effect.

Magistrates' concerns in Manchester and its satellites were repeated in other parts of the country. A café in Hastings, for example, was granted a fourteen-day juke box licence for a trial period 'pending inspection of the cellar premises by the Borough Engineers and the fire authorities'. A spate of music licence applications marked the early stages of rejuvenations of old shop and café premises, bringing them into use as new youth venues. In the Hastings case it was the proprietor's intention 'to have dancing in the café cellar to music relayed from the juke box upstairs'.[23]

An 'Establishment' recognition of the crossover from arcade to high street as well as mainstream acceptance of juke box technology was noted by the Manchester Recorder: 'He had visited the premises concerned and saw nothing which led him to believe that any of these premises where juke boxes were installed led to the assembly of undesirable customers'.[24] Here the Recorder questioned the perceived link between juke boxes and 'undesirable customers' that was culturally pervasive. There was an urban/suburban/rural split in viewpoints and city attitudes were more cosmopolitan than those in outlying areas. By mid-1957 resistance to granting music licences to potential juke box operators had faded away in London and the major cities. However, some anti-juke-box forces existed in the small towns where 'there are still prejudices among magistrates, civic dignitaries and others that tend to discourage would-be operators'.[25] These prejudices were attributed in most cases to simple ignorance of the 'facts' on the part of magistrates, and *World's Fair* suggested a positive approach for the courts focusing on the benefits to the Exchequer and ease of volume control as the best way of promoting the cause:

> Fortunately this attitude [prejudice] is showing signs of passing. By the right type of psychological approach it can sometimes be banished completely. In a recent test case at Aylesbury the matter of noise nuisance was answered by a full explanation of how the volume control operated, and the fact that, in addition to tax revenue from records, the Customs and Excise were benefiting to the extent of about £200 per machine, swayed the justices to a friendly view.

By 1957 favourable publicity had been gained through using juke boxes in TV programmes and 'the winning over of the press by interesting articles and letters, and the wise use of posters and other visual aids'. However, as with the Ditchburn Company, respectability would be 'gained by even greater care being taken in siting and using boxes to avoid noise or other nuisances'.[26]

II: Venues and style

After World War II a close relationship between young people and juke boxes began in traditional magnets for adolescents like amusement arcades, fairgrounds and seaside resorts.[27] Juke boxes between 1945 and 1960, however, were increasingly sited in high street cafés, and coffee and milk bars. Youth and juke box venues need to be viewed within a regional context and this section draws on sources from England's industrial north-west, particularly Manchester and its surrounds.

Juke box numbers in Britain grew from probably a few hundred at the beginning of the period to an estimated 13,000 in 1958, when they were increasing by around 400 per month.[28] Throughout this time the juke box industry had fought a continual battle for mainstream acceptance and respectability but some hostility to them was always present. Throughout the 1950s, however, juke box appeal widened and became part of mainstream popular culture. In 1956 the *Manchester Guardian* reported on the changes affecting juke box venues:

> A few years ago the juke-box was the plaything of youth alone. 'The kid who handled the music-box' with a threepenny bit was … alien to the life of the adult Englishman. … But now, its advocates claim, the juke-box is becoming part of social life. It has graduated from a corner of the amusement arcade, through the milk and snack bars, chip shops and transport cafés to some pubs and clubs.[29]

Milk bars, which had been established between the wars, were positioned predominantly in urban areas and were meeting places for young people.[30] Their design influences were often modernist, using materials like stainless steel to convey a clean, modern and American image. Britain's first milk bar was opened in London's Fleet Street in 1935; within a year there were 420 in the country and by 1938 there were more than a thousand.[31] Moreover, they were popular across Britain: in 1938 the *Milk Trade Gazette* reported 18 in Manchester, 120 in Lancashire as a whole and 90 in Yorkshire.[32]

After the war milk bar development and growth was lent impetus by E.E.F. Colam's *Practical Milk Bar Operation* of 1946 and Joan N. Marks' *Café and Milk Bar Catering* of 1952. Both books helped in the industry's expansion by providing practical, step-by-step instruction guides for the would-be caterer.[33] Milk developed a clean and healthy image: 'There can be few things more refreshing and sustaining than a glass of cold, rich, creamy milk served attractively with, say, a biscuit and a straw in a spotless glass on a spotless saucer.'[34] In 1952 Marks defined a milk bar as

> a catering establishment mainly concerned with the provision of milk drinks, milk soups, ice cream and other milk dishes. It is styled a 'bar' by reason of the fact that its service is performed at a bar counter, thereby facilitating speed and economy in operation. Usually its front is open to the pavement and the approaches and exterior of the premises should be as such as to leave no doubt in the mind of the passer-by as to the nature of the establishment. The minimum equipment requirements should comprise refrigerated milk and ice cream storage, milk and soup heating appliances, electric drink mixers, milk and syrup pumps, milk menu boards, glassware and crockery and the necessary washing and sterilising apparatus for same. Light snack catering and soda fountain service may be added to the above.[35]

The new design styles, the unfamiliar surroundings and the introduction of 'fast food' was criticised by George Orwell in the 1930s through his fictional anti-American anti-hero, George Bowling. Bowling delivered a vindictive tirade at what he saw as American design influences in pre-jukebox days. It is a reflection of perceived hostility towards American popular cultural influences:

> Behind the bright red counter a girl in a tall white cap was fiddling with an ice-box, and somewhere at the back a radio was playing, plonk-tiddle-tiddle-plonk, a kind of tinny sound. Why the hell am I coming here I thought to myself as I went in. There's a kind of atmosphere about these places that gets me down. Everything slick and shiny and streamlined; mirrors, enamel, and chromium plate whichever direction you look in. Everything spent on the decorations and nothing on the food. No real food at all. Just lists of stuff with American names, sort of phantom stuff that you can't taste and can hardly believe in the existence of. Everything comes out of a carton or a tin, or it's hauled out of a refrigerator or squirted out of a tap or squeezed out of a tube. No comfort, no privacy. Tall stools to sit on, a kind of narrow ledge I eat off, mirrors all round you. A sort of propaganda floating round, mixed up with the noise of the radio, to the effect that food doesn't matter, comfort doesn't matter, nothing matters except slickness and shininess and streamlining.[36]

Shortages of milk in World War II provided the impetus for milk bars to offer a wider menu; the label 'milk bar' therefore was not always descriptive.[37] Numbers of milk bars increased in the post-war period in line with an overall expansion of the catering industry. In 1951 the catering industry was expanding 'faster than any other in the country. Between 1946 and 1948 no fewer than 40,300 new catering outlets were opened, bringing the total to 203,600. These included 10,600 restaurants and cafés, 8,300 hotels and boarding houses, and nearly 5,000 snack bars, milk bars and other outlets.'[38]

Trade directory records as well as marketing surveys raise issues of definition. Typically catering establishments were grouped together: a Lancaster directory for 1956–57, for example, had twenty-one entries under the heading 'Restaurants, Cafes and Snack Bars'.[39] Some of these would have been milk bars but we do not know how many. Moreover, most directory entries had to be paid for and probably under-report the actual numbers. Chisholm gives 'official figures' for milk bars and states that they are a 'new channel of distribution ... for soups, biscuits, confectionary, ices, and other lines'. Between 1947 and 1949 there were twenty-seven in Blackpool, four in Lancaster and forty-five in Manchester.[40] Photographs provide a visual record.[41]

Sociologist T.R. Fyvel made the distinction between three types of café, though, as his observations were from the London area, they should not be taken as definitive for the rest of Britain. Firstly, he described 'the original rough working men's caff' that had developed partly into a youth venue by extending its hours and introducing coffee and juke box music. Secondly, he highlighted the milk bar that was based on the American drugstore counter but was considerably less successful or widespread than in the USA. The third type was the espresso bar, which had 'cultural significance' in its décor that, although disparaged by the 'sophisticated', introduced a certain amount of 'glamour' to the working-class scene. 'While the sophisticated may deride espresso-bar glamour, to the majority of British working-class youth this glamour ... seems precisely part of that modern life they want to aspire to.'[42]

Fyvel's descriptions provide a rough guide to the type of affordable café available in a British city or large town. There were regional variations, however. Interviewee Harry Isaacs, for example, describes Manchester's coffee bars as being frequented by students,[43] and in Manchester temperance bars and herbalists' counters (Figure 7.1) were part of the catering infrastructure selling soft drinks (although these were in decline following

World War II). Sarsaparilla and Vimto were among the best known and were concocted from herbal ingredients.[44] Placing juke boxes in these small establishments sometimes incurred opposition and legal challenges, as a report from 1948 demonstrates: 'A juke box which is operated in a shop and temperance bar … in Long Street, Middleton (Lancs.) was mentioned in the Lancashire Chancery Court on Friday, when a next door neighbour … asked for an interlocutory injunction. He complained about the use of the machine in the evenings …'[45]

Isaacs describes some of the variety in 1940s and 1950s Manchester. The 'snack bars were more like what the Cockneys call caffs – cups of tea and a sarny – sandwich for the workmen in the area and people dropping in' (Figures 7.2 and 7.3), and Manchester's milk bars tended to be owned by Italian families 'Supporis, Grinellis and so on' (Figure 7.4). Some of these places were 'big', 'more like the American soda bar, soda fountain, with a lot more chrome and the hiss of steam and that', but *coffee bars* were

> very different from milk bars. Milk bars were essentially – well in my view – milk bars were in working class areas in Manchester. The coffee bars opened

7.1   Herbalist and Surgical Stores, 1960. Upper Moss Lane, Hulme, Manchester in the centre of the town and once again were mainly … in the centre of the town I would say [frequented] by the studenty … Manchester has always had a very very large student population, so they were frequented by the student population.[46]

Manchester's relatively expensive city-centre coffee bars were also remembered as being part of a 'cosmopolitan' scene. Terry Mitchell recalls that with his friends he

started to go down into Manchester to the various coffee bars. One at the top end of the street was Macarlo's which I think was on Brazennose Street just off Deansgate. I don't know how much a coffee cost, it was quite expensive, something like 1s. 6d. It was something outrageous at that time so you only went and had one and tried to make it stretch out.[47]

For Isaacs the coffee bars in Manchester were not American-influenced but the milk bars were: 'The milk bar reminded me of America but the coffee bars … I just thought of them as being continental. … I don't think there were the Gaggia machines in those days, but it was good, you could get espresso. … I never ever thought of it as being American, the coffee bar.'[48] Barry Stott explains of Blackpool's coffee bars that 'in those days you

Regent Snack Bar, 1958. Collyhurst Road, Collyhurst, Manchester   **7.2**

7.3   Snack Bar, 1958. Ardwick, Junction of Hyde Road and Marshland Road, Manchester

had to make your coffee last at least an hour and if you had enough money for a record as well that was a bonus'.[49]

Introducing stylish décor to the new youth cafés indicates a process whereby imported design influences were adapted in part and mixed with the existing café aesthetic. This created individual British and regional style fusions that could be particularly mundane. The new youth cafés brought into use old shop premises and rooms that had been in decline since the beginning of the war and this helped to revitalise and update Britain's catering infrastructure. Coffee bars 'were initially built for other purposes, necessitating much masking of original features and clever exploitation of awkward spaces. Refits often required that ceilings be lowered, cornices be hidden or staircases be screened.'[50]

In 1952 Marks wrote about the importance of a café's appearance:

The new customer is often attracted as much by the look of the café as by the tariff. It is so depressing to see a dark, badly lit café decorated in heavy colours, with windows concealed by dirty net curtains. The impression is amplified in the winter by water running down the windows in dreary rivulets and steam condensing on the shiny surface of the walls.[51]

A. Chiappe, Italian Café, 1958. Stockport Road, Ardwick, Manchester   **7.4**

Preferably milk bars and café interiors would have looked something like the contemporary advertising ideals, but this was rarely the norm. Some milk bars may have appeared to be American-styled and glamorous at the time but in most cases they did not reach Marks' ideal. Indeed, most would have been more mundane. Valerie Tome, speaking of the Yorkshire side of the Pennines, describes the *C and D Milk Bar* in Heckmondwyke in Yorkshire's West Riding that was known among the local youth as 'Cold and Dead':

> because that's really what it was, because it was very cold and very dead, not many people in it at a time. I don't know if there was coffee, but I know we always drank Oxo and, although it was called a milk bar, I don't think there was anything as exotic as milk shakes or anything like that.

She recalls that authority at the C and D was maintained by a very fierce woman behind the counter determined to keep order in spite of falling standards and the job she was expected to do behind a pile of curling sandwiches and scones and hot cross buns, and brewing up cups of Oxo from a kettle on a gas stove, no electric kettles.[52]

Terry Mitchell's vivid account of Ron's Snack Bar in Manchester echoes Valerie Tome's humorously grim and austere descriptions:

Again in retrospect the atmosphere was non-existent because it was really quite bleak. The floors were sort of linoleumy type presumably which could be easily mopped over. Again the tables and chairs were the simplest structure. I don't know whether they were metal or … There was nothing on the walls. The walls as I remember them were … just sort of painted. … There was no atmosphere in there at all other than a bit of steam that came out of the tea and coffee making machines. But we thought it was wonderful. It had great big windows along the front like I was describing for the temperance bar. It was really like that only on a bigger scale. These great plated glass windows that were painted half way up …[53]

These northern snack-cum-milk bars with their 'gritty' atmospheres have since been adopted into popular memory and folklore. Here any imported cultural influences had been so nuanced by the local conditions and environment that they had become part and parcel of the 'way of life' for young people of the period. Keith Waterhouse's novel *Billy Liar* defines a moment in the late 1950s in the fictional northern town of Stradhoughton:

The Kit-Kat was another example of Stradhoughton moving with the times, or rather dragging its wooden leg about five paces behind the times. … The Kit-Kat was now a coffee bar, or thought it was. It had a cackling espresso machine, a few empty plant-pots, and about half a dozen glass plates with brown sugar stuck all over them. The stippled walls, although redecorated, remained straight milkbar: a kind of Theatre Royal backcloth showing Dick Whittington and his cat hiking it across some of the more rolling dales. Where the coffee-bar element really fell down, however, was in the personality of Rita, on whom I was now training the sights of my anxiety. With her shiny white overall, her mottled blonde hair, and her thick red lips, she could have transmogrified the Great Northern Hotel itself into a steamy milkbar with one wipe of her tea-cloth.[54]

III: Social uses

Traditionally amusement arcades provided mechanical entertainments for young people as well as social space. They were ideal meeting places and areas for courtship and male display and one of the primary reasons for this was that young people were distanced from the parental gaze.[55] Teenagers viewed the arcades as entertaining and exciting venues, and the original juke boxes were tied in with these feelings. People who were teenagers in the 1940s and 1950s regularly cite amusement arcades as the places where they heard their first juke box and they would gather round the machines in groups. Interviewee Dave Fagan recalls that the arcades were 'where the juke boxes were, and you always used to get a crowd round the juke box, boys and girls, all stand round the juke box. They used to sort of make a beeline for it.' In Manchester:

> the first memory I've got of an amusement arcade was. … I was about fourteen and a half … we used to go to a dancehall in Manchester called the Plaza and they used to have dancing, but not to records it was to a band. I mean the band played popular songs but it was not what you'd class as rock and roll, you know real rock and roll or anything. I mean just for an example, they'd play the Ballad of Davy Crockett which was out in the charts at the time and things like that. And what we used to do, we used to get a pass out from this dancehall, and you could get a pass out from 7.30 to 9.30 or something and we used to go a few doors away from the dance place at the Plaza. There used to be an amusement arcade, we used to go in there to listen to the juke box in between the dance.[56]

Blackpool played a prominent role in disseminating popular culture and bringing popular music to young ears and here Barry Stott remembers the arcades as being 'magical':

> All the slot machines were really exciting. You wanted to go on them all, but if you'd only twopence, you walked around for an hour or so and then chose what to spend your money on. To go on a juke box would be threepence in those days for one record. You had to really choose your record very carefully because you wouldn't have the money for more than maybe one and you'd hope other people would put money in and listen to their records first.[57]

As youth venues included more and more milk bars and cafés containing juke boxes so the social needs that had been catered for by amusement arcades were transferred to the youth café. This change in social space inevitably attracted comment. On the whole contemporary intellectual observation positively appraised youth cafés for providing much-needed social space. Fyvel wrote glowingly on the positive aspects of what he saw as a new 'café society'. Although his conclusions were 'not meant to be expert and exhaustive', his descriptions are unusually extensive and highlight the importance of juke box music to teenagers. The new cafés provided 'an atmosphere of garish gaiety, warm coffee steam, contemporary décor, …

[where] the noise of the juke box seems to have become for many young people an antidote against the emptiness of their lives'.[58]

For Fyvel urban life in Britain before 1950 did not provide the facilities to satisfy youth's social needs. The new 'café society' provided a space where teenagers could come and socialise, listen to music and find identity. They could turn up

> when they feel the need for gregariousness and for places where they could come together informally, to meet the opposite sex, to drift, to experiment, to feel their own way towards adult life, and this without supervision from their elders.
> ... the average little café answers their demands ... there may be music, and above all the ordinary café is a small enough place for a group of young people to be able to regard it as 'theirs'. When a bloke goes to the same café every night, well, I mean he's known – he's somebody.[59]

Gerge Melly is another positive commentator whose retrospective observations, like Fyvel's, are drawn from a London experience. He wrote that the coffee bars were 'the first exclusive teenage meeting-places. A nation-wide network of cells where, above the fierce gurgling and hissing of the Gaggia machine, the secret codes and passwords were formulated.'[60] Youth cafés provided a similar function across Britain but the 'Gaggia' coffee machines were expensive and, like juke boxes, probably worth more than the rest of the contents of the café. They were uncommon in the north of England outside the cosmopolitan city centres.

Ethnographic research by Pearl Jephcott from 1954 observed the milk bars of the Robin Hood area of Nottingham and noted that they were somewhere that her young respondents could find their own social space. In this area there were 'half a dozen cafés of the shake-and-cake brand. Cliques of boys and girls frequent their own particular cafe and some of the boys always spend the dead hour between Sunday dinner and [the] five o' clock picture queue in one or other of them.'[61] Youth cafés could provide a sense of identity stemming from this 'own space': 'Sometimes a set of friends could be identified as the idle but vigilant little group which haunted a particular spot, a corner doorway of a juke-drenched milk bar.'[62] Jephcott's, Fyvel's and Melly's views are clear and stand in stark contrast to those of their contemporary cultural commentator, Richard Hoggart. Though Hoggart noted the same functions of the youth café (that of providing social space and popular music) writing from his experiences in England's north, Hoggart voiced current fears of the uptake of

American mass-cultural influences and was apparently unsympathetic to the new cultural needs of post-war British youth. He further defined the milk bar and explained that his comments were not about 'those milk-bars which are really quick-service cafés where one may have a meal more quickly than in a café with table service. I have in mind rather the kind of milk-bar – there is one in almost every northern town with more than, say, fifteen thousand inhabitants – which has become the regular evening rendezvous of some of the young men.'[63] In his section on the 'Juke-Box Boys' he expressed strong criticism of perceived American influences in youth culture and café décor and observed that they were predominantly places where young men met:

> Girls go to some … [but] most of the customers are boys aged between fifteen and twenty, with drape suits, picture ties and an American slouch. Most of them cannot afford a succession of milk shakes, and make cups of tea serve for an hour or two whilst – and this is their main reason for coming – they put copper after copper into the mechanical record-player. … the 'nickelodeon' is allowed to blare out so that the noise would be sufficient to fill a good-sized ballroom rather than a converted shop in the high street. The young men waggle one shoulder or stare, as desperately as Humphrey Bogart, across the tubular chairs.[64]

These views, however, were not culturally dominant; indeed, a more negotiated attitude towards young people, youth cafés and juke boxes was more common. The mass-tabloid *Daily Mirror*, for instance, maintained a positive attitude towards teenagers and reported in 1955 on a 'Teen Canteen' that claimed to be Britain's first 'Teddy Boys-only' café. Situated at 'London's Elephant and Castle, birthplace of the Teddy gangs' it contained a 'rainbow-coloured juke-box' where 'youths with Slim Jim ties beat time on the table with their combs'. The teen canteen was an example of regeneration in run-down areas: 'in a derelict eating-room facing a bombed site [it was an] oasis of colour and light for the lads in grimy St Georges Road. … It's as gay and modern as any Mayfair coffee bar.' It was established to attract the 'hundreds of teenagers' who did not go to youth clubs and who had nowhere to go before the Teen Canteen. Jimmy, a brewery worker of sixteen, was asked what he did previously and he replied, 'hung around. We'd walk up "West" to the Strand and hang around. Sometimes we'd go to the South Bank and hang around.'[65]

The youth café became widespread and socially important in the 1950s. Brian Jackson reveals a teenage coffee bar, the 'Santa Maria', as being central to the Huddersfield schoolgirl social scene, where the girls and young workers socialised. There were American-style influences such as 'blue neon'[66] and young people mixed, disregarding occupational and class barriers:

> Four or five fifth-form girls ... turn off for the Santa Maria – a teenage coffee bar. Bright blue neon lights, already lit, point the way up a disused yard between the shoe shops. Girls from Glossop Road, St John's, Aggridge and Park End secondary modern schools will soon be at the 'Santa', together with the odd office junior slipping in for ten minutes instead of delivering letters – and then, after five o'clock, boys from the mills and engineering works.[67]

There was a class barrier that some grammar school girls were reluctant to cross. In this respect, 'Many of the older girls ... would have delighted in a kind of superior coffee bar life, but not for anything would they have turned off into the "Santa Maria"'.[68]

Young people wanted their own space and used youth cafés as alternatives to the unwelcoming, older-generation-dominated public houses. Though exceptions did exist, pubs on the whole did not house juke boxes, were not places where teenagers wanted to socialise and did not welcome young people. The 1958 case in Rochdale showed that they were not seen as suitable places for juke box music.[69] In Birmingham the 'number of boys and girls who mention a visit to a public house' was 'extremely small';[70] and Colin MacInnes, eleven years later, simply maintained of youth that they 'don't drink' and that this had 'thus created another industry, that of the non-alcoholic beverage'.[71]

Nonetheless, there was some public concern about teenage drinking which was not necessarily in pubs. A 1955 survey by the Economic Research Council[72] asked 'Do teen-agers spend too much on drink?' and concluded that teenage drunkenness might have been responsible for illegitimate babies and violent crimes by boys aged between seventeen and twenty. The tone of the feature was softened, however, by comments from Salford's Chief Constable: 'It is our experience that far more immorality among young people comes from milk bars than from pubs. My officers know that dances and milk bars, where the girls and boys gather, are the place where they tend to go astray.'[73] A front-page report the following week revealed Government concern over 'a marked increase in drunkenness' among young people;[74] and in September because of a 'Flaw in the Law', under-eighteens had been obtaining drinks at town hall dances.[75]

Although oral testimony and written evidence suggests it was widely ignored, the law prohibited young people under the age of eighteen from buying alcohol. The main barriers to teenage use of public houses, however, were more tied up with generational and cultural issues. In the late 1940s and 1950s teenagers perceived pubs as old fashioned, lacklustre and dreary, and frequented by old men playing outdated pub games.[76] They were not distinguished as entertainment places for young people who, for their part, avoided them for their 'older generation' connotations and because the under-eighteens were unlikely to be served. The main brewers did not attempt to change this image until many years later. Indeed, modernity and change were resisted, with juke boxes not becoming widespread in pubs until the 1960s. The milk and snack bars with their juke boxes were seen as modern and glamorous by comparison. Juke boxes targeted the 'teens and twenties', an age band that sat uneasily with the public house customer. Some pubs in Manchester in the early 1950s, however, did seek music licences for juke boxes. In one case 'it was submitted that the music played by the juke boxes was an inducement to the public to visit licensed premises'.[77]

Public houses were socially inhibiting for young men and women who might want to assess their romantic possibilities. They were places whose primary function was to provide space for men to drink alcohol:

> To be sure, there were pubs, but it is probably time that the brewers' legend of the public house as a modern community centre was done away with. By today the majority of public houses have become little more than commercialised outlets for a few multi-million brewery combines, ... The pub was not a place to which a young man ordinarily took his girl.
>
> Youths of today who believe themselves mature at sixteen or seventeen are put off by licensing restrictions and the fact that they cannot take their girls to public bars. In most pubs they are not welcome in groups and the pub is not the place for their kind of noise, which is connected with the world of juke boxes and 'pop' records.[78]

Growing up in Manchester, Terry Mitchell recalls of his friends that they

> quite obviously didn't go to pubs because we were too young. But even in those times, in that sort of area, pub going was not a particularly social or sociable activity. Pubs had a myriad of different rooms ... the tap room for the workman in his working clothes, a saloon bar or the snug or whatever where anyone who ventured forth, generally older ones, would go.[79]

And Laura Dowding, who lived in east Lancashire, notes that pubs were not places for young women to visit:

I can't remember anybody going in a pub. In fact my friends have said none of them went in a pub before they were of age unless it was for a wedding, and then they went in the back room. But under age certainly wasn't a thing that happened. So the clientele in pubs … yes you'd get some attracting the twenty-year-olds that era group kind of thing … eighteen to twenty, but it was always mixed. I can't remember a pub that just catered for the younger generation.[80]

In London it was less socially proscribed for young women to drink in pubs. Jephcott connected an increase in young women drinking in pubs with relatively high wages for women after the war and suggested that 'young people who are earning "the big money" do not like the idea of having money and not spending it'. She also drew attention to some of the problems identified with increased drinking: 'More boys and girls are going into public-houses now than before the war, and drinking adds to the difficulties that may arise in their relationships with each other.'[81] In Huddersfield pub visits were uncommon for Jackson's schoolgirls, who did go into pubs but saw this as being a daring gesture and not a regular activity: 'a little frightened and quite illegally, they explore the pubs.'[82]

Over the period 1945 to 1960 youth cafés housing juke boxes entered the mainstream of British cultural life and were generally welcomed by most sections of society. Some of these, like milk and temperance bars, had been present in the inter-war years but in the post-war period, in parallel with a general expansion of the catering trade, their numbers increased dramatically and they began to house juke boxes. By 1960, despite a confusing legal situation regarding music licensing, the youth café had become an inescapable part of British towns and cities. These cafés have since entered popular memory as a key feature of the period.

Notes

1 Joan N. Marks, *Café and Milk Bar Catering* (London: Heywood & Co., 1952), p. 6.
2 Juke boxes were invented after the law was written. Several companies, inventors and designers claim to have produced the first juke box in the first quarter of the twentieth century: see Frank Adams, *Jukeboxes 1900–1992: Obscure, Mysterious and Innovative American Jukeboxes*, Vol. 1 (Seattle: AMR Publishing, 1992), pp. 9–30.
3 Copyright Act 1911, pp. 183–4.
4 WF, 11 January 1958.
5 WF, 17 September 1955, p. 25.

6 WF, 7 August 1957, p. 1.

7 Lancashire Record Office refs: PSBL 9/1 and PSK 7/2.

8 'The Top Twenty Come to the Public Bar: Remorseless March of the Juke Box', *Manchester Guardian* (30 November 1956).

9 WF, 29 March 1958: A report on a Phonograph Operators Association meeting.

10 See chapter 1.

11 H.D. Wilcox, *Report on Juvenile Delinquency* (London: Falcon Press, 1949), pp. 12–13.

12 'Juke Box Needs a Licence / Judgement in Test Case', WF, 7 October 1950, p. 1.

13 WF, 7 October 1950, p. 1.

14 Taking the case of Lancaster as an example, the first café to receive a music licence was the Harlequin Espresso Café in 1956, a further three were issued for cafés in 1957, 1958 and 1959. From the licensing records they all appear to have been granted without comment, controversy or fuss. Lancashire Records office ref. PSLA 2/3 1949–58.

15 'Juke box Firm's New Policy is "Sell" Now', WF, 25 January 1958, p. 33.

16 President of the Board of Trade, Mr Heathcoat Amory quoting Mr Norman Ditchburn in WF, 17 July 1954, p. 26.

17 'Rochdale Ban On All Forms of Automatic Music', WF, 13 September 1958, p. 35.

18 WF, 13 September 1958, p. 35.

19 Rochdale's recreational facilities and local attitudes towards them have received some academic attention concerning the years leading up to World War II: see chapter 1; Wild, 'Recreation in Rochdale'.

20 WF, 13 September 1958, p. 35.

21 WF, 13 September 1958, p. 35.

22 WF, 23 May 1953, p. 1.

23 WF, 29 March 1958, p. 34.

24 WF, 23 May 1953 p. 1.

25 Bingo Beaufort, 'Britain's Juke Industry Takes Shape', WF, 27 July 1957, p. 31.

26 Beaufort, WF, 27 July 1957, p. 31.

27 Amusement arcades in this setting were less exciting to visit than might be imagined, often being no bigger or more glamorous than a small shop. See for example images from Manchester Central Library, Archives and Local Studies.

28 See chapter 1; WF, 6 December 1958, p. 36; Krivine, *Juke Box Saturday Night*, p. 128 estimates fewer than 100 machines before 1938.

29 'The Top Twenty Come To The Public Bar: Remorseless rise of the juke box', *Manchester Guardian* (30 November 1956).

30 From 1935 the National Milk Publicity Council promoted milk as a healthy drink as part of regional publicity campaigns that included 'Milk Weeks'. For

these the media were coordinated using 'posters, window displays, house to house distribution of leaflets, local press publicity and the establishment of Milk Bars. By 1936, there were more Milk Bars, in Liverpool, Hastings, and other towns, especially at seaside places where the ice cream market was also attractive.' Alan Jenkins, *Drinka Pinta: The Story of Milk and the Industry that Serves it* (London: Heinemann, 1970), pp. 105–6.

31 Joan N. Marks, *Café and Milk Bar Catering* (London: Heywood & Co., 1952), p. 6.

32 *Milk Trade Gazette*, 16 April 1938, p. 3, in Fowler, *First Teenagers*, p. 108.

33 E.E.F. Colam, *Practical Milk Bar Operation* (London: 1946); Marks, *Café and Milk Bar*.

34 Marks, *Café and Milk Bar*, p. 105.

35 Marks, *Café and Milk Bar*, pp. 103–4.

36 George Orwell, *Coming up for Air* (London: Penguin, 1986), p. 22 (first published 1939).

37 Marks, *Café and Milk Bar*, p. 104.

38 Cecil Chisholm (ed.), *Marketing Survey of the United Kingdom* (London: Business Publications Ltd, 1951), p. 13.

39 *Lancaster and District Directory 1956–1957* (Carlisle: County Publicity Ltd), p. 314.

40 Chisholm, *Marketing Survey*, pp. 17, 126, 203, 221.

41 See for example images from Manchester Central Library, Archives and Local Studies.

42 T.R. Fyvel, *The Insecure Offenders: Rebellious Youth in the Welfare State* (Harmondsworth: Penguin, 1963), p. 70.

43 Harry Isaacs, b. 1938, interviewed 27 July 2001, tape ref: T.02.

44 See www.sarsaparilla.co.uk/bar.html (acessed on 24 April 2003) and www.nicholsplc.co.uk/hist/vimhist.htm (accessed on 11 April 2003).

45 'Court Action over Juke Box', WF, 3 July 1948.

46 Isaacs, tape ref: T.02.

47 Terry Mitchell, b. 1940, interviewed 2 November 2001, tape ref: T.06.

48 Isaacs, tape ref: T.02.

49 Barry Stott, b. 1941, interviewed 11 July 2001, tape ref: T.01.

50 Adrian Maddox, *Classic Cafes* (London: Black Dog Publishing, 2003), p. 82.

51 Marks, *Café & Milk Bar Catering*.

52 Valerie Tome, 'Trouble at the Copper Kettle', BBC Radio North, Produced by Amanda Mares, 1994.

53 Terry Mitchell, Tape ref: T.06.

54 Keith Waterhouse, *Billy Liar* (Harmondsworth: Penguin, 1962), p. 44.

55 Research carried out by Pearl Jephcott in early 1940s London suggested that boys went to arcades primarily to use the machines and when girls went it was to mix with boys rather than from an interest in the mechanical amusements. Jephcott, *Girls Growing Up*, p. 124.

56 Dave Fagan, b. 1941, interviewed 22 October 2001, Tape ref: T.03.

57 Barry Stott, tape ref: T.01.
58 Fyvel, *Insecure Offenders*, p. 67.
59 Fyvel, *Insecure Offenders*, pp. 68–9.
60 Melly, *Revolt Into Style*, p. 48.
61 Jephcott, *Some Young People*, p. 34.
62 Jephcott, *Some Young People*, p. 89.
63 Richard Hoggart, *The Uses of Literacy* (Harmondsworth: Penguin, 1960), p. 248.
64 Hoggart, *Uses of Literacy*, p. 248. 'Nickelodeon' is an incorrect word for juke box or automatic phonograph.
65 Tony Miles, 'There's hope among the teacups in … The Teen Canteen', DM, 5 July 1955, p. 9.
66 Actually Europeans pioneered neon tubes – the first appeared in London's Leicester Square in 1913. See Rayner Banham, 'Mediated Environments *or*: You can't build that here', in *Superculture: American Popular Culture and Europe*, ed. by C.W.E. Bigsby (London: Paul Elek, 1975), pp. 69–82.
67 Brian Jackson, *Working Class Community* (London: Routledge & Kegan Paul, 1968), p. 139.
68 Jackson, *Working Class Community*, p. 150.
69 WF, 13 September 1958, p. 35.
70 Bryan H. Reed (director), *Eighty Thousand Adolescents: A Study of Young People in the City of Birmingham by the Staff and Students of Westhill Training College for the Edward Cadbury Charitable Trust* (London: Allen & Unwin, 1950), p. 39.
71 Colin MacInnes, *England, Half English* (London: Macgibbon & Kee, 1961), p. 58.
72 Conducted on behalf of the temperance organisation – The United Kingdom Alliance.
73 DM, 21 July 1955, p. 8.
74 DM, 29 July 1955, p. 1.
75 DM, 3 September 1955, p. 8.
76 Retrospective academic accounts of the situation regarding pubs include Dave Harker, *One for the Money: Politics and Popular Song* (London: Hutchinson, 1980), p. 73 and Peter Wicke, *Rock Music: Culture, Aesthetics and Sociology* (Cambridge: Cambridge University Press, 1990), pp. 55–9.
77 WF, 9 August 1952, 'Automatic Gossip by Edward Graves', p. 22.
78 Fyvel, *Insecure Offenders*, p. 69.
79 Terry Mitchell, tape ref: T.06.
80 Laura Dowding, b. 1939, interviewed 18 November 2001, tape ref: T.07.
81 Jephcott, *Rising Twenty*, p. 136.
82 Jackson, *Working Class Community*, pp. 139 and 141.

Conclusion

Juke box Britain set out to explore and examine the influence of American popular culture on British teenagers between the approximate dates of 1945 and 1960. It has done this through a variety of disciplinary approaches that include cultural studies and cultural, social, design and economic histories. *Juke box Britain* provides a reassessment of the subject of style and youth culture in the first fifteen years after World War II. Its findings show that the period was not, as has been commonly thought, one where young people significantly adopted American popular cultural influences, except, that is, in the area of popular music.

I chose for my research the general areas of design, music and social history. Youth culture has been an exciting field of study because it is enlivened by the spirit and enthusiasm of the teenage years, and this would be the case in any time period. All of the people I formally interviewed, and those to whom I talked informally, who were teenagers in the late 1940s and 1950s, conveyed the impression that it was a magical and thrilling point in their lives. It is possible that some of their youthful *joie de vivre* has enthused parts of the book.

Future researchers might chose to employ more theoretical approaches to music and youth culture and I would direct them toward Dick Hebdige, Sarah Thornton, Andy Bennett, Paul Willis and Matt Hills.[1] Also of great importance to this debate is the vast body of work that came out of the Centre for Contemporary Cultural Studies (CCCS) in the late 1960s and 1970s under the directorships of Richard Hoggart and Stuart Hall.[2] Hall and Jefferson's *Resistance Through Rituals*, though routinely criticised, is particularly relevant.[3]

Before I conducted this extensive research I had assumed that the period was especially glamorous and exciting for young people because of increasing popular cultural influences from America that revolutionised the visual and aural world for teenagers. What I uncovered, however, was a more humdrum way of life in which young people found their 'kicks'; the legacy of which I now view as quaint.

Much of the research has been involved with a study of juke boxes and their style influences, the music that was played on them, the teenagers who used them and the venues where they were sited. Young people's positive receptions of American cultural influences in this period occurred against a backdrop of established cultural attitudes that were very often wary of, but not substantially antagonistic to, American influences.

Import of American popular culture into Britain since at least the beginning of the twentieth century was far from being a cultural 'take-over'. There was no widespread defence of 'traditional' culture against imported American mass or popular culture, which had, in fact, been the subject of wide popular appeal in Britain. Indeed, mass enthusiasm for American popular music, disseminated through sheet music and gramophone records, for example, was well established before the end of World War II. The war aided this musical dissemination as large numbers of US troops and ancillary workers were stationed in Britain from the beginning of 1942. In Blackpool, for instance, troops from a number of countries as well as the local population were entertained by British dance bands playing American tunes. It is a key point of this book that British renditions of American popular music as well as British cultural receptions in British venues negotiated the American product creating musical modifications.

Juke boxes were a commodity that contained many peculiarly American popular-cultural associations. The juke boxes that were imported into Britain from America in the few years before the outbreak of World War II in 1939 were predominantly taken up by amusement arcade and fairground operators. This did not indicate, however, a change of use for juke boxes in Britain compared to America, but it did point to a change in their reception. Juke boxes in Britain were absorbed into a tradition of cheap mechanical entertainments enjoyed by the working classes. Before World War II juke boxes received little attention outside of the mechanical entertainments industry.

Between the end of World War II and June 1959 Britain was cut off from imports of American 'luxury' goods, and a British juke box industry (for which manufacturing began in Blackpool in 1945) developed in its own particularly British way. A detailed investigation into the British juke box industry in this period reveals that, even with this archetypal example of Americana, direct American style-influences were very few.

Visual comparisons between American and British juke boxes between 1945 and 1954 make clear that the dominant American styles of industrial Art Deco and Streamline as seen in the Filben Maestro and the Wurlitzer 1015 (Plates 3 and 4) did not influence designs in Britain. Here juke box design followed its own distinctive path as seen in the Hawtin/Ditchburn Music Makers and the Acadia Minstrel (Plate 2 and Figure 2.8). The British industry developed independently of American design influences for four main reasons: firstly, direct imports of American juke boxes were prohibited by law; secondly, restricted supplies of raw materials like wood for the cabinets meant that more accessible materials like aluminium were used instead; thirdly, Britain's economy was exhausted from the war effort and production costs had to be kept to a minimum; and fourthly, flamboyance was seen by the design establishment and much of society as being in bad taste.

American design influences did, however, enter the British market following licensed juke box manufacturing by Automatic Musical Instruments (AMI) in 1954 through Balfour Engineering in Essex. These BAL-AMIs (Plates 5–7), though American-designed and containing features such as illuminated cabinets in a variety of finishes, had comparatively small record selections (no more than 80) and the styles were more subdued than more mainstream American models of the period. The output of the BAL-AMI factory was a prime example of the design mediation process. American-designed machines built in Britain were made to sell in a British economic climate that also had less flamboyant tastes.

American and European juke boxes did enter Britain later in the decade, introducing new styles. By this time, however, American juke box design had become more subdued, losing most of its Art Deco and Streamline influences, and the look of American and European juke boxes was remarkably similar. If we compare the American 'Wurlitzer 1900' and 'Seeburg 100 EL' with the West German 'Fanfare' (Figure 2.11), for example, there is no significant difference in style between the models. By the time that American imports directly entered the British market following the resumption of Sterling convertibility in June 1959 there was little to choose between the look of American- and European-styled machines.

Juke boxes helped the spread of undiluted forms of American popular music by circumventing broadcasting restrictions imposed by the BBC. The BBC generally resisted broadcasting popular or mass-cultural music on ideological grounds. The reasons for this are to be found in its past, where a remit for public service broadcasting was interpreted as a responsibility to educate the listeners in what the BBC perceived as 'good music' of a high cultural value, which was inevitably classical.

Parallels can be drawn with the role that juke boxes played in America whereby they bypassed the racist restrictions of white-owned radio stations to spread black music across the country. In Britain the American music played on juke boxes was unmediated just as black music was in America. The venues for juke box reception were, however, British in nature and subject to regional differences. The look of juke boxes was less flamboyant and the young listeners had a social and economic status that was particular to the UK.

Teenagers in Britain, contrary to popular belief, were not a uniquely post-war phenomenon. Subcultural groups and styles had been part of working-class youth, in an urban setting, since at least the late nineteenth century. Research by David Fowler, for example, has made clear that there was a distinctive teenage market and identity in the 1920s and 1930s. Following World War II, however, social conditions changed for young people who, in general throughout the period, left school at fifteen and entered paid employment, where they enjoyed increasing levels of discretionary expenditure.

Teenager definitions vary and, as my concern has been mainly with juke box users, I have interpreted the teenager in a broad way that includes the age bands of young people who enjoyed juke box music; what the *World's Fair* called 'teens and twenties'. There is evidence from *World's Fair* that the age band for juke box listeners widened, especially toward the over-twenties, steadily through the 1945 to 1960 period.[4]

Juke boxes allowed young people to satisfy their need to socialise and communicate with their peers; they provided a central and visible place for communication and identification and were a point of intersection between American popular culture and the British teenage audience. Here regional interpretations were made and American and American-style music was absorbed into a mainstream, predominantly working-class and British youth culture. Teenage receptions of American popular culture after the war necessarily mediated its cultural impact in areas like music, design and fashion.

Because of the process of accelerated social and cultural change brought about by World War II and due to the social, cultural, educational and economic changes affecting young people in the post-war period a wide 'generation gap' was reported. This led to a perception, far from the truth, of a rebellious younger generation.

British youth culture developed regionally as well as nationally. The strength of regional identity, however, though strong, was arguably less after than before the war as transport and communication improved through the 1950s, and this is an area that should prove fruitful for future researchers.

Although, for the most part, middle- and working-class teenagers visited the same venues, where they enjoyed juke box music together, there were social divisions that were difficult to bridge. The effect of children being segregated into grammar and secondary modern schools at the age of eleven added to these barriers. On the whole, middle-class youth, although leaving school at a similar age earned less in the workplace due to training on the job and were subject to more parental control than their working-class compatriots. Popular contemporary arguments, consolidated in the views of economist Mark Abrams, claiming that youth was becoming classless because they were becoming more affluent, are hard to sustain.[5] Life style and life chances are more significant factors in constructing class inequalities.[6]

Although in its first recorded incidences the Teddy Boy style of the mid-1950s was eye catching and flamboyant, the move toward expression in style by young men was not a new phenomenon but part of an historic continuum of youthful male display. From its first sightings in the south and east of London, in 1952 and 1953, the Teddy Boy style became popular among young men as it spread from London to the rest of Britain. In this period the Teddy Boy, following a murder on Clapham Common in London, became a 'folk devil' for some sections of the national and local press. This led, through other reported incidents and scapegoating over the next five years, particularly after alleged rioting following the release in 1956 of the film *Rock Around the Clock*, into a media-led 'moral panic'. Much of the press coverage, however, was more sympathetic towards Teddy Boys and teenagers in general than has been recognised within cultural studies. The *Daily Mirror*, for example, maintained an indulgent attitude toward the Teddy Boy phenomenon noting, as this book maintains, that Teddy Boys posed no real threat to the established order.

There is evidence that the Teddy Boy phenomenon spread from this country to mainland Europe. Fyvel looks at this movement in his chapter 'Europe: the Bourgeois Resistance' and notes that '[I]n different forms –

and in different degrees – the Teddy boy problem and a serious increase in youthful lawlessness have in recent years affected a large part of the world. Most Western European countries as well as Communist Eastern Europe, or, further afield, Japan, have all had their share of it…'[7] As this Continental and global discussion falls outside of *Juke box Britain*'s research area it is yet another region of study that could be profitably taken up by other researchers.

The Teddy Boy regalia was a fusion of British and American influences and signifiers and, as the fashion spread across the UK, these meanings changed as the style fused further, adapting to local conditions. Through this process the strength of its initial rebellious meaning was diluted as young men and boys, often still at school, would adopt and often adapt perhaps one or two significant parts of the dress, say the 'Tony Curtis' hairstyle or 'drainpipe' trousers. In this context of style dispersion the Teddy Boy fashion could no longer connote the levels of perceived violence and 'gang' mentality attributed to London's first expressions of the style. Like the juke box and youth café the Teddy Boy style was soon absorbed into British mainstream popular culture.

Young women's fashions over the same period were mediated through availability and the economic constraints of low incomes. The widespread use of home dressmaking meant that teenage girls could adapt dress patterns to take on board the style influences that were illustrated in magazines and the cinema. Mainstream styles were made individual as these fashion tips were adapted in the home. There is no convincing evidence to suggest that British teenagers wholeheartedly took on the American 'college girl' look in the post-war period.

Social researchers, with the notable exception of Pearl Jephcott, have generally ignored the teenage girl of the 1940s and 1950s. This is, perhaps, because their behaviour and style was not perceived as a threat to prevailing cultural values. Young women's styles have traditionally been drawn from the mainstream with non-confrontational modifications and this is one of the reasons why they were not perceived as a threat. There is evidence, however, of working-class women using 'consumer skills' in an original way, and more research could profitably be directed to this area. Toward the end of the 1950s members of the 'intelligent' and 'artistic' middle classes did, however, challenge accepted dress styles for young women and these can be seen in photographic records of, for example, CND (Campaign for Nuclear Disarmament) protests. These sartorial challenges were constructed by adopting alternative fashions that gave the impression of an unkempt or 'scruffy' appearance. Significant stylistic influences on this trend came from a Continental chic as depicted by Hollywood, and the stars Juliette Greco, Audrey Hepburn and Leslie Caron are good examples of individual influences.

There was a significant expansion of the British catering industry following World War II, and *Juke box Britain* charts the increase in small-scale catering establishments frequented by teenagers for which I have used the collective description of 'youth café'. Young people who might in previous times have congregated on street corners, 'monkey racks' and amusement arcades started to frequent the youth cafés where juke box music could be heard.

Juke boxes needed to be licensed by the PPL (Phonographic Performance Limited) and the PRS (Performing Rights Society) and were often the subject of the further restrictions of local by-laws requiring another licence issued by local Magistrates. The situation regarding by-laws meant that debates about the suitability or otherwise of siting juke boxes in youth cafés were conducted on a local level in Magistrates' courts. These discourses provide insight into some of the attitudes of the time towards perceptions of 'undesirable elements' and noise nuisances, as well as the more mundane considerations of fire and safety regulations.

Contemporary differences in British society were highlighted in the style and type of youth cafés, which were becoming more visible over the period. In the industrial northwest, which, for example, contained a range of venues like amusement arcades, temperance, milk, snack and coffee bars, imported design influences were limited and the cafés and décor may now be viewed as typically British and of the period. Those who visited them in their youth frequently remember these youth cafés vividly and are aware, in retrospect, that the décor appeared to be 'glamorous' only because of their limited expectations. The juke box, however, did provide a window to a glamorous, more American world through music largely unavailable on radio.

The youth cafés provided young people with their own space away from the parental gaze and the interference of well-meaning adults that was available through youth clubs and organisations like the Boy Scouts and Girl Guides. It was in the youth cafés that they could behave like teenagers in a world of imagined sophistication. Indeed, by 1960 the youth café had become part of the British social fabric and retail infrastructure synonymous with the period's 'way of life'.

Due to inevitable time constraints *Juke box Britain* has necessarily neglected several important areas for research. Although the background to the Americanisation debate among British intellectuals was discussed in chapter 2 a reappraisal might certainly reveal more high-profile pro-American attitudes. The claimed intellectual jeremiad in Britain against the perceived detrimental influence of American culture need not, as is so often stated, have started with Matthew Arnold.[8] Work by Lesley Johnson, for example, has shown that a thorough trawl through the writings of nineteenth- and twentieth-century thinkers can reveal previously unnoticed attitudes.[9] John Stuart Mill, for instance, has written profusely on the subject of America mostly in response to Tocqueville's essay 'Democracy in America' from 1835.[10]

The regionality of American popular culture's reception by young people in Britain is one that could be pursued much further. Some regions, however, should prove to be particularly fruitful for the cultural historian: Northern Ireland and Scotland spring to mind in both their urban and rural aspects because they would present a non-English view. Oral archives, and I have consulted several,[11] that exist across Britain could be added to in respect of the 'rock 'n' roll era, whilst the people who experienced its effects are still alive and willing to share their recollections.

Ethnographic research could usefully be extended further to include the experiences of the two million or so young men who were 'called up' into National Service between 1948 and 1960. The training camps where they were sent were places where attitudes and musical tastes from all over Britain mixed and were subsequently circulated to local populations. This mixing process would have direct relevance to, for example, popular music's dissemination and the spread of Teddy Boy styles.

Comparisons of America's reception in Europe and the rest of the world could shed more light on the creation of post-war youth identities through fusions of imported and existing design influences. Everywhere that the American military went in World War II, for example, they brought their mass-cultural trappings like chewing gum, nylon stockings, Lucky Strike cigarettes and, of course, juke boxes and 'hot' dance music. World War II, then, was a global trades exhibition for American mass-cultural products. The level of acceptance and rejection of what in 1951 Sam Aaronovitch called 'coca-colonization'[12] has provided much debate, and interested readers should consult Richard Pells, Rob Kroes, Bertrand Russell, Duncan Webster, George McKay and C.W.E. Bigsby to name but a few.[13]

Juke box Britain has explored the extent of the assimilation of American design influences in Britain in the period 1945 to 1960 with particular reference to juke boxes, contemporary popular music, the young people who played and enjoyed the juke box music, and the youth cafés where they would congregate and socialise. Moreover, it has taken a detailed look at the meanings and spread of youthful male flamboyance in the Teddy Boy styles of the mid-1950s as well as teenage girls' and young women's dress styles. It has also examined an evident regionality within youth experience. *Juke box Britain* concludes that imported American and mass-cultural influences were not part of a cultural domination or infringement but were influences that combined, in varying degrees, with existing dominant British regional styles to create style fusions that may now be viewed as distinctly British and of the period.

Notes

1 Dick Hebdige, *Subculture: The Meaning of Style* (London: Methuen, 1979); Sarah Thornton, *Club Cultures: Music, Media and Subcultural Capital* (Cambridge: Polity Press, 1995); Andy Bennett, *Cultures of Popular Music* (Buckingham, Philadelphia: Open University Press, 2001); Paul Willis, *Profane Culture* (London: Routledge & Kegan Paul, 1978); Matt Hills, *Fan Cultures* (London: Routledge, 2002).

2 Richard Hoggart was appointed Director in 1964 and Stuart Hall in 1968.

3 Stuart Hall and Tony Jefferson (eds), *Resistance Through Rituals* (London: Hutchinson, 1976).

4 WF, 19 October 1957, p. 31.

5 See Mark Abrams, *The Newspaper Reading Public of Tomorrow* (London: Oldhams, 1964).

6 Graham Murdock and Robin McCron, 'Youth and Class: The Career of a Confusion', in *Working Class Youth Culture*, ed. by G. Mungham and G. Pearson (London: Routledge & Kegan Paul, 1976), pp. 10–26.

7 Fyvel, *Insecure Offender*, p. 138.

8 Matthew Arnold, *Culture and Anarchy* (London: Cambridge University Press, 1960), first published 1868.

9 Lesley Johnson, *The Cultural Critics: From Matthew Arnold to Raymond Williams* (London: Routledge and Kegan Paul, 1979).

10 Alexis de Tocqueville, 'Democracy in America' translated by Henry Reeve in 2 volumes (London: Saunders and Otley, 1835). John Stuart Mill, 'De Tocqueville on Democracy in America', [I] and [II], 'State of Society in America' in John Stuart Mill, *Essays on Politics and Society* (London: Routledge and Kegan Paul, 1977), pp. 47–90, 153–204, 91–116.

11 For example, the North West Sound Archive in Clitheroe, Lancashire and Manchester's Jewish Museum.

12 Sam Aaronovitch, 'The American Threat to British Culture' in *The American Threat to British Culture*, Communist Party of Great Britain, National Cultural Committee Conference 1951 (London: Arena, 1952), pp. 3–22, p. 13.

13 Richard Pells, *Not Like US: How Europeans Have loved, Hated, and Transformed American Culture since World War II* (New York: Basic Books, 1997); Rob Kroes et al (eds), *Cultural Transmissions and Receptions: American Mass Culture in Europe* (Amsterdam: Vu University Press, 1993); Bertrand Russell et al., *The Impact of America on European Culture* (Boston: Beacon Press, 1951); Duncan Webster, *Looka Yonda: The Imaginary America of Populist Culture* (London: Routledge, 1988); George McKay (ed.), *Yankee Go Home (& Take Me With You)* (Sheffield: Sheffield Academic Press, 1997); C.W.E. Bigsby (ed.), *Superculture: American Popular Culture and Europe* (London: Paul Elek, 1975).

Bibliography

Abbreviations

WF   *World's Fair*
DM   *Daily Mirror*

Primary sources

Oral testimony: references T.01 to T.07 interviewed by Adrian Horn

Tape Ref: T.01
Informant: Barry Stott
Year of Birth: 1941
Location: Informant's Home, Thornton Cleveleys, Lancashire
Date: 11 July 2001

Tape Ref: T.02
Informant: Harry Isaacs
Year of Birth: 1934
Location: Informant's Home, Bury, Lancashire
Date: 27 July 2001

Tape Ref: T.03
Informant: Dave Fagan
Year of Birth: 1941
Location: Informant's Home, Rhodes Middleton, Manchester
Date: 22 October 2001

Tape Ref: T.04
Informant: John Farmery
Year of Birth: 1939
Location: Informant's Home, Longridge, Lancashire
Date: 29 October 2001

Tape Ref: T.05
Informant: Jim Cheetham

Year of Birth: 1929
Location: Informant's Home, Hale, Cheshire
Date: 2 November 2001

Tape Ref: T.06
Informant: Terry Mitchell
Year of Birth: 1940
Location: Informant's Home, Mobley, Cheshire
Date: 2 November 2001

Tape Ref: T.07
Informant: Laura Dowding
Year of Birth: 1939
Location: Informant's Home, Padiham, Lancashire
Date: 18 November 2001

Oral testimony from other sources
North West Sound Archive
Tape Ref: 2001.0723a
Informant: Gwynneth Broadbent
Year of Birth: 1938
Location: —
Date: 15 May 2001

University of Sussex
Tape Ref: 14: A: I, 14: A: ii
Informant: T. Web
Year of Birth: —
Location: Informant's Home, Portslade
Date: 15 March 1989

BBC Radio North
Programme: Trouble at the Copper Kettle
Informant: Valerie Tome
Location: —
Producer: Amanda Mares
Broadcast: 1994

Manchester Jewish Museum
Tape Ref: MJM: T. 214
Informant: Benny Segal
Year of Birth: 1902
Location: —
Date: 23 June 1976

Archives

Blackpool Reference Library
Hulton Archive (now Getty Images)
Ilkley Public Library
Jack Hylton Archive, Lancaster University
Jewish Museum
Lancashire Records Office
Manchester Central Library
National Fairground Archive
NW Sound Archive
World's Fair, Oldham

Reports and surveys

Abrams, Mark, *The Teenage Consumer* (London: London Press Exchange, 1959).
Abrams, Mark *Teenage Consumer Spending in 1959 (part II): Middle Class and Working Class Boys and Girls* (London: London Press Exchange, 1961).
Abrams, Mark, *The Newspaper Reading Public of Tomorrow* (London: Oldhams, 1964).
Chisholm, Cecil (ed.), *Marketing Survey of the United Kingdom* (London: Business Publications Ltd, 1951).
Jephcott, Pearl, *Girls Growing Up* (London: Faber & Faber, 1942).
Jephcott, Pearl, *Rising Twenty* (London: Faber & Faber, 1948).
Jephcott, Pearl, *Some Young People* (London: Allen & Unwin, 1954).
Jephcott, Pearl, *Time of One's Own* (London: Oliver & Boyd, 1967).
Reed, Bryan H. (director), *Eighty Thousand Adolescents: A Study of Young People in the City of Birmingham by the Staff and Students of Westhill Training College for the Edward Cadbury Charitable Trust* (London: Allen & Unwin, 1950).
Report of the Committee on Broadcasting 1960 (presented June 1962) ix–x, p. 271.
Rowntree, B.S., *Poverty and Progress: A Second Social Survey of York* (London: Longmans, Green, 1941).
Rowntree, B.S. and Lavers, G.R., *English Life and Leisure: A Social Study* (London: Longmans, Greenman & Co., 1951).
Titmuss, Richard M., *Problems of Social Policy* (London, 1950).
Vaness, Thelma, *School Leavers: Their Aspirations and Expectations* (London: Methuen, 1962).
Wilcox, H.D., *Report on Juvenile Delinquency* (London: Falcon Press, 1949).
Wilkins, Leslie T., *Delinquent Generations* (London: Home Office, 1960).
Young, Michael and Willmott, Peter, *Family and Kinship in East London* [1957] (London: Routledge & Kegan Paul, 1986).

Secondary sources
National newspapers

Daily Mirror
Daily Mail
Daily Telegraph
News Chronicle
The Observer
Picture Post
The Times

Local newspapers

Blackpool Gazette and Herald
Evening Argus
Ilkley Gazette
Lancaster Guardian
London Evening Standard
Manchester Evening News
Manchester Guardian
Nottingham Journal

Periodicals

Billboard
Melody Maker
Milk Trade Gazette
New Musical Express
The Performer
Picture Post
World's Fair

Journals

Annals of the American Academy of Political and Social Science
The Architects' Journal
Architectural Association Quarterly
Camera Obscura
Economic History Review
Economy and Society
Educational Review
Employment and Productivity Gazette
Gender and History
History Workshop Journal
Howard Journal of Penology and Crime Prevention
International Economic Review
Journal of Design History
Journal of Popular Culture

Local Historian
Media, Culture and Society
New Left Review
New Society
Popular Music
Scottish Journal of Political Economy
Screen
Youth and Society

Directories

Lancaster and District Directory 1956–7 (Carlisle: County Publicity Ltd).
Lancaster, Morecambe and Suburban Directory 1934 (Lancaster: Frank N. Shires Ltd).
The North West Counties of England Trades' Directory 1955–56 (Manchester: Trades' Directories Ltd).

Novels

MacInnes, Colin, *Absolute Beginners* (Harmondsworth: Penguin, 1964).
Orwell, George, *Coming Up for Air* (London: Penguin, 1962).
Waterhouse, Keith, *Billy Liar* (Harmondsworth: Penguin, 1962).

Autobiographies

Greenwood, Jack, *Blackpool Entertains the Troops* (Clevelys: J. Greenwood, 1986).
Hiranandani, S, *Blackpool Memories: Early 1940's and Now* (Bolton: Stylus Press, 1991).
Roberts, Robert, *The Classic Slum: Salford Life in the First Quarter of the Century* (Manchester: University of Manchester Press, 1971).
Roberts, Robert, *A Ragged Schooling: Growing up in the Classic Slum* (Manchester University Press, 1976).

Pamphlets

Briggs, Asa, *Mass Entertainment: The Origins of a Modern Industry* (Adelaide: Griffin Press, 1960).
Communist Party of Great Britain. National Cultural Committee Conference 1951, *The American Threat to British Culture* (London: Arena, 1952).
Design Council, *Leisure in the Twentieth Century* (London: Design Council, 1977).
The Institute of Contemporary Arts, *The British Edge* (Boston: ICA, 1987).
Jefferson, Tony, *The 'Teds' – A Political Resurrection* (Centre for Contemporary Cultural Studies, University of Birmingham, April 1973).

Films and TV programmes

BBC, *Special Enquiry* no. 5: 'A Report for Television on Issues of National Importance'. 5. Leisure, 30 January 1953, commentator Robert Reid. Transcript from BBC Archives, Caversham Park, Reading, ref: T21–D421–17-218.
Brooks, Richard, *The Blackboard Jungle* (MGM, 1955).

Good, Jack, *6.5 Special* (BBC, 1957).

Katzman, Sam, *Rock Around The Clock* (Columbia, 1956).

Reisz, Karel, *We are the Lambeth Boys* (Graphic Films, for the Ford Motor Company, 1959).

Wilder, Billy, *Sabrina Fair* (Paramount, 1954).

Photographic essays

Ken Russell, *Photo Essay on London Teddy Girls* (www.teddygirl.co.uk).

Records

Berry, Chuck, *Maybelline* (Chess, 1955).

Haley, Bill, *(We're Gonna) Rock Around The Clock* (Brunswick, 1954).

Haley, Bill, *Shake Rattle and Roll* (Brunswick, 1954).

Lee, Brenda, *Sweet Nuthins* (Brunswick, 1960).

Martino, Al, *Here in My Heart* (Capitol, 1952).

Presley, Elvis, *That's All Right* (Sun, 1954).

Presley, Elvis, *Heartbreak Hotel* (HMV, 1956).

Books

Adams, Frank, *Rock-Ola Jukeboxes 1935–1989* (Seattle: AMR Publishing, 1983).

Adams, Frank, *Wurlitzer Jukeboxes 1934–1974* (Seattle: AMR Publishing, 1983).

Adams, Frank, *Rowe – AMI Jukeboxes 1927–1988* (Seattle: AMR Publishing, 1988).

Adams, Frank, *Jukeboxes 1900–1992: Obscure, Mysterious and Innovative American Jukeboxes*, Vol. 1 (Seattle: AMR Publishing, 1992).

Addison, Paul, *Now the War is Over: A Social History of Britain 1945–51* (London: BBC, 1985).

Almind, Gert J., *'Golden Age' Juke-Box Design: American Juke-Box Design Patents 1934–1951* (Denmark: Almind, 1994).

Arnold, Matthew, *Culture and Anarchy* (London: Cambridge University Press, 1960).

Ash, Juliet and Elizabeth Wilson (eds), *Chick Thrills: A Fashion Reader* (London: Pandora, 1992).

Banham, Mary et al. (eds), *A Critic Writes: Essays by Reyner Banham* (London: University of California Press, 1996).

Banham, Reyner, *Theory and Design in the First Machine Age* (London: The Architectural Press, 1960).

Barfe, Louis, *Where Have All the Good Times Gone? The Rise and Fall of the Record Industry* (London, Atlantic, 1988).

Barnard, Stephen, *On The Radio: Music Radio in Britain* (Milton Keynes: Open University Press, 1989).

Bayley, Stephen (ed.), *In Good Shape: Style in Industrial Products 1900–1960* (London: Design Council, 1979).

Bayley, S., Garner, P. and Sudjic, D., *Twentieth Century Style and Design* (London: Thames & Hudson, 1986).

Belson, W.A., *The Impact of Television: Methods and Findings in Program Research* (London: Crosby Lockwood, 1967).

Bennett, Tony, et al. (eds), *Popular Culture and Social Relations* (Milton Keynes: Open University Press, 1986).

Benson, John (ed.), *The Working Class in England 1875–1914* (London: Croom Helm, 1985).

Berlin, Edward A., *Ragtime: A Musical and Cultural History* (London: University of California Press, 1980).

Bibby, Cyril, *Scientist Extraordinary – T.H. Huxley* (Oxford: Pergamon, 1972).

Bigsby, C.W.E. (ed.), *Superculture: American Popular Culture and Europe* (London: Paul Elek, 1975).

Bogdanor, V. and Skidelsky, R. (eds), *The Age of Affluence 1951–64* (London: Macmillan, 1970).

Bourdieu, Pierre, *Distinction: A Social Critique of the Judgement of Taste*, translated by Richard Nice (London: Routledge & Kegan Paul, 1984).

Brake, Michael, *Comparative Youth Culture: The Sociology of Youth Cultures and Youth Subcultures in America, Britain and Canada* (London: Routledge & Kegan Paul, 1985).

Bramah, Edward, *Tea & Coffee: A Modern View of Three Hundred Years of Tradition* (London: Hutchinson, 1972).

Briggs, Asa, *Governing the BBC* (London: BBC, 1979).

Briggs, Asa, *The BBC: The First Fifty Years* (Oxford: Oxford University Press, 1985).

Brivati, Brian and Jones, Harriet (eds), *What Difference Did The War Make?* (London: Leicester University Press, 1993).

Brown, Ian, Hutchins, Nigel and Mizera, Gerry, *The Ultimate Jukebox Guide 1927–1974* (Brighton: Pla-mor, 1994).

Carpenter, Humphrey, *The Envy of the World: Fifty Years of the BBC Third Programme and Radio 3, 1946–1996* (London: Phoenix, 1997).

Cash, Tony (ed.), *Anatomy of Pop* (London: BBC, 1970).

Chambers, Iain, *Urban Rhythms: Pop Music and Popular Culture* (London: Macmillan, 1985).

Chambers, Iain, *Popular Culture: The Metropolitan Experience* (London: Methuen, 1986).

Clarke, John and Critcher, Chas, *The Devil Makes Work: Leisure in Capitalist Britain* (London: Macmillan, 1985).

Clarke, John et al. (eds), *Working Class Culture* (London: Hutchinson, 1979).

Cohen, Stanley, *Folk Devils and Moral Panics: The Creation of the Mods and Rockers* (New York: St Martins Press, 1980).

Cohn, Nik, *Today There Are No Gentlemen* (London: Weinfield & Nicolson, 1971).

Cohn, Nik, *Awopbopaloobop Alopbamboom: Pop from the Beginning* (London: Mandarin, 1996).

Colam, E.E.F., *Practical Milk Bar Operation* (London: Binstead and Sons, 1946).

Collins, Richard, et al. (eds), *Media, Culture and Society* (London: SAGE, 1986).

Cross, Gary (ed.), *Worktowners at Blackpool: Mass Observation and Popular Leisure in the 1930s* (London: Routledge, 1990).

Cummings, Tony, *The Sound of Philadelphia* (London: Methuen, 1975).

Curran, James et al. (eds), *Impacts and Influences: Essays on Media Power in the Twentieth Century* (London: Methuen, 1987).

Davies, Stella C., *North Country Bred* (London: Routledge, 1963).

Dormer, Jane, *Fashion: The Changing Shape of Fashion Through the Years* (London: Galley Press, 1979).

Dow, J.C.R., *The Management of the British Economy 1945–60* (Cambridge: Cambridge University Press, 1965).

Escort, Colin with Hawkins, Martin, *Good Rockin' Tonight: Sun Records and the Birth of Rock 'n' Roll* (London: Virgin, 1992).

Everett, Peter, *You'll Never Be 16 Again: An Illustrated History of the British Teenager* (London: BBC, 1986).

Faulkner, T. (ed.), *Design 1900–1960: Studies in Design and Popular Culture of the 20th Century* (Newcastle Upon Tyne: Newcastle Upon Tyne Polytechnic, 1976).

Fowler, David, *The First Teenagers: The Lifestyle of Young Wage-earners in Interwar Britain* (London: Woburn Press, 1995).

Frith, Simon, *The Sociology of Rock* (London: Constable, 1978).

Frith, Simon, *Sound Effects: Youth, Leisure, and the Politics of Rock* (London: Constable & Co., 1983).

Frith, Simon, *The Sociology of Youth* (Ormskirk: Causeway Press, 1984).

Frith, Simon, *Music for Pleasure: Essays in the Sociology of Pop* (Oxford: Blackwell, 1988).

Frith, Simon, *Performing Rites* (Oxford: Oxford University Press, 1998).

Frith, Simon and Goodwin, Andrew (eds), *On Record:Rock, Pop, and the Written Word* (London: Routledge, 1990).

Fyvel, T.R., *The Insecure Offenders: Rebellious Youth in the Welfare State* (Harmondsworth: Penguin, 1963).

Gambaccini, Paul, Rice, Tim and Rice, Jonathan, *British Hit Singles*, 8th edition (Enfield: Guinness, 1991).

Gelatt, Roland, *The Fabulous Phonograph 1877–1977* (London: Cassell, 1977).

George, Nelson, *The Death of Rhythm and Blues* (London: Omnibus, 1988).

Gillett, Charlie, *Sound of the City: The Rise of Rock and Roll* (London: Souvenir Press, 1971).

Gillis, John R., *Youth and History: Tradition and Changes in European Age Relations, 1770–Present* (London: Academic Press, 1981).

Gramsci, Antonio, *Selections from the Prison Notebooks*, trans. and ed. by Quintin Hoare and Geoffrey Nowell-Smith (London: Lawrence & Wishart, 1971).

Green, Benny, *Yesterday: A Photographic Album of Daily Life in Britain 1953–1970* (London: Dent, 1982).

Hall, G.S., *Adolescence* (New York: Appleton, 1916).

Hall, Stuart, and Jefferson, Tony (eds), *Resistance Through Rituals* (London: Hutchinson, 1976).

Halsey, A.H. (ed.), *Trends in British Society Since 1900: A Guide to the Changing Social Structure of Britain* (London: Macmillan, 1972).

Halsey, A.H., *Change in British Society* (Oxford: Oxford University Press, 1978).

Harker, Dave, *One for the Money: Politics and Popular Song* (London: Hutchinson, 1980).

Hazzard-Gordon, Katrina, *Jookin: The Rise of Social Dance Formations in African-American Culture* (Philadelphia, PA: Temple University Press, 1990).

Hebdige, Dick, *Subculture: The Meaning of Style* (London: Methuen, 1979).

Hebdige, Dick, *Hiding The Light* (London: Routledge, 1988).

Higgins, Patrick, *Before Elvis There Was Nothing* (New York, Carroll & Graff, 1994).

Hills, Matt, *Fan Cultures* (London: Routledge, 2002).

Hoggart, Richard, *The Uses of Literacy* (Harmondsworth: Penguin, 1960).

Hopkins, Harry, *The New Look: A Social History of the Forties and Fifties in Britain* (London: Secker & Warburgh, 1963).

Jackson, B., *Working Class Community* (London: Routledge & Kegan Paul, 1968).

Jenkins, Alan, *Drinka Pinta: The Story of Milk and the Industry that Serves it* (London: Heineman, 1970).

Johnson, B.S. (ed.), *All Bull: The National Servicemen* (London: Quartet, 1973).

Johnson, Lesley, *The Cultural Critics: From Matthew Arnold to Raymond Williams* (London: Routledge and Kegan Paul, 1979).

Jones, LeRoi, *Blues People* (Edinburgh: Payback Press, 1995).

Krivine, John, *Juke Box Saturday Night* (London: Bucklebury, 1988).

Kroes, Rob et al. (eds), *Cultural Transmissions and Receptions: American Mass Culture in Europe* (Amsterdam: Vu University Press, 1993).

Laing, Dave, *The Sound of Our Time* (London: Sheed and Ward, 1969).

Laurie, Peter, *The Teenage Revolution* (London: Anthony Blond, 1965).

Leavis, F.R., *For Continuity* (Cambridge: Minority Press, 1933).

LeMahieu, D.L., *A Culture for Democracy: Mass Communication and the Cultivated Mind in Britain Between the Wars* (Oxford: Clarendon, 1988).

Lévi-Strauss, Claude, *The Savage Mind* (Wiedenfeld & Nicolson, 1966).

Low, Rachael and Manvel, Roger, *British Film 1906–1914* (London: Allen & Unwin, 1948).

Lynch, Vincent, *American Jukebox: The Classic Years* (San Francisco: Chronicle Books, 1990).

McAleer, Dave, *The Ultimate Hit Singles Book* (Bristol: Siena, 1998).

MacInnes, Colin, *England, Half English* (London: Macgibbon & Kee, 1961).

MacInnes, Colin, *Sweet Saturday Night* (London: MacGibbon & Kee, 1967).

McKay, George (ed.), *Yankee Go Home (& Take Me With You)* (Sheffield: Sheffield Academic Press, 1997).

McRobbie, Angela (ed.), *Zoot Suits and Second-Hand Dresses* (London: Macmillan, 1989).

Maddox, Adrian, *Classic Cafes* (London: Black Dog Publishing, 2003).

Marks, Joan N., *Café and Milk Bar Catering* (London: Heywood & Co., 1952).

Marsh, David C., *The Changing Social Structure of England and Wales 1871–1961* (London: Routledge, 1965).

Mead, Margaret, *Coming of Age in Samoa: A Study of Adolescence and Sex in Primitive Societies* (London: Random House, 1928).

Mead, Margaret, *Sex and Temperament in Three Primitive Societies* (London: Routledge & Kegan Paul, 1935).

Melly, George, *Revolt Into Style* (Harmondsworth: Penguin, 1970).

Mill, John Stuart, *Essays on Politics and Society* (London: Routledge and Kegan Paul, 1977).

Moore, Bob and van Neirop, Henk, *Twentieth-Century Mass Society in Britain and the Netherlands* (Oxford: Berg, 2006).

Mungham, Geoff and Pearson, Geoff (eds), *Working Class Youth Culture* (London: Routledge & Kegan Paul, 1976).

Nott, James J., *Music for the People: Popular Music and Dance in Interwar Britain* (Oxford: Oxford University Press, 2002).

Oliver, Paul, *The Story of the Blues* (London: Barrie & Jenkins, 1978).

Orwell, George, *Coming up for Air* (London: Penguin, 1986), first published 1939.

Orwell, George, *The Penguin Essays of George Orwell* (Harmondsworth: Penguin, 1994).

Osgerby, Bill, *Youth in Britain Since 1945* (Oxford: Blackwell, 1998).

Parker, Tony, *The Plough Boy* (London: Hutchinson, 1965).

Parsons, Talcott (ed.), *Essays in Sociological Theory* (New York: The Free Press, 1964).

Pearce, Chris, *Vintage Jukeboxes* (London: Apple, 1988).

Pearce, Chris, *Jukebox Art* (London: Blossom, 1991).

Pearsall, Ronald, *Popular Music of the 1920s* (Newton Abbot: David & Charles, 1976).

Pearson, Geoffrey, *Hooligan: A History of Respectable Fears* (New York: Schocken, 1983.

Pells, Richard, *Not Like US: How Europeans Have Loved, Hated, and Transformed American Culture since World War II* (New York: Basic Books, 1997).

Perks, Robert and Thomson, Alistair (eds), *The Oral History Reader* (London: Routledge, 1998).

Pollard, Sidney, *The Development of the British Economy 1914–1967* (London: Edward Arnold, 1973, 2nd edition).

Priestley, J.B., *English Journey* (London: Heinemann, 1984).

Reynolds, David, *Rich Relations: The American Occupation of Britain, 1942–1945* (London: Harper Collins, 1995).

Richards, Jeffrey, *The Age of the Dream Palace: Cinema and Society in Britain 1930–1939* (London: Routledge and Kegan Paul, 1984).

Roberts, Kenneth, *Leisure and Recreation Studies 3: Youth and Leisure* (London: George Allen & Unwin, 1983).

Rose, Clare, *Children's Clothes Since 1750* (London: Batsford, 1989).

Russell, Bertrand et al., *The Impact of America on European Culture* (Boston: Beacon Press, 1951).

Russell, Dave, *Popular Music in England 1840–1914: A Social History* (Manchester: Manchester University Press, 1997).

Rust, Frances, *Dance in Society* (London: Routledge & Kegan Paul, 1969).

Scott, Derek, *The Singing Bourgeois: Songs of the Victorian Drawing Room and Parlour* (Milton Keynes: Open University Press, 1989).

Seebury, William Marston, *The Public and the Motion Picture Industry* (New York: Macmillan, 1926).

Sissons, M. and French, P. (eds), *Age of Austerity 1945–1951* (Harmondsworth: Penguin, 1964).

Smith, Cyril S., *Adolescence: An Introduction to the Problems of Order and the Opportunities for Continuity Presented by Adolescence in Britain* (London: Longmans, 1968).

Smith, Graham, *When Jim Crow met John Bull: Black American Soldiers in World War II Britain* (London: I.B. Tauris, 1987).

Springhall, John, *Coming of Age: Adolescence in Britain 1860–1960* (Dublin: Gill & Macmillan, 1986).

Stead, W.T., *The Americanisation of the World or The Trend of the Twentieth Century* (London: The 'Review of Reviews' Office, 1902).

Steele-Perkins, Chris and Smith, Richard, *The Teds* (Stockport: Dewi Lewis, 1979).

Storey, John, *Cultural Theory and Popular Culture* (London: Harvest Wheatsheaf, 1993).

Storey, John, *Cultural Theory and Popular Culture: A Reader* (London: Harvest Wheatsheaf, 1994).

Strinati, Dominic and Wagg, Stephen (eds), *Come on Down? Popular Media and Culture in Post-War Britain* (London: Routledge, 1992).

Thornton, Sarah, *Club Cultures: Music, Media and Subcultural Capital* (Cambridge: Polity Press, 1995).

Tocqueville, Alexis de, *Democracy in America* translated by Henry Reeve in 2 volumes (London: Saunders and Otley, 1835).

Trilling, Lionel, *Matthew Arnold* (London: Unwin, 1963).

Tunstall, Jeremy, *The Media are American* (London: Constable, 1977).

Turner, B. and Palmer, S., *The Blackpool Story* (Cleveleys: Blackpool Corporation, 1976).

Waites, Bernard et al. (eds), *Popular Culture: Past and Present* (London: Croom Helm, 1982).

Waldo, Terry, *This is Ragtime* (New York: Da Capo, 1991).

Walton, John, K., *The Blackpool Landlady: A Social History* (Manchester: Manchester University Press, 1978).

Walton, John, K. and Walvin, James (eds), *Leisure in Britain 1780–1939* (Manchester: Manchester University Press, 1983).

Walvin, James, *Leisure and Society 1830–1950* (London: Longman, 1978).

Webster, Duncan, *Looka Yonda: The Imaginary America of Populist Culture* (London: Routledge, 1988).

Whitcomb, Ian, *After the Ball: Pop Music from Rag to Rock* (Baltimore, MD: Penguin, 1974).

Wicke, Peter, *Rock Music: Culture, Aesthetics and Sociology* (Cambridge: Cambridge University Press, 1990).

Williams, Raymond, *The Long Revolution* (London: Chatto & Windus, 1961).

Williams, Raymond, *Culture and Society 1780–1950* (London: Penguin, 1962).

Wilson, Elizabeth, *Adorned in Dreams: Fashion and Modernity* (London: Virago, 1985).

Wilson, Elizabeth and Taylor, Lou, *Through the Looking Glass: A History of Dress from 1860 to the Present Day* (London: BBC, 1989).

Young, Michael and Willmott, Peter, *Family and Kinship in East London* [1957] (London: Routledge & Kegan Paul, 1986).

Zweig, Ferdynand, *The Student in the Age of Anxiety* (London: Heinemann, 1963).

Zweiniger-Bargielowska, Ina, *Austerity in Britain: Rationing, Controls, and Consumption 1939–1955* (Oxford: Oxford University Press, 2000).

Essays

Aaronovitch, Sam, 'The American Threat to British Culture' in *The American Threat to British Culture*, Communist Party of Great Britain. National Cultural Committee Conference 1951 (London: Arena, 1952), pp. 3–22.

Banham, Reyner, 'Mediated Environments *or*: You can't build that here' in *Superculture: American Popular Culture and Europe*, ed. by C.W.E. Bigsby (London: Paul Elek, 1975), pp. 69–82.

Banham, Reyner, 'Detroit Tin Revisited' in *Design 1900–1960: Studies in Design and Popular Culture of the 20th Century*, ed. by T. Faulkner (Newcastle Upon Tyne: Newcastle Upon Tyne Polytechnic, 1976), pp. 120–40.

Banham, Reyner, 'Vehicles of Desire' in *A Critic Writes: Essays by Reyner Banham* ed. by Mary Banham et al. (London: University of California Press, 1996), pp. 3–6.

Bennett, Tony et al. 'Class, Culture and Hegemony – 1 Antonio Gramsci' in *Culture, Ideology and Social Process: A Reader*, ed. by Tony Bennett et al. (Milton Keynes: Open University Press, 1983), pp. 185–219.

Bigsby, C.W.E., 'Europe, America and the Cultural Debate', in *Superculture: American Popular Culture and Europe*, ed. by C.W.E. Bigsby (London: Paul Elek, 1975), pp. 1–28.

Cardiff, David, 'The serious and the popular: aspects of the evolution of style in the radio talk 1928–1939' in *Media, Culture and Society*, ed. by R. Collins et al. (London: SAGE, 1986), pp. 228–46.

Clarke, John and Jefferson, Tony, 'Working Class Youth Cultures', in *Working Class Youth Culture*, ed. by G. Mungham and G. Pearson (London: Routledge & Kegan Paul, 1976).

Clarke, John et al., 'Sub Cultures, Cultures and Class' in *Culture, Ideology and Social Process: A Reader*, ed. by Tony Bennett et al. (Milton Keynes: Open University Press, 1983), pp. 53–81.

Cohen, Phil, 'Subcultural Conflict and Working Class Community' [1972], in *The Subcultures Reader*, ed. by K. Gelder and S. Thornton (London: Routledge, 1977), pp. 90–9.

Cooper, Martin, 'Revolution in musical taste' in *The Impact of America on European Culture*, Bertrand Russell et al. (Boston: Beacon Press, 1951), pp. 67–78.

Corrigan, Paul and Frith, Simon, 'The Politics of Youth Culture', in *Resistance Through Rituals*, ed. by Stuart Hall and Tony Jefferson (London: Hutchinson, 1976), pp. 231–42.

Cunningham, Hugh, 'Leisure' in *The Working Class in England 1875–1914* ed. by John Benson (London: Croom Helm, 1985), pp. 133–64.

Frith, Simon, 'The Making of the British Record Industry 1920–64' in *Impacts and Influences: Essays on Media Power in the Twentieth Century*, ed. by J. Curran et al. (London: Methuen, 1987), pp. 278–90.

Frith, Simon, 'Packeting The Lot: Notes on Art and Pop' in *The British Edge* (Boston: ICA, 1987), pp. 70–84.

Frith, Simon, 'The Industrialization of Music' in *Music for Pleasure: Essays in the Sociology of Pop* (Oxford: Blackwell, 1988), pp. 11–23.

Frith, Simon, 'Playing with Real Feeling – Jazz and Suburbia' in *Music for Pleasure: Essays in the Sociology of Pop* (Oxford: Blackwell, 1988), pp. 45–64.

Frith, Simon, 'The Pleasures of the Hearth' in *Music for Pleasure: Essays in the Sociology of Pop* (Oxford: Blackwell, 1988), pp. 24–43.

Frith, Simon, 'The Good, The Bad and the Indifferent: Defending Popular Culture from the Populists' in *Cultural Theory and Popular Culture – A Reader*, ed. by John Storey (London: Prentice Hall, 1994), pp. 570–85.

Hall, Stuart and Whannel, Paddy, 'The Young Audience' in *Cultural Theory and Popular Culture: A Reader*, ed. by John Storey (London: Prentice Hall, 1994), pp. 61–7.

Hebdige, Dick, 'Towards a Cartography of Taste, 1935–1962' in *Hiding The Light* (London: Routledge, 1988), pp. 45–77.

Howlett, Peter, 'The War Economy', in *Twentieth Century Britain: Economic, Social and Cultural Change*, ed. by Paul Johnson (London: Longman, 1994), pp. 283–99.

Hughes, David, 'The Spivs', in *Age of Austerity 1945–1951*, ed. by M. Sissons and P. French (Harmondsworth: Penguin, 1964), pp. 86–105.

Jefferson, Tony, 'Cultural Responses of the Teds: The Defence of Space and Status' in *Resistance Through Rituals*, ed. by Stuart Hall and Tony Jefferson (London: Hutchinson, 1976), pp. 76–81.

Kroes, Rob, 'Americanisation: What are we Talking About?' in *Cultural Transmissions and Receptions: American Mass Culture in Europe*, ed. by Rob Kroes et al. (Amsterdam: Vu University Press, 1993), pp. 302–18.

Leavis, F.R., 'Mass Civilisation and Minority Culture', in *For Continuity* (Cambridge: Minority Press, 1933).

Lehmann, John, 'The Lesson of the Pupil' in *The Impact of America on European Culture*, Bertrand Russell, et al (Boston: Beacon Press, 1951), pp. 23–33.

MacInnes, Colin, 'Young England, Half English: The Pied Piper from Bermondsey', *Encounter*, December 1957, in *England, Half English* (London: Macgibbon & Kee, 1961), pp. 11–18.

McRobbie, Angela, 'Settling accounts with subcultures: a feminist critique', in *Culture, Ideology and Social Process: A Reader*, ed. by Tony Bennett et al. (Milton Keynes: Open University Press, 1983), pp. 111–25.

McRobbie, Angela, 'Second-hand Dresses and the Role of the Ragmarket' in *Zoot Suits and Second-Hand Dresses*, ed. by Angela McRobbie (London: Macmillan, 1989), pp. 23–49.

Mead, Margret, 'Social Change and Cultural Surrogates' in *Personality in Nature, Society and Culture*, ed. by C. Kluckholm and H.A. Murry (New York: Alfred A. Knoph, 1948).

Mill, John Stuart, 'De Tocqueville on Democracy in America', [I] and [II] in *Essays on Politics and Society* (London: Routledge and Kegan Paul, 1977), pp. 47–90, 153–204.

Mill, John Stuart, 'State of Society in America' in *Essays on Politics and Society* (London: Routledge and Kegan Paul, 1977), pp. 91–116.

Miller, Perry, 'The Reimportation of Ideas' in *The Impact of America on European Culture*, by Bertrand Russell et al. (Boston: Beacon Press, 1951), pp. 80–95.

Mitchell, David, 'What's Wrong With the Teddy Girls', *Picture Post* (4 June 1955), pp. 37–40.

Morpurgo, J. E., 'Hollywood: America's Voice' in *The Impact of America on European Culture*, by Bertrand Russell, et al (Boston: Beacon Press, 1951), pp. 37–47.

Mungham, Geoff and Pearson, Geoff, 'Introduction: Troubled Youth, Troubling World' in *Working Class Youth Culture*, ed. by G. Mungham and G. Pearson (London: Routledge & Kegan Paul, 1976), pp. 1–9.

Mungham, Geoff, 'Youth in Pursuit of Itself' in *Working Class Youth Culture*, ed. by G. Mungham and G. Pearson (London: Routledge & Kegan Paul, 1976), pp. 82–106.

Murdock, Graham and McCron, Robin, 'Youth and Class: The Career of a Confusion' in *Working Class Youth Culture*, ed. by G. Mungham and G. Pearson (London: Routledge & Kegan Paul, 1976), pp. 10–26.

O'Faolain, Sean, 'Look Homeward Angel' in *The Impact of America on European Culture*, by Bertrand Russell, et al (Boston: Beacon Press, 1951), pp. 37–47.

Oppenheimer, Peter, 'Muddling Through: The Economy, 1951–1964' in *The Age of Affluence 1951–64*, ed. by V. Bogdanor and R. Skidelsky (London: Macmillan, 1970).

Osgerby, Bill, 'From the Roaring Twenties to the Swinging Sixties: Continuity and Change in British Youth Culture, 1929–59' in *What Difference Did The War Make*, ed. by Brian Brivati and Harriet Jones (London: Leicester University Press, 1993), pp. 80–98.

Parsons, Talcott, 'Age and Sex in the Social Structure of the United States (1942)' in *Essays in Sociological Theory*, ed. by Talcott Parsons (New York: The Free Press, 1964), pp. 89–103.

Partington, Angela, 'Popular Fashion and Working Class Affluence' in *Chick Thrills: A Fashion Reader*, ed. by Juliet Ash and Elizabeth Wilson (London: Pandora, 1992), p. 151.

Pells, Richard, 'American Culture Abroad: The European Experience Since 1945' in *Cultural Transmissions and Receptions: American Mass Culture in Europe*, ed. by Rob Kroes et al. (Amsterdam: Vu University Press, 1993), pp. 67–83.

Phillips, Pearson, 'The New Look' in *Age of Austerity 1945–1951*, ed. by M. Sissons and P. French (Harmondsworth: Penguin, 1964), pp. 132–54.

Reisman, David, 'Listening to Popular Music' in *On Record: Rock, Pop, and the Written*

Word, ed. by Simon Frith and Andrew Goodwin (London: Routledge, 1990), pp. 5–13.

Roberts, Elizabeth, 'The Family' in *The Working Class in England 1875–1914*, ed. by John Benson (London: Croom Helm, 1985), pp. 1–35.

Roberts, Elizabeth, 'Woman's Place' in *The Working Class in England, 1875–1914*, ed. by John Benson (London: Croom Helm, 1985), pp. 1–35.

Rock, Paul and Cohen, Stanley, 'The Teddy Boy', in *The Age of Affluence 1951–64*, ed. by V. Bogdanor and R. Skidelsky (London: Macmillan, 1970), pp. 289–319.

Russell, Bertrand, 'The Political and Cultural Influence' in *The Impact of America on European Culture*, by Bertrand Russell et al. (Boston: Beacon Press, 1951), pp. 3–22.

Scannell, Paddy, 'Broadcasting and the Politics of Unemployment' in *Media, Culture and Society*, ed. by R. Collins et al. (London: SAGE, 1986), pp. 214–27.

Steadman Jones, Garreth, 'History: The Poverty of Empiricism' in *Ideology in Social Science: Readings in Critical Social History*, ed. by Robin Blackburn (London: Fontana, 1972), pp. 96–119.

Street, John, 'Shock Waves: The Authoritative Response to Popular Music' in *Come on Down? Popular Media and Culture in Post-War Britain*, ed. by Dominic Strinati and Stephen Wagg (London: Routledge, 1992), pp. 302–24.

Strinati, Dominic, 'The Taste of America: Americanization and popular culture in Britain' in *Come on Down? Popular Media and Culture in Post-War Britain*, ed. by Dominic Strinati and Stephen Wagg (London: Routledge, 1992), pp. 46–81.

Wild, Paul, 'Recreation in Rochdale, 1900–40' in *Working Class Culture*, ed. by John Clarke et al. (London: Hutchinson, 1979).

Essays in journals

Biven, B. and Holden, Dr. H.M., 'Informal Youth Work in a Café Setting', *Howard Journal of Penology and Crime Prevention*, 12/1 (1966), pp. 13–25.

Breward, Christopher, 'Style and Subversion: Postwar Poses and the Neo-Edwardian Suit in Mid-Twentieth Britain', *Gender and History*, 14 (November 2002), pp. 560–83.

Chibnall, Steve, 'Whistle and Zoot: The Changing Meaning of a Suit of Clothes', *History Workshop Journal*, 20 (Autumn 1985), pp. 56–81.

Cosgrove, S., 'The Zoot Suit and Style Warfare', *History Workshop Journal*, 18 (Autumn 1984), pp. 77–91.

Fletcher, Colin, 'Beat and Gangs on Merseyside', *New Society*, 3/73 (February 1964), pp. 11–15.

Forty, Adrian, 'Wireless Style, Symbolic Design and The English Radio Cabinet 1928–33', *Architectural Association Quarterly*, 4/2 (Spring 1972), pp. 23–31.

Gronow, Pekka, 'The Record Industry: The Growth of a Mass Medium', *Popular Music*, 3, Producers and Markets (1983), pp. 53–75.

Hancock, A. and Wakeford, J., 'The Young Technicians', *New Society*, 5 (14 January 1965), pp. 13–14.

Jones, Michelle, 'Television and the British Broadcasting Corporation's Promotion of "Good Design"', *Journal of Design History*, 16/4 (2003), pp. 307–18.

Leysham, A.M., 'Import Restrictions in Post War Britain', *Scottish Journal of Political Economy*, 4 (1957), pp. 177–93.

Metcalf, David, 'The Determinants of Earnings Changes: A Regional Analysis for the UK, 1960–68', *International Economic Review*, 12/2 (June 1971), pp. 273–82.

Morris, Terence, 'The Teenage Criminal', *New Society*, 1/28 (1963), pp. 13–16.

Musgrove, Frank, 'The Problem of Youth and the Social Structure of Society in England', *Youth and Society*, 1 (1966), pp. 38–58.

North, C.J., 'Our Foreign Trade in Motion Pictures', *Annals of the American Academy of Political and Social Science*, 128 (1926), p. 102.

Scannell, Paddy, 'Music for the Multitude', *Media, Culture and Society*, 3 (1981), pp. 243–60.

Smith, C.S., 'The Youth Service and Delinquency Prevention', in *Howard Journal of Penology and Crime Prevention*, 12/1 (1966), pp. 42–51.

Sparke, Penny, 'From Lipstick to a Steamship: the Growth of the American Design Profession' in *Design Council: Fad or Function?*, ed. by Terry Bishop (London: Design Council, 1978), pp. 10–16.

Williams, Raymond, 'Base and Superstructure in Marxist Cultural Theory', *New Left Review*, 82 (1973), pp. 1–16.

Wright, D.S., 'A Comparative Study of the Adolescent's Concepts of His Parents and Teachers', *Educational Review*, 14 (1962), pp. 226–32.

PhD theses

Brader, Christopher, *Timbertown Girls: Gretna Female Munitions Workers in World War 1*, PhD dissertation, Warwick University, 2001.

Demetriadi, J., *English Seaside Resorts 1950–74*, Lancaster PhD thesis T2235 (history), 1995.

Horn, Adrian M., *Americanisation and Youth Culture: Juke Boxes and Cultural Fusions, with special reference to Northwest England 1945–1960*, PhD dissertation, Lancaster University 2004.

Osgerby, W.J., *One for the Money, Two for the Show: Youth, Consumption and Hegemony in Britain in 1945–70, with special reference to a South East coastal Town*, PhD dissertation, Sussex University, 42-2586, A9F, 1992.

Websites

International Gramsci Society: www.internationalgramscisociety.org

The Raymond Williams Society: www.nottingham.ac.uk/~aezrwmts/society

The Rise and Fall of the Temperance Bar: www.sarsaparilla.co.uk/bar.html

VIMTO: The Story of a Soft Drink: www.vimto.co.uk/history

The Journal of Cinema and Media: www.frameworkonline.com/index2.htm

Classic Cafés: www.classiccafes.co.uk

Leigh, Spencer, 'Coal in the Bunker, Burning Up Bright': www.spencer.demon.co.uk/Feature 6.5Special

Teddy Girls: www.teddygirl.co.uk

Index

advertising 4, 6, 43, 83–4, 175
  of gramophones 24–6
  of juke boxes 27–8, 35–8, 40,
    45–6, 48–9, 51–8
aircraft, juke box design and 36, 37,
    38–9, 42, 44, 132
alcohol 73, 92, 166, 180–1
  see also public houses
American culture
  juke boxes disseminate 66, 188–9
  perceived dominance of 2–3, 98,
    186–7
  praise of 1945–1960 3
  and social venues 172–6
  synonymous with mass culture 3
  see also rock 'n' roll, American;
    Teddy Boys
American football 119
American Graffiti 146
American Look 118–19, 123, 137
American soldiers in Britain 20–4, 98,
    116, 118
amusement arcades 36, 40, 67–8, 100,
    176
  behaviour in 104, 163–5, 177
  juke boxes in 9–11, 24–5, 29–30,
    46, 49, 77, 131, 161, 168, 177,
    189, 192
  and music licences 74
Amusement Caterer's Association
    (ACA) 75–6
Arnold, Matthew 3, 14–15, 193

Art Deco 9, 27, 34, 40–1, 54, 188

BAL-AMI 58, 61, 188
  advertises 55
  anglicised jukeboxes 49–50,
    52–3
BBC
  distrusts juke boxes 67
  ideology of 66–70
  ignores popular music 50, 66,
    68–9, 73, 83, 85, 188–9
  Light Programme 68, 71, 75
  near-monopoly on broadcasting
    10, 20, 66
  relaxes attitude to popular music
    70–1, 75–6, 78
  resists commercialisation 75
  as voice of establishment 3, 9–10,
    66, 70–1, 188–9
  see also television
be-bop 69–74, 133
Berry, Chuck 2, 81
Big Band Sound 24
Blackbottom 14
black music 14–16, 82–3, 124
Blackpool 19–20, 104, 122, 171, 173,
    177, 187
  and beginnings of British juke box
    industry 34–6, 44–5, 54
blues 2, 81, 83, 85
British Broadcasting Corporation *see*
    BBC

Broadbent, Gwynneth 144

cafés 1
    types of 192
    see also coffee bars; milk bars;
        public houses; temperance bars
Campaign for Nuclear Disarmament
    151–4, 191
Caron, Leslie 142, 155–7, 192
catalogues, clothes 142
censorship 83
    see also licences, music
Centre for Contemporary Cultural
    Studies (CCCS) 5–6, 148, 186
Charleston 14, 16, 20
charts, music 81, 83–4, 177, 192
Cheetham, Jim 21–2, 73, 136
childhood 91, 99, 103
church 11, 17, 19, 20, 22, 24, 73–4,
    78, 161
cinema 2, 9–10, 17–20, 78–80, 92,
    100, 142, 145, 158, 191
    American 9, 14, 18, 23–4
    and imperialism 20
    music and 19, 68
classical music 14, 18, 68–70, 83,
    189
class, middle 14, 16, 66–7, 70, 102,
    124, 142, 158, 190, 191
    and fashion 151–5, 158, 191
    record industry targets 18
class system 16
    and youth culture 102–5
    see also class, middle; class, upper;
        class, working
class, upper 10, 16, 66, 70, 123, 125
class, working
    American influences on 15
    and fashion 119, 123, 125–6, 137
    girls 145, 149–50, 191
    increasing affluence of 16, 96–7,
        100, 102, 171–2, 187, 191
    teenagers 189–90
coffee bars 103–4, 138, 169, 171–81,
    192

Cohen, Stanley 5, 8–9, 123, 125, 132,
    136
Cohn, Nik 78, 115, 124, 125, 127,
    138
communism 3, 7, 79, 191
copyright 11, 77, 161–3
cosmetics *see* make-up
cost of living 16, 97
country and western music 82–3
culture *see* youth culture
Curtis, Tony 10, 124–5, 134, 137

Dad's Army 122
dance schools 20
dancing 92, 98, 100, 103, 108, 163,
    177, 180
    American influences on 9, 14–17,
        19–20, 69, 71–5, 118, 182, 193
    in American military bases 23–4
    see also Blackbottom; Charleston;
        jive; jitterbug; waltz
delinquency 5, 8, 18, 29, 153, 191
    and amusement arcades 163–5
    and music 67, 78
    and Teddy Boys 121, 124–7, 129,
        130–1, 135–6
    and World War II 105–7
Ditchburn 45–50, 52–3, 56–62, 165,
    169, 188
dominant culture 5, 7–8, 14–16, 149,
    165
Dowding, Laura 76, 104, 181–2
drainpipe trousers 10, 127, 133, 137,
    153, 191
drape suits 10, 116–123, 126, 137–8,
    179
dressmaking 10, 142–4, 146, 158, 191

economics 188
    cost of living 16, 97
    income 16
    and record industry 80–1
    and Teddy Boys 124
    and youth culture 81, 92–8
    see also employment

Edwardian Look 115–16, 123–5, 127, 133–4, 137–8, 150
emergent culture 7–8, 68, 77–8
Empire Windrush 116–17
employment 94–6, 99, 101–5, 108–9, 189
    see also economics

Fagan, Dave 177
fairgrounds 3, 36–7, 73
    juke boxes in 9, 23–5, 29–30, 40, 46, 49, 77, 169, 187
Farmery, John 77, 100, 136
fashion 10–11, 100
    and class 119, 123, 125–6, 137, 151–5, 158, 191
    see also American Look; drape suits; drainpipe trousers; dressmaking; Edwardian look; fashion, women's; haircuts; ratters; shoes; sideburns; Spivs; Teddy Boys; ties; Trilby hats
fashion, women's
    catalogues 142
    changes in 143–4
    and cinema 145–6
    clothing clubs 142–3
    cost of 142–3, 191
    diversity 146
    dressmaking 10, 142–4, 146, 158, 191
    haircuts 23, 143, 146, 155, 176
    hire purchase 142
    lack of research into 142, 146–8, 191
    and magazines 10, 145
    make-up 2, 91, 98, 144
    and middle class 151–5, 158, 191
    New Look 148–9
    and parental control 144–5
    regionalism 145
    'scruffy' clothes 151–6
    and trousers 157–8
    and Teddy Boys 142, 148
    Teddy Girls 142, 149, 151

Vicky Girls 150–1
    and World War II 143
flick knives 124
Fowler, David 5, 94, 96, 100, 189
Fyvel, Tosco R. 5, 105, 130–1, 135–6, 171, 178, 190

Gable, Clarke 119
gender 16, 94–6, 148
generation gap 3, 78–80, 82–3, 100, 189–90
Givenchy, Hubert de 155–6
gramophones 2, 14–18, 20, 24–6, 53, 68, 72, 80, 92, 162–7, 187
Gramsci, Antonio 7–8
Grant, Cary 119
Gréco, Juliette 142, 154–6, 192

haircuts
    female 23, 143, 146, 155, 176
    male 10, 122, 124–5, 129–30, 132–4, 137–8, 191
Haley, Bill 51, 74–5, 78–81, 133, 147, 190
Happy Days 146
Hawtins 35–9, 44–5, 188
Hebdige, Dick 3, 5, 134, 186
Heartbreak Hotel 83
Hepburn, Audrey 142, 155–7, 192
Here in my Heart 81
HMV 15, 83
Hoggart, Richard 3, 123, 178, 186
Hollywood *see* cinema
homosexuality 124
Hylton, Jack 37–9, 44–5

imperialism
    and cinema 20
    and World War II 38
import restrictions 27, 43–4, 50, 53–4, 56, 60, 142, 161, 187
Isaacs, Harry 73, 122, 136–7, 150, 171–3

Jackson, Brian 72, 103, 179

jazz 14–18, 69–73, 78, 83–4, 153–4, 157
jitterbug 24, 118
jive 24, 79, 118
juke boxes, British
    American influence on 59–61
        lack of 35, 39, 188
    British compared to American jukeboxes 58
    as cultural icons 3
    design 37–49
        and obsolescence 40–2
    development of 1, 24–7
    disc size 17, 47–8, 61, 81
    growth in popularity of 28–9, 49–56
    imported 53, 58, 60–2, 187
    and import restrictions 27, 43–4, 50, 53–4, 56, 60, 187
    literature on 5
    first manufactured in Britain 35–9
    numbers of 169
    second hand 61–2
    suspicion of 67
    see also selections, number of
Juke Box Jury 82

Laurie, Peter 5, 91, 145
Leavis, F.R. 3, 14, 18
Lee, Brenda 81
Leigh 71, 80
licences, juke box importing 43, 60
licences, juke box manufacturing 50, 52
licences, music 5, 67–9, 72–6, 80, 161–8, 181, 192
Light Programme 68, 71, 75
Liverpool 164
London 17, 23–4
    dominates studies of youth culture 1–2, 93
Lynn, Vera 81

magazines 10
Magistrates' courts 69–76, 78, 80, 161, 164–8, 192
make-up 2, 91, 98, 144

Manchester 73, 77, 115, 136, 150, 154, 166–77, 181
    and fashion 122
    juke boxes made in 45, 47–8, 61
    juke box licenses refused in 67–8
    photos of 6
    riots in 80, 136
    see also Leigh; Rochdale
Martino, Al 81
Mass-Observation reports 4, 6, 72, 118–19, 143, 164
Melly, George 5, 127, 132, 136
milk bars 50, 52, 68, 100, 104, 176–9
    American influences on 171, 173
    décor 161, 169–71, 175
    defined 170
    and milk shortages 171
    and music licences 163–4, 167
    see also delinquency
Miller, Glenn 24
Mitchell, Terry 77, 103, 137, 173, 176, 181
music
    blues 2, 81, 83, 85
    country and western music 82–3
    see also black music; jazz; rock 'n' roll, American
music charts 81, 83–4, 177, 192
music halls 15, 19
Musician's Union 77–8
Music Maker 37–8, 42, 44–7, 50–3, 56–61, 165, 188

National Service 107–8, 125, 193
New Look 148–9
north/south divide 2, 95, 115, 182
    see also regionalism

Orwell, George 170

parental authority 72–3, 78, 91, 98–101, 103, 144, 162, 177, 190
Picture Post 6, 120–1, 128, 130, 149
PPL (Phonographic Performance Limited) 162–3, 192

Presley, Elvis 2, 81–4, 137
PRS (Performing Rights Society)
    162–3, 192
puberty 91, 98–9, 176
    see also sex
public houses 15, 19, 23, 67, 162–3,
    166–7, 180–2

racial issues 19, 83, 116–18, 189
    see also black music
Radio Luxembourg 73, 75–7
radios, scarcity of 76
radio *see* BBC
ragtime 14–16, 18
ratters 131
record companies 16–18, 84–5
recorded sound, history of 17
regionalism 2, 7, 16, 97, 101–2, 115,
    182
    see also north/south divide
religion 73–5
residual culture 7, 66, 100
revolutions per minute 27, 40, 47–9,
    52–3, 56, 59, 61, 81
Richard, Cliff 81–2
Rochdale 19–20, 166–7, 180
Rock Around the Clock 51, 74–5, 78–
    81, 133, 190
rock 'n' roll, American
    arrival in Britain 17, 51, 76, 78, 81
    broadcasting restrictions 78
    and class 70–1
    development of 84–5
    disapproval of 3, 10, 78–80, 82–3
    dissemination of 49, 187
    dominance of 2
    and fashion 134, 138
    'filtering' of 9
    popularity of 1–2, 9, 50, 83
    as rebellion against older gener-
        ation 16
    see also BBC
rpm *see* revolutions per minute
Russell, Bertrand 3, 193
Russell, Ken 142, 149

St. Trinians 122
Salford 15, 16, 18–19
Sarsaparilla 172
Savile Row 125
schools 70, 92–4, 96, 101–3, 107–9,
    137, 180
    Borstal 104
    dance 20
    leaving age 101, 107, 109
    types of 73, 101–3, 137, 180, 190
science, Americans dominate
seaside towns 16, 19, 24–5, 29, 46, 49,
    74, 77, 125
Seeburg 24, 54–6, 188
selections, number of 27, 46–8, 50,
    52–3, 56, 58, 61–2, 188
sex 22–3, 98–9, 176–7
    see also puberty
sheet music 14, 18, 187
shoes 115, 124, 127, 137, 157
sideburns 10, 82, 124, 126–7, 137
skating rinks 20
snack bars *see* cafés; coffee bars; milk
    bars; public houses; temperance
    bars
Spivs 118–23
    and American culture 119, 122–3
    as dandies 118, 123
    as 'media folk devils' 8–9, 116, 119
    origins of 119
    and Teddy Boys 10, 116, 121
Springhall, John 5, 90
Steele, Tommy 81–2
Stott, Barry 104, 136–7, 173, 177
Streamlining 9, 34, 39, 41, 43, 170,
    188
Sweet Nuthins 81

Teddy Boys 2, 190–1
    acceptance of 131–2, 134–8
    cafés for 179
    cost of being 124
    described 124
    development of 115–16, 123–4
    in Europe 190–1

and homosexuality 123–4
as 'media folk devils' 8–9, 116, 127–9, 132–3
numbers of 115, 130
panic caused by exaggerated 8–9, 130–4
and petty crime 121, 124–7, 129, 130, 136
regionality of 115, 132, 134, 135–6
and rock 'n' roll 80
and Spivs 10, 116, 121
as subculture 134–5
and Teddy Girls 142, 148–9, 151
unoriginality of 10, 115, 126
see also Edwardian Look; Spivs
temperance bars 80, 161, 171–2, 176, 182, 192
taste 9, 15, 20, 34, 41–3, 55–6, 68–71, 75, 188, 193
television 5, 67, 82, 122, 145–6, 169
see also BBC
That's All Right 83
ties 119, 123, 124, 126–7, 132, 138, 179
Tome, Valerie 76–7, 175–6
Tonomat Automaton 58–60
Trilby hats 118, 122

university 73, 101–2, 151
urban/rural split 2, 168, 193

venues *see* cafés; coffee bars; delinquency; licences, music; milk bars; public houses; temperance bars
Victorian Britain 14–15, 66, 73, 100, 119, 132
Vicky Girls 150–1
Vimto 172

waltz 14, 20
'war babies' 105
women's fashion *see* fashion, women's

World's Fair 4–5, 25, 27, 29, 46–50, 61, 72, 74, 84, 91
advertising in 24, 35, 53, 60
and age of jukebox users 189
reports on copyright laws 163–4, 166, 168
World War II
America enters 25, 83
American soldiers in Britain 20–4, 98, 116, 118
and Imperialism 38
import restrictions 27, 43–4, 50, 53–4, 56, 60, 142, 161, 187
'war babies' 105
Wurlitzer 23–5, 27–8, 36–7, 47, 55–6, 61–2
'1015' model 40
advertisements 24, 36, 55, 57
sets up agencies in Britain 24–5

youth culture
and class 102–5
diversity of 2
and economics 81, 92–8
and employment 99, 101–2, 108
and gender 94–6
and hooliganism 104–8
London dominates study of 1–2, 93
in northwest England 7
origins of 90–1, 99 , 101
and puberty 98–9
size of 92
and socialising 11, 25, 98–100, 161, 170–2
study of neglected 5, 191
terminology of 91, 98, 189
see also dominant culture; emergent culture; generation gap; regionalism; residual culture

zoot suits 116–17, 119, 124, 132, 133, 137